T0084000

GUITAR LESSON DICTIONARY

AN A-Z GUIDE TO TIPS, TECHNIQUES & MUCH MORE

BY WOLF MARSHALL

HAL•LEONARD®

7777 W. BLUEMOUND RD. P.O. BOX 13819 MILWAUKEE, WI 53213

ISBN: 978-1-5400-1589-1

In Australia Contact:
Hal Leonard Australia Pty. Ltd.
4 Lentara Court
Cheltenham, Victoria, 3192 Australia
Email: ausadmin@halleonard.com.au

Visit Hal Leonard Online at
www.halleonard.com

CONTENTS

INTRODUCTION

The guitar is one of the most diverse and ubiquitous instruments in music, arguably *the most*. Its ascendance and preeminence in the twentieth century is a remarkable success story. The guitar, in all its wondrous forms and incarnations, has exerted a monumental influence and left an indelible mark on the world's cultures and traditions. Though I am obviously biased, it is hardly over-reaching or chauvinistic to cite the instrument's sweeping significance across all genres today. Consider the following.

The body of work for gut-string acoustic guitar in classical music alone is enormous, ranging from Segovia's Bach transcriptions, Bream's Renaissance lute arrangements, and a host of original Spanish genre pieces by Sor, Tarrega, Carcassi, Albeniz, and Granados to modern concert compositions by Rodrigo, Ponce, de Falla, Moreno Torroba, Villa Lobos, Castelnuovo-Tedesco, Brouwer, and many others.

In rock, pop, and metal the guitar is supreme, underscored by the never-ending cavalcade of guitar heroes since its inception. A selective list of lionized players includes Chuck Berry, Les Paul, Bo Diddley, Scotty Moore, Buddy Holly, Cliff Gallup, James Burton, Duane Eddy, Steve Cropper, Dick Dale, George Harrison, Keith Richards, Pete Townshend, Eric Clapton, Jeff Beck, Jimi Hendrix, Jimmy Page, Neil Young, Ritchie Blackmore, Carlos Santana, Billy Gibbons, Tony Iommi, Duane Allman, Steve Howe, David Gilmour, Brian May, Angus Young, Larry Carlton, Allan Holdsworth, Robben Ford, Steve Morse, Mark Knopfler, Michael Schenker, Andy Summers, Eddie Van Halen, Randy Rhoads, Yngwie Malmsteen, James Hetfield, Steve Vai, Joe Satriani, Eric Johnson, Brian Setzer, Slash, The Edge, Kurt Cobain, Dimebag Darrell, and John Mayer. There are *many* more.

Jazz very nearly matches the rock pile with its own long line of formidable guitar exponents. Charlie Christian, Django Reinhardt, Eddie Lang, George Van Eps, Freddie Green, Barney Kessel, Johnny Smith, Jimmy Raney, Tal Farlow, Jim Hall, Howard Roberts, Wes Montgomery, Kenny Burrell, Herb Ellis, Grant Green, Joe Pass, Pat Martino, George Benson, Charlie Byrd, Ed Bickert, Antonio Carlos Jobim, John McLaughlin, Larry Coryell, Al Di Meola, John Scofield, Pat Metheny, Henry Johnson, Jimmy Bruno, and Mike Stern are exemplary voices purveying a plethora of approaches.

Blues is dominated by its great guitar players. Names like Robert Johnson, Charlie Patton, Leadbelly, Blind Lemon Jefferson, Lightnin' Hopkins, Elmore James, T-Bone Walker, Muddy Waters, John Lee Hooker, Guitar Slim, Howlin' Wolf, Clarence "Gatemouth" Brown, Hubert Sumlin, the three "kings" (B.B., Freddie, and Albert), Albert Collins, Otis Rush, Magic Sam, Buddy Guy, Mike Bloomfield, Rory Gallagher, Peter Green, Johnny Winter, and Stevie Ray Vaughan are forever embedded in guitar lore. These players represent a hardy tradition, which has influenced virtually every contemporary music style.

And, last but not least, what would country music be without its revered pickers: Merle Travis, Chet Atkins, Hank Garland, Joe Maphis, Jimmy Bryant, Jerry Reed, Phil Baugh, Buck Owens, Tony Rice, Albert Lee, Danny Gatton, Scotty Anderson, Ricky Skaggs, Brent Mason, Keith Urban, and Brad Paisley?

Suffice it to say that every major form of music has a prominent role for the guitar: classical, folk, country, flamenco, blues, jazz, R&B, rock, bossa nova, funk, metal, reggae, fusion, and pop. These are powerful assertions, but you can't argue with the evidence.

What does all this have to do with you, the reader and ever-inquisitive guitarist seeking new sounds and modes of expression? Just this. If every major form of music has a prominent role for the guitar, then every aspiring guitarist must be ready to fill that role. It follows that today's player must be prepared, knowledgeable, and conversant with a variety of established styles and sounds—the stuff that guitar players should know. That's where *The Guitar Lesson Dictionary* comes in. This is not an instruction book, but you will find it very instructive. This is not a reference book, but you will find a wealth of reference material covering essential styles, sounds, tips, and gear. This is not a play-along licks book, but you are cordially invited to home in on any one of the over 100 audio examples and play along.

The Guitar Lesson Dictionary is none of those and happily all of the above and more. Enjoy.

—Wolf Marshall

ABOUT THE AUDIO

All audio examples played by Wolf Marshall

Recorded at Marshall Arts Music Studios
San Diego, California

Special thanks to: Fender Music Instruments, Gibson USA, Heritage Guitars, Roger Sadowsky, Jazz Kat amplifiers

ABOUT THE AUTHOR

Wolf Marshall is a respected and prolific performer/author who has been an influential force in music education since the 1980s. *Guitar Player* as well as *Guitar World France* and *The Wall Street Journal* have interviewed him. Wolf's voluminous magazine credits include articles, transcriptions, and columns in *Guitar World*, *Guitar for the Practicing Musician*, *Guitar School*, *Guitar Extra*, *Guitar Edge*, and his own creation *Guitar One*. His current "Fretprints" series has appeared monthly in *Vintage Guitar* since 2001.

Over the years, companies as diverse as The Experience Music Project, World Vision and Floresta charities, Tri-Star films, Line 6 Guitar Port Online, and Sibelius software have employed Wolf's professional services. Wolf is an endorser and spokesman for Fender Music Instruments and has also partnered with manufacturers such as Gibson USA, Epiphone, Heritage, Sadowsky Guitars, National Resophonic, Jim Dunlop, Digitech, Thomastik-Infeld strings, Acoustic-Image, Raezer's Edge, Jazz Kat, and Polytone amps for numerous notable projects.

Wolf has worked closely with Hal Leonard over the last three decades. Under that association, his eight-volume series *The Wolf Marshall Guitar Method* established new standards for guitar pedagogy. Moreover, Wolf authored such acclaimed works as *The Guitar Style of Stevie Ray Vaughan*, *The Beatles Favorites*, *B.B. King: The Definitive Collection*, *The Essential Albert King*, *The Rolling Stones*, *Best of The Doors*, *Blues Guitar Classics*, *Guitar Instrumental Hits*, *Eric Clapton Unplugged*, *The Guitars of Elvis*, *The Guitar Style of Mark Knopfler*, *Best of Queen*, *Best of Cream*, *Best of Wes Montgomery*, *Best of Jazz Guitar*, *101 Must-Know Rock Licks*, and the DVD *Lead Guitar* for Hal Leonard. Their latest cooperative venture is an exciting online guitar series for the worldwide web.

Wolf was invited to join the music faculty at his alma mater UCLA in 2007. He currently teaches advanced jazz guitar studies in the department of ethnomusicology alongside long-time mentor Kenny Burrell and Anthony Wilson.

ACOUSTIC GUITAR

General stuff: An acoustic guitar produces its sound from the string vibrations resonating through the body and soundboard. Acoustic guitars come in numerous shapes and sizes, from small parlor-style instruments to large dreadnaughts and jumbos, and are often chosen for the timbral characteristics associated with body types and sizes.

Acoustic guitars fall into two basic categories: flat-top acoustics and arch-top acoustics. Within this division are sub-categories like steel-string acoustics, 12-string acoustics, wooden and metal resonator guitars, gypsy-jazz guitars, nylon-string classical, and flamenco guitars.

Martin 000-28   Martin D-28   Guild 12-string

Dobro resonator guitar   Ramirez classical guitar   Taylor cutaway acoustic

Sonic stuff: Acoustic guitar styles are as numerous as the types of instruments available. Classical, bluegrass, flamenco, gypsy-jazz, country blues, and folk music are played exclusively on acoustic guitars. Some pop, country, and rock players use acoustic guitars as the preferred medium for composition and the basis of an arrangement, while others add acoustic guitar(s) to an electric combo for different texture.

Playing stuff: Acoustic guitar techniques range from strummed rhythm-guitar work and flat-picked single-note licks to country picking and intricate classical fingerstyle. Here are two illustrative, contrasting examples:

This typical strummed figure is played on a six-string acoustic guitar and is characteristic of country, folk, and pop rhythm styles. The phrase is based on three first-position chords (G, C, and D) and a consistent, driving strum pattern.

TRACK 2

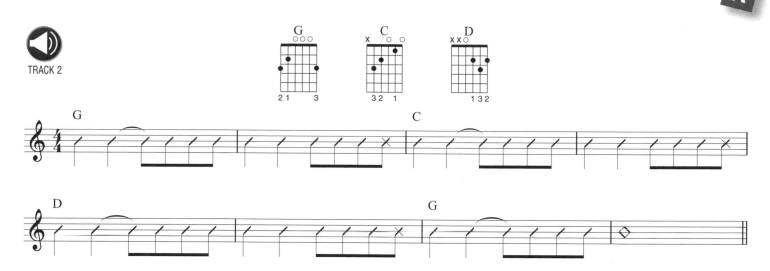

Classical guitar has arguably the oldest tradition in the acoustic-guitar family. The guitar competed with the lute during the Baroque period. Guitarist-composers like Fernando Sor, Mateo Carcassi, and Francisco Tarrega furthered the Spanish-guitar's lexicon and playing techniques in the eighteenth and nineteenth centuries. Musicians like Segovia began to build the classical concert repertory in the early twentieth century. Several of his transcriptions are standard performance fare, like this Bach lute piece adapted to the guitar. This phrase depicts the typical arpeggiation technique of the idiom. The plucking hand follows the mandatory *p–i–m–a* (alternating thumb–index–middle–ring fingers) picking pattern.

TRACK 2
(0:14)

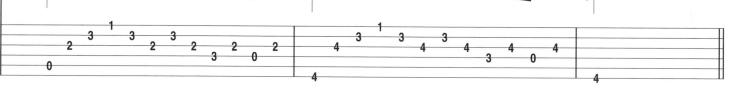

ACOUSTIC-ELECTRIC GUITAR

General stuff: Acoustic-electric guitars retain the acoustic appearance, timbre, and design but are fitted with pickups, which allow the guitars to be amplified. The Gibson J-160E, introduced in 1954 and made popular by John Lennon and George Harrison a decade later in the Beatles, was an early jumbo flat-top with a surface-mounted, built-in P-90 pickup.

Arch-top guitars use both built-in and suspended pickups. The Gibson ES-175 is an example of the built-in style, while the Gibson Johnny Smith is the best-known acoustic arch-top with a stock suspended pickup.

Most popular acoustic-electrics (like Ovations) made from the 1970s to the present are amplified via a piezo pickup that is mounted in the bridge. This is now a standard method for acoustic guitar amplification. Many acoustic-electrics today use a piezo pickup in conjunction with an interior microphone apparatus, which makes for an overall warmer, more natural tone.

Gibson J-160E

Gibson ES-175

Ovation classic with piezo

Playing stuff: Acoustic-electric guitars entered the musical mainstream and pop culture with the Beatles in the 1960s. This telling phrase is played on an electrified jumbo flat-top, a Gibson J-160E, into a Vox amp, typical of the kind of sound John Lennon employed.

TRACK 3

The arch-top acoustic-electric guitar is the de facto standard for jazz. From Charlie Christian in the early swing period to Wes Montgomery in hard bop to George Benson and Pat Metheny in the modern era, the amplified arch-top is immediately identifiable and the right tool for the job. This chord-melody passage exemplifies the sound and stylistic application of the arch-top acoustic-electric jazz guitar.

TRACK 3
(0:15)

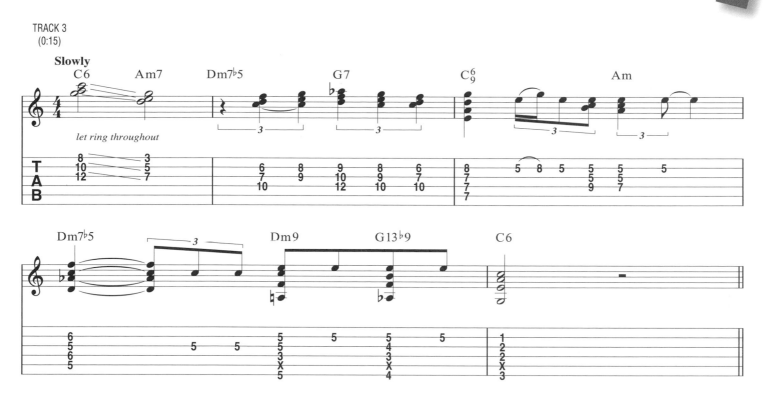

ACTION

General stuff: Action refers to the height of the strings from the fretboard. If the action is too low, the strings will buzz, generate false tones, and even fret out. If the action is too high, the instrument will be uncomfortable to play and may have intonation problems when the strings are pressed down in higher positions.

Technical stuff: Action is determined by a combination of the bridge, nut, and truss rod. Action can be changed to suit a performer's personal playing style by increasing or decreasing the height of the bridge, replacing or deepening the grooves in the nut, and/or adjusting the tightness of the neck's truss rod.

It goes without saying that the tools needed to adjust the bridge (screwdriver) and truss rod (hex wrench) on your guitar should be at hand whether you're at home or at the gig. Many neighborhood hardware stores sell small double-sided screwdrivers (standard blade and Phillips head), which are ideal for the job. While you're shopping, don't forget to pick up a hex-head cap-style wrench for the truss rod.

> *"I like a high action. I like a guitar to give me pull and I like something to pull against."*
>
> —Michael Bloomfield, *Heroes of the Electric Blues*, 2004

> "[My action] *is pretty high. It has to be, because if you have it too low on a Strat it plunks like a banjo.*"
>
> —Jeff Beck, *Guitar Player*, 1980

ALTERNATE TUNINGS

General stuff: Alternate tunings are those that deviate from standard tuning. Alternate tunings have been used by guitarists of practically every genre; proponents include Jimmy Page, Eddie Van Halen, Bonnie Raitt, and Eric Clapton in rock and pop styles; classical artists Andres Segovia and Christopher Parkening; country performers Chet Atkins and Jerry Reed; jazz guitarists Johnny Smith and George Benson; and blues players Robert Johnson, Skip James, John Lee Hooker, and Albert Collins.

Technical stuff: Alternate tunings generally fall into two categories: dropped (also called "slack") tunings and raised tunings. The former is achieved by lowering one or more strings in pitch to create a different fretboard layout. Conversely, the latter is achieved by raising the pitch of one or more strings. Common dropped tunings include Drop D, Open G, and Open D. Common raised tunings are Open A and Open E, the counterparts to open dropped tunings.

> *"Open tunings are great because you hit something you're familiar with, like an E shape, and it's a weird chord and blows your mind."*
>
> —Peter Townshend, *Guitar Player*, 1972

Modal tunings are a subset of the alternate-tuning family. While most open tunings tend to spell open chords like G major, D major, C6, and E minor, modal tunings are harmonically ambiguous and often incorporate suspensions. The DADGAD tuning of Led Zeppelin fame is an example of a Dsus4 chord made into an alternate tuning. Other variations of alternate tunings include unison tunings (two or more strings tuned to the same pitch) and hybrid tunings (a combination of any of the above).

Playing stuff: Drop D is arguably the most popular and pervasive alternate tuning. It is accomplished by lowering the sixth string one whole step, from E to D. Drop D has been found in the repertories of John Denver, Andres Segovia, and Pete Seeger (linking pop, classical, and folk), jazz guitarists Johnny Smith and George Benson, and hard-rock bands like Van Halen and Tool. This example is from Segovia's transcription of J.S. Bach's "Chaconne for Solo Violin" and is played on nylon-string acoustic guitar.

TRACK 4

Drop D Tuning:
(low to high) D–A–D–G–B–E

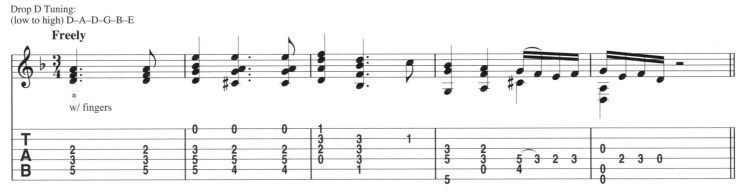

Open G is one of the most versatile and ubiquitous alternate tunings. It is created by lowering the sixth, fifth, and first strings down one whole step to D, G, and D, respectively. Open G is indigenous to the music of Muddy Waters, the Rolling Stones, Eric Clapton, James Taylor, Hot Tuna, Led Zeppelin, Rory Block, and Moses Kahumoko, which encompasses urban and rural blues, rock, folk, country, metal, and Hawaiian music. This is a classic blues phrase that is played with a slide.

TRACK 4
(0:21)

Open G tuning:
(low to high) D–G–D–G–B–D

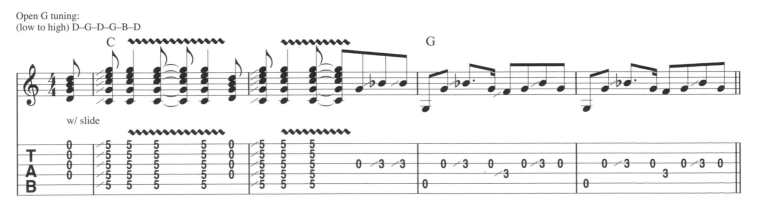

AMPLIFIER

General stuff: An amplifier (amp) is the instrument and means by which an electric guitar is made louder. Guitar amps come in many sizes, shapes, and configurations. Their power output and decibel level can vary drastically from small living-room setups like the Emery Sound 2-watt Microbaby to the gargantuan 200-watt-plus Marshall Major stacks of Ritchie Blackmore.

Amps come in three basic configurations: the combo, the stack, and the rack-mount model. The combo combines speaker(s) and amplifier in one cabinet. Stevie Ray Vaughan and Wes Montgomery were both users of the combo type. The stack, originally called "piggy-back" by Fender, places the amplifier in its own cabinet, on top of a speaker cabinet(s). Jimi Hendrix, Jimmy Page, and Eddie Van Halen are well-known users of amp stacks. The rack-mount type is a pre-amplifier that is housed in a rack unit and generally feeds its output to a power amp. The latter, popular in the 1980s, was used by guitarists such as Steve Vai and Steve Lukather. Choices in amplification have affected the tone of countess guitar-driven recordings.

> *"I've never found the Stones or anyone else made great records by using huge stacks in the studio and blasting away. You can get very powerful-sounding records playing very quietly and with relatively small amps. Small amps turned way up have the tension you're trying to get anyway and it sounds big."*
>
> —Keith Richards, *Guitar Player*

Technical stuff: Electronically, amplifiers consist of three sections: a preamp, a power amp, and the power supply. A preamp receives the guitar's output signal and provides initial tone-shaping. The power amp takes the weak signal from the preamp, makes it louder, and turns it into a high-watt form that can power speakers. In the power amp, the output transformer acts as the final stage, changing the electrical signal of the amp into a signal for the speakers. An amp's final tone quality is affected by the power amp and transformer. The power transformer converts electricity from the wall socket into different voltage levels for different parts of the amp circuit. High voltage (about 300 to 500 volts) is needed for the plates in power tubes. The preamp tubes require less (in the neighborhood of 200 volts), and the filaments and pilot light need even less (approximately 6 or 12 volts). Though not part of the audio circuit, the power transformer also has an effect on the amp's overall feel.

Sonic stuff: In virtually every form of music, the amp is not only responsible for volume, but also for the tone of the electric guitar. It is instructive to take an amplifier through its paces, from clean to heavy distortion.

- Clean amp tone is what the amp is capable of producing without distortion. Paradoxically, a clean guitar tone is enhanced with a little natural overdrive. In fact, that small amount of distortion is essential to the warm tone and sustain of pop, jazz, rockabilly, and country guitar music. Clean tone is generally set with low preamp settings and high power-amp settings on amps with a master volume, and with the tone controls at midway or less. This ratio assures the cleanest sound for chords and heavily attacked notes. The higher the power, the greater the potential is for clean and loud response with the least undesirable distortion.

- Semi-dirty (or semi-clean) tone is the sound of blues, early rock 'n' roll, and various modern rock and pop styles. On an amp with a master volume, turn up the preamp for greater gain, dialing in the appropriate amount of overdrive. On older amps with no master volume like the tweed Bassman, Twin, and blackface Super-Reverb, the volume hits a sweet spot past the half-way point. Higher tone settings (treble, bass, middle) shape the semi-dirty tone favorably. The key is to experiment and use your ear to dial in just the right amount of drive.

- Heavy overdrive takes you into hard rock and heavy metal territory. In those genres, the gain is "maxed" for an extreme result. In tube amps, generally, the preamp tubes are mostly overdriven, while the output tubes are fairly clean and are simply amplifying the distorted tone generated in the preamp section. Sometimes the preamp and power amp tubes are overdriven. Most players use much higher tone settings in conjunction with increased distortion to boost and define treble, middle, and bass frequencies. These adjustments enhance sustain, emphasize stylistic upper-partial harmonics of rock timbre, and facilitate guitar-amp pairing.

1957 Fender Deluxe

Emery Sound Microbaby

1961 Fender Showman

Marshall Stack

Vox AC30

1965 Fender Super Reverb

BARRE CHORD

General stuff: The barre chord is one of the most useful resources in the guitarist's toolbox—make that, all guitarists' toolboxes. Barre chords are essential in classical, punk, jazz, country, rock, folk, metal, funk, reggae, pop… Well, you get the idea. The barre chord is the origin of the hard-rock power chord. You also need to develop barre-chord technique to play chord-melody solos in jazz, as well as traditional classical and flamenco pieces. And what about punk and garage-band parallelism? Suffice it to say, the barre chord is truly ubiquitous.

Technical stuff: The barre chord is formed by using one or more fingers to create a "bar" across several strings. Depending on the barre-chord type, it is common to apply any of the four fretting fingers and even the thumb to barre strings on the fingerboard. The barre chord makes possible the movement of common-fingered shapes to different positions on the neck and instant transposition.

Playing stuff: To get a grip on barre chords, it is important to visualize them relative to their un-barred (i.e., open-position) forms.

Every chord in open position is a viable candidate for conversion to a barre chord. To experience this, begin with a fingering shape for a common E major chord in open position, but finger this shape without the index finger. Then, scoot the entire shape up one fret and lay the index finger down to barre at the first fret. This process creates an F major barre chord based on the E form.

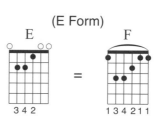

Barre chords can similarly be created from any basic open-position form. In this next example, the other most common barre chords, based on sixth- and fifth-string roots, are presented. Note the use of major, minor, and seventh chord types.

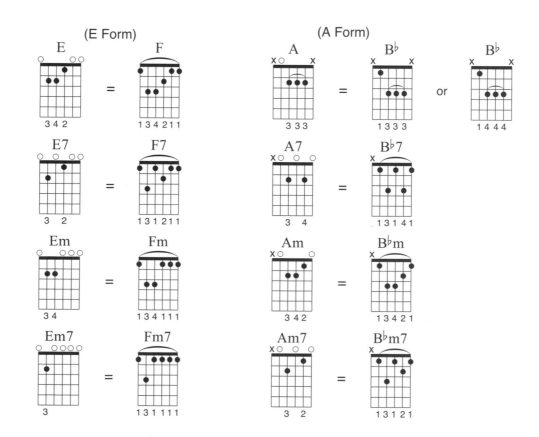

There are many barre chord forms beyond conventional major, minor, and seventh types.

In more sophisticated applications, different fingers can be used to barre within the same phrase. The following progression has three jazz barre-chord forms. Each has a different barring finger.

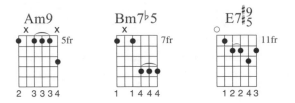

Kenny Burrell used these two enriched seventh-chord forms in "Chitlins Con Carne." This is a blues application. Note the C7♯9/E. This is an inverted chord with an altered tone that employs the barring technique.

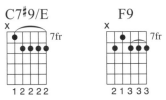

Thumb-fretted barre chords are found in the playing of Barney Kessel, Chet Atkins, Wes Montgomery, Jimi Hendrix, Merle Travis, and Howard Roberts. This V–I progression includes two typical jazz barre chord forms. The final chord, E♭maj9/B♭, is a thumb-fretted barre chord. The thumb is used to press down the sixth and fifth strings.

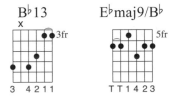

This rhythm figure is a staple of garage-band fare. It is a striking case of the barre chord and parallelism. Compact and portable, the barre chord lends itself to this sort of application. Check out the shapes. The progression is made entirely of major barre chords, with the same shape moved in parallel motion. Similar moves are found in rock, blues, punk, pop, and folk.

TRACK 5

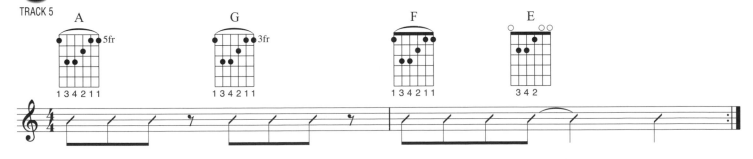

The barre chord figures prominently in classical and flamenco guitar styles. This characteristic passage exploits a finger-picked arpeggiation of a B7 chord in the key of E minor. The symbol "CVII" is typical of classical-guitar notation; it means to fully barre all six strings at the VII (seventh) fret. C=*Capotasto*, the Spanish term for "barre."

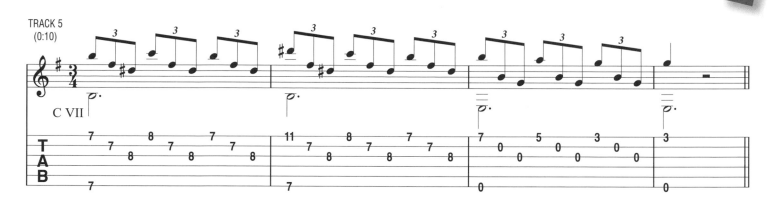

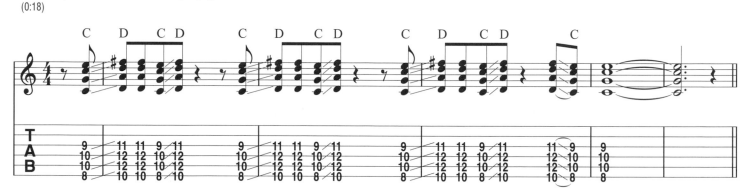

The barre chord riff, as purveyed by the Kinks and others, took parallelism to another level. With its semi-dirty tone and aggressive rhythmic delivery, this parallel pattern uses the partial forms that gave rise to the almighty power chord.

BLUES

General stuff: What is the blues? The blues is Ray Charles, Lightnin' Hopkins, Joe Williams, John Lee Hooker, B.B. King, Kenny Burrell, Otis Rush, and Buddy Guy. It is also the Rolling Stones, Eric Clapton, Jeff Beck, Mike Bloomfield, ZZ Top, Johnny Winter, Robben Ford, and Stevie Ray Vaughan. That's a short answer.

Historic stuff: Blues is a uniquely American music. The blues has its origins in a regional form developed by black musicians in the Old South. The style evolved from field hollers and work songs to become one of the most influential global musical styles, with numerous sub-genres, cross-overs, and spin-offs. Today, blues is played by musicians of every race and socioeconomic background.

Blues has a hardy lineage. The music was established and codified in the early twentieth century by first-generation blues artists like Jelly Roll Morton, Ma Rainey, and Reverend Gary Davis. Pre-World War II innovations came from guitarists Charlie Patton, Son House, Robert Johnson, and others in the Mississippi Delta region. Post-war blues saw the rise of such important guitar performers as T-Bone Walker, Elmore James, Muddy Waters, and B.B. King. Later, blues upheavals included blues-oriented forms of rock and R&B and the "white blues revival" in America and England in the sixties.

The blues permeates and informs practically all styles of contemporary music. From George Gershwin's blues-tinged "classical" compositions and show tunes in the thirties to swing and bebop jazz, rock 'n' roll, country, hard rock, heavy metal, and pop, blues is a common denominator in America and worldwide.

Many blues artists are categorized by the style and sound of their region: Robert Johnson and Charlie Patton in the Mississippi Delta; T-Bone Walker, Freddie King, and Stevie Ray Vaughan in Texas; Muddy Waters, Howlin' Wolf, and Elmore James in Chicago; B.B. King and Albert King in Memphis; and Eric Clapton, Peter Green, and John Mayall in the U.K.

15

Playing stuff: Blues is a highly expressive music. On the guitar, a primary objective is to convey the sound of the human voice. A lexicon of string bends, slurs, vibrato, specific scale usage, and idiomatic licks have been developed over the years by iconic players, all must-know ingredients of the blues language. Once these elements are learned, assimilated, and internalized, the player addresses larger concerns of phrasing and producing a unique personal statement.

> *"The blues has to be felt through your body and soul, and there's no way you can fake it."*
>
> —Buddy Guy, *Heroes of the Electric Blues*, 2004

> *"The blues isn't a sad thing. When I'm down, it still picks me right back up again."*
>
> —John Lee Hooker, *The Guitarist Book of the Blues*, 2003

> *"In the blues format I can just almost lose consciousness; it's like seeing in the dark."*
>
> —Eric Clapton, *Guitar Player*, 1976

> *"Blues is a real tasty, feel type of thing, so I copped that in the beginning."*
>
> —Eddie Van Halen, *Guitar Player*, 1980

This stylistic figure has country blues origins but has followed a true "round robin" path in the genre. Variants are found in the music of Robert Johnson, Freddie King, Eric Clapton, Johnny Winter, Jimmy Page, and Stevie Ray Vaughan. The phrase is played fingerstyle and is a favorite turnaround lick of many great players.

TRACK 6

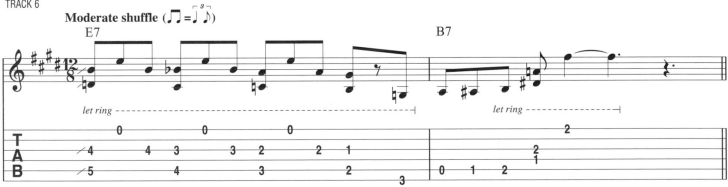

Texas blues giant T-Bone Walker brought a swing-oriented lead-guitar approach to the blues. His predominately single-note style had a fluid, horn-like feel and influenced virtually every blues-based soloist to follow, from B.B. King, Chuck Berry, and Buddy Guy to Jimi Hendrix and Stevie Ray Vaughan. This T-Bone lick in the key of G presents several aspects of his style: seminal string-bending sounds, triplet riffing, and a combination of minor and major blues melody, all harbingers of future blues.

TRACK 6
(0:08)

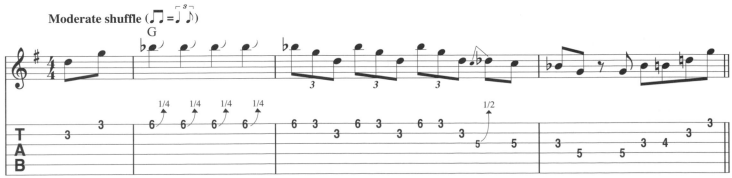

B.B. King perfected many of T-Bone's innovations. Among his modern blues contributions are singing hand vibrato and more evolved string bending. This slow-blues phrase contains some of his trademark sounds: a slurred shift, typical string bending in the "B.B. Box," chromatic passing tones, and that unmistakable "hummingbird" vibrato.

TRACK 6
(0:17)

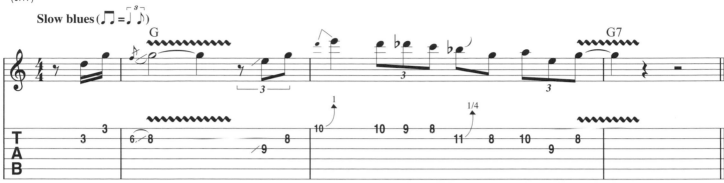

Also see: *Blues Scale* (p. 17) and *Twelve-Bar Blues* (p. 132).

BLUES SCALE

General stuff: The blues scale is a six-note scale that is used frequently in—what else?—blues and blues-related music such as rock, jazz, and western swing.

Technical stuff: The blues scale is identical to the minor pentatonic scale in melodic structure, with the addition of a flatted 5th (or raised 4th), the "blue note." In the key of C, the blues scale is spelled C–E♭–F–F♯/G♭–G–B♭.

The most common form of the blues scale is similar to the most common form of the minor pentatonic scale, referred to in guitar parlance as the "blues box." This is the shape and note content of the C blues scale in the blues-box shape at the eighth position.

Blues box form

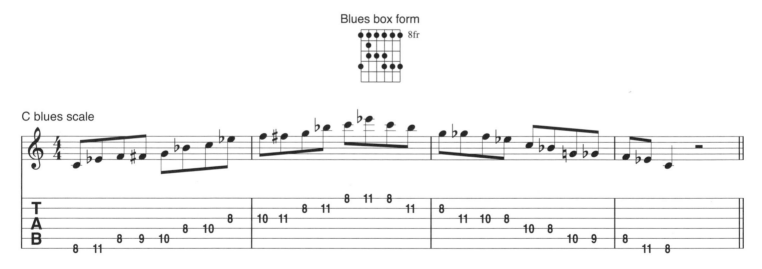

Playing stuff: If you want to play the blues, knowing the blues scale isn't enough. The blues language should inform a blues musician's playing more than scalar structures and theory. Even simple refinements like rhythmic placement and slurred phrasing can make a big difference in a scalar blues lick. As a simple demonstration, the following phrase begins on beat 3 and has a slide into the blue note G♭.

String bending, triplet phrasing, and changes of scalar direction can produce even more soulful results. This winding line contains all three refinements.

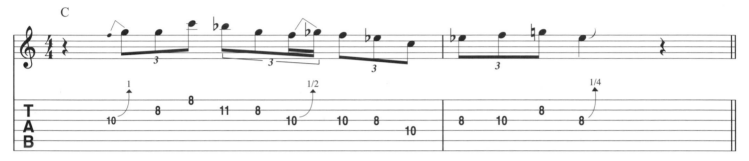

Buddy Guy is fond of milking the ♭5 blue note with double stops and repetition. This phrase contains a soulful wide-triplet feel and is played with the fingers or hybrid picking.

BOSSA NOVA GUITAR

Historic stuff: Bossa Nova is a regional Brazilian musical style that combines the native samba and American jazz. Bossa Nova (literally "New Stream" in Portuguese) was introduced to America in the late fifties and popularized worldwide in the early sixties. The seminal figures in Bossa Nova were Brazilian nationals Antonio Carlos Jobim, Joao and Astrud Gilberto, Luis Bonfa, and Sergio Mendes, and American jazz musicians Charlie Byrd and Stan Getz. The repertory of Bossa Nova has yielded a number of immortal must-know standard songs, most notable among them are "The Girl from Ipanema," "One Note Samba," "Desafinado," "Meditation," "Corcovado," "Wave," "Trieste," "Manha de Carnaval," "How Insensitive," "Dindi," and "Samba de Orfeo."

Sonic stuff: Bossa Nova has a distinct guitar approach, underscored by the fact that it is the fundamental instrument in the rhythm section and a favored medium for composition. Classic Bossa Nova is usually played on a nylon-string acoustic guitar and performed fingerstyle. This sound transcended the Brazilian genre post-1964 and is now found in many forms of jazz, pop, and soft rock, where it is often played on an electric guitar.

"The hands move differently on the guitar and piano and act differently, and the guitar is the greatest instrument for accompaniment things and the human voice. For writing songs, it's ideal."

—Antonio Carlos Jobim, *Guitar Player*

Playing stuff: Bossa Nova is guitar-driven and distinguished by its pulsating rhythm patterns, distinctive syncopations, and hypnotic accents. This figure is played fingerstyle in the typical Bossa Nova manner. The thumb plucks bass notes in the phrase while the fingers (or thumb and fingers) attack the alternating chord partials.

TRACK 8

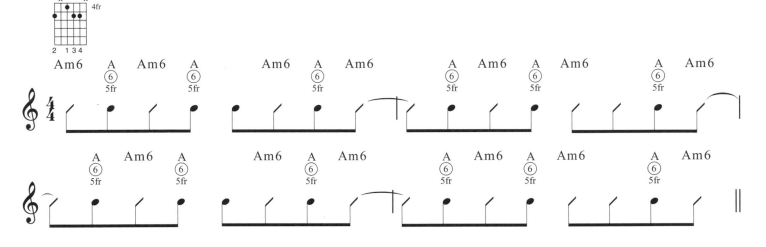

Bossa Nova chord progressions make extensive use of jazz chords. This phrase includes minor-seventh and dominant-seventh chords, as well the extended chord Cm11 and the altered chord B7♭5. Note the use of pedal point in the top voice of each chord; the F tone is maintained throughout the changes.

TRACK 8
(0:12)

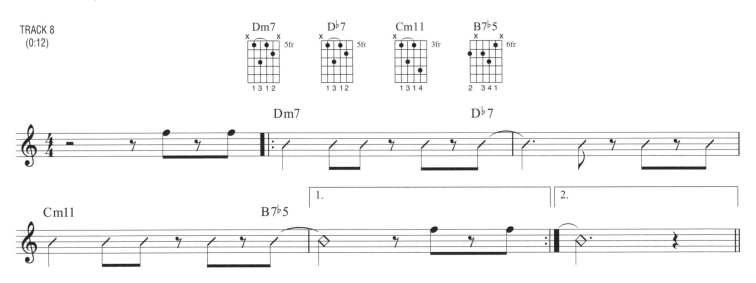

BRIDGE (HARDWARE)

General stuff: A bridge is the point at which the strings break (i.e., arch) on the guitar's body, and where string vibrations and energy are transmitted to the soundboard. Archtops employ movable bridges. Flattop acoustic and most solidbody electric guitars use fixed bridges that are either glued to the top of the soundboard or screwed into the body. The bridge is also a crucial part of the guitar's action and its overall intonation.

Sonic stuff: On the bridge, the string rests on a saddle, from which the vibrations pass to the body. Saddles are notched to form a groove in which the string is seated, and are made of various materials: wood, bone, ivory, plastic, or metal. The materials can significantly affect guitar tone. Compare the woody, more muted timbre of an archtop with a wooden bridge versus a similar archtop with a Tune-O-Matic bridge and metal saddles.

Technical stuff: Bridge height is adjusted by manually turning the serrated-edge thumb wheels on a traditional archtop's wooden bridge, or a metal Gibson-style Tune-O-Matic. On a standard Fender bridge/tailpiece with individual saddles, such as Teles and Strats, a small hex wench is used for adjustments. Some bridges can be adjusted with a flat-head screwdriver, while others must be moved manually with the strings loosened. Fixed bridges should only be adjusted by professionals. See *Intonation* (p. 55).

Gibson combination bridge/stop tailpiece

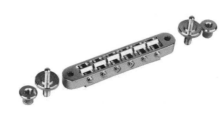

Gibson tune-o-matic bridge

Fender Tele bridge

Strat bridge

BRIDGE (MUSIC)

General stuff: A bridge is also part of a song form, usually a contrasting section (B section). Many pop songs are in the AABA form. Consider the song "A Hard Day's Night," by the Beatles. The 12-bar verses are the A sections, the middle section (beginning with the line, "When I'm home…") is the eight-bar B section, or bridge (sometimes called a "channel" or "release"). John Lennon used the old term "middle eight" to refer to this section.

On a related note, the song name "Badge" (from Cream's *Goodbye* album) came about from a misunderstanding between Eric Clapton and George Harrison, the songwriters. During the collaboration process, George had scrawled the word "bridge" on a piece of paper, referring to the song's famous middle section. Eric misread it, to his amusement, as "Badge"—and the name stuck. Consequently, one of the greatest classic-rock songs was titled by accident.

CAPO

General stuff: The capo is a mechanical device that attaches to the guitar neck and clamps down strings on the fingerboard, forming a barre at various positions. This works like a moveable nut, allowing guitarists to transpose music instantly while retaining the same chord forms and fingerings. Many guitarists rely on the capo to play simple open-position chords and riffs in different keys, while other players use the capo to produce a unique timbre, as well as to change keys.

Historic stuff: John Lee Hooker, Albert Collins, Gatemouth Brown, Keith Richards, the Beatles, REM, Joni Mitchell, and innumerable country blues and folk acoustic players have used the capo regularly, often in conjunction with alternate tunings. Notable capo tunes include the Rolling Stones' "Tumbling Dice," the Beatles' "Here Comes the Sun," Albert Collins' "Frosty," and John Lee Hooker's "Boogie Chillen."

Technical stuff: While a capo is simple to use, a few basic points are essential to bear in mind. Attach the capo just behind the chosen fret. For example, if you want a D chord to sound as an A chord, you will clamp the capo at the seventh fret and then play the chord as if the seventh fret was the new nut. This raises the pitch seven semitones, or a 5th interval.

Oftentimes, the guitar must be retuned after seating and properly clamping the capo. Make sure the capo is as straight as the nut. Check the tuning with the capo on. Tune to the correct pitches and then pull lightly on each string to dislodge it from a pinched position. Check the tuning again. You may notice that one or more of the strings has drifted. Retune and repeat the process until all six strings remain in tune with the capo seated and clamped.

Clamp with screw fastener

Elastic strap and spring
attachment

Kyser style

Playing stuff: This characteristic capoed phrase sounds in A but is fingered as if the guitarist were thinking in D. The capo is attached at the seventh fret. Note the directions in the music. The symbols in parentheses represent chord names respective to the capoed guitar. The symbols above reflect the actual sounding chord.

TRACK 9

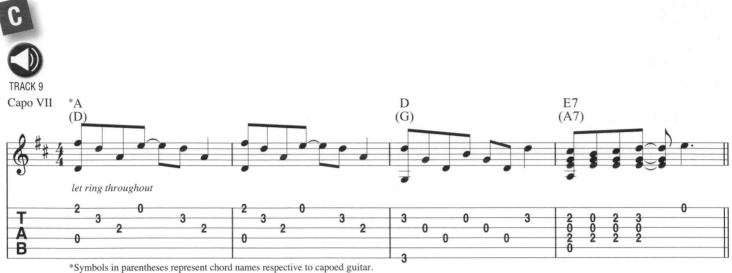

*Symbols in parentheses represent chord names respective to capoed guitar.
Symbols above reflect actual sounding chords. Capoed fret is "0" in tab.

CHORD CHART

General stuff: A chord chart is a musical road map that shows the chord progressions in a song or arrangement. On a typical chord chart, chords are given letter names and described as major, minor, seventh, diminished, augmented, etc.

Technical stuff: On a professional chart, the rhythm of specific figures is indicated. On a casual chart, the meter is written as a time signature; it is up to the player to interpret and to play stylistically within the implied rhythm structure.

An example of the latter type of chord chart will presume that a given style will dictate where the player will go within the road map. Consider the use of the 4/4 time signature, a quarter-note pulse as the basic rhythm structure (notated as slashes), and that the style is jazz. Each slash represents a quarter-note strum. Within these parameters, the chord name is indicated as G7. A seasoned jazz player who uses his/her ears may choose to color the chord and instead play a G13. It is assumed that the player would already know the correct chord voicing, have the right tone, and produce an appropriate rhythm pattern.

If the chart called for a hard-rock style, the G chord would likely become a G5 power chord, and the player would again use his/her ears to create an appropriate rhythm part. Though a quarter-note pattern is written, the feel may prompt the player to play steady eighth notes with downstrokes.

A more professional chart would show deliberate accents and syncopated figures, as well as requisite chord types. These are notated on a staff as letter names above slashes that indicate the required rhythms. This example depicts a chord chart for a section of "Stompin' at the Savoy," a classic swing tune. Note the more explicit chord names, like A♭13 and D♭maj7, and the accents that emphasize specific syncopated figures.

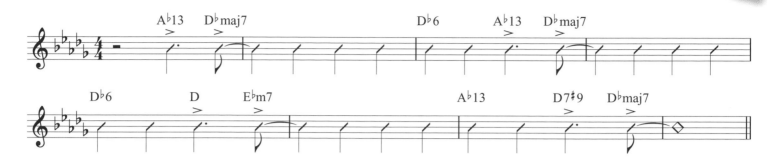

Playing stuff: A typical chord chart for a rocking 12-bar blues in G would look like this. Note the use of G5 and G6 to indicate the basic changes, the steady eighth-note rhythm, and the rising cadence figure in the turnaround: C5–C#5–D5. The words "shuffle feel" mean that the eighth notes are to be swung. See *Shuffle* (p. 101).

TRACK 10

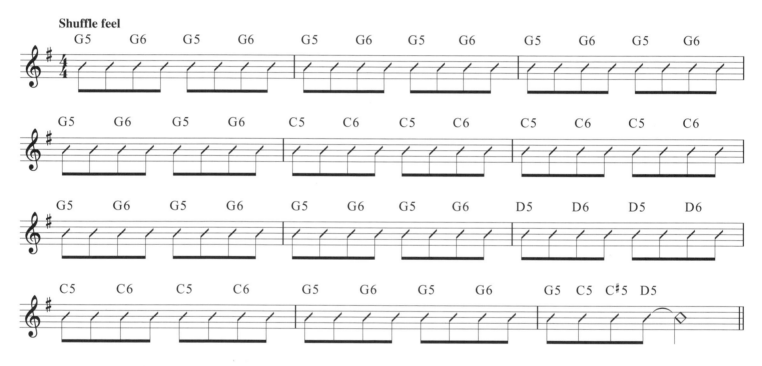

CLASSICAL GUITAR

Historic stuff: Classical guitar has a long and proud heritage. It's a broad term that encompasses Elizabethan lute traditions, true Baroque, Classical, Romantic, and Impressionistic transcriptions, various regional Spanish styles, and modern developments of the last century. Early composer/innovators of the classical guitar in the eighteenth and nineteenth centuries established the seminal repertory, including Mauro Giuliani, Fernando Sor, Francisco Tarrega, Matteo Carcassi, Federico Moreno Torroba, and Joaquin Turina. Subsequent important composers of the literature are Heitor Villa Lobos, Joaquin Rodrigo, Manuel De Falla, and Mario Castelnuovo Tedesco.

Andres Segovia is universally acknowledged as the performer who built the reputation of classical guitar in the twentieth century. Though he was not a composer (aside from technical pieces), he single-handedly brought the classical guitar to the fore as a serious concert instrument. His transcriptions of music by J.S. Bach are among the most revered pieces in the repertory, and his performances and recordings remain the yardstick by which all subsequent players are judged, including guitarists Julian Bream, John Williams, Christopher Parkening, Elliot Fisk, and Oscar Ghiglia, many of whom were his students.

Sonic stuff: Classical guitar is generally played solo on a nylon-string guitar. Segovia, Bream, Williams, and others are essentially soloists who only rarely concertize with an ensemble or orchestra. Working closely with builders to improve and perfect the nylon-string guitar, the problem of volume was solved by Segovia in the early twentieth century. Segovia also codified many of the right- and left-hand techniques and positions that produce the timbre and projection necessary for performance in large auditoriums.

Technical stuff: Classical guitar is played *fingerstyle*, using the *p–i–m–a* fingers (thumb–index–middle–ring; no pinky). The *rest stroke* (finger rests on the adjacent string after attack) is used to play certain single-note melodies, while the *free stroke* (no resting) plays most every other type of passage, from chord arpeggiation and plucking to complex counterpoint. The picking-hand's wrist is slightly arched, and the hand itself is held suspended over the strings, without resting on the face of the instrument, as in folk and country styles.

Playing stuff:

One of the most definitive examples of classical-guitar counterpoint is found in Bach's "Bourree" from *Lute Suite No. 1 in E minor*. With its prominent independent melodies, this excerpt exemplifies the Baroque idiom. This phrase was not originally written or conceived for the guitar; instead, it was transcribed from extant classical literature. The thumb plays all of the down-stemmed bass melodies, while the fingers articulate the treble strings.

TRACK 11

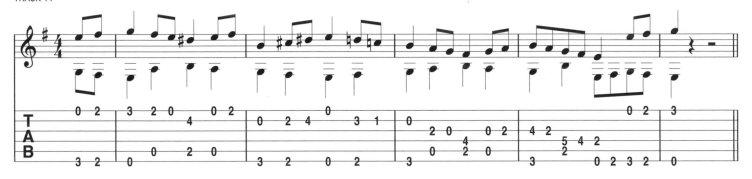

The filigree texture of this familiar Spanish piece presents the traditional Andalusian folk roots of classical guitar. Here, the guitar establishes a haunting repetitive figure with an E minor scale melody and a B pedal tone that is played on the open second string.

TRACK 11
(0:11)

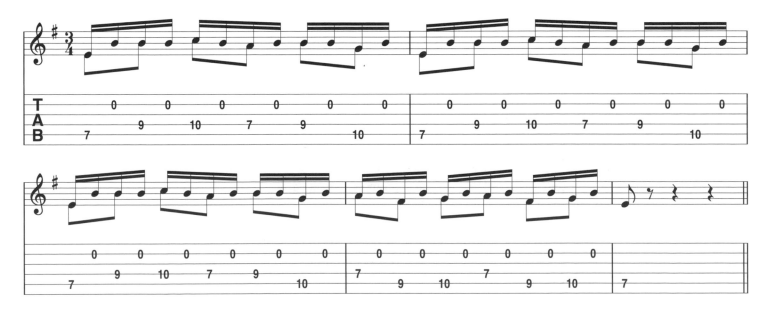

COMBO AMP

General stuff: "Combo amp" is an abbreviation for "combination amplifier." This is an amp with speakers and electronics combined in the same cabinet. It's a broad category covering everything from the 1937 Gibson EH-150 to the current computer-friendly Fender Cyber-Twin.

Combo amps vary considerably in output and configuration, from small low-wattage models with a single speaker to large high-powered cousins with as many as four speakers. Combo amps can be all-tube types, solid-state transistor types, or a hybrid style (i.e., a combination of tube and solid-state design).

The classic Fender combo amps of the fifties and sixties are all-tube models, while the Standel Custom used by Wes Montgomery, the Acoustic 134 favored by Pat Metheny, and the Yamaha G-100 in Mike Stern's rig are solid-state combo amps. The Music Man line of the seventies was a hybrid design with a solid-state preamp and a tube power amp. The Fender Cyber-Twin employs tubes in the preamp with digital sound processing and a solid-state power amp, and has a SPDIF output for direct connection to computers.

Sonic stuff: Many combo amps are "famous" (i.e., sought after by musicians for their specific desirable tones). Knowledgeable players pick amp tones like painters select colors. The vintage tweed Fender Bassman and the blackface Fender Super-Reverb (both with four 10-inch speakers) are prized by innumerable blues guitarists for their smooth distortion and distinctive timbre. The blackface Fender Twin-Reverb, with its greater power, clean sound, and increased headroom, is a perennial favorite among country, jazz, R&B, and pop players, as well as blues virtuoso Mike Bloomfield and Robby Krieger of the Doors in the sixties. The Vox AC-30 was made popular by the Beatles, Rolling Stones, and Yardbirds during the British Invasion. It has an unmistakable amp voice and remains an industry standard across genres—both Tom Petty and John Scofield have found it suitable for their music. Similarly, the Marshall Model 1962 "Blues Breaker" combo amp set the stage for the greater distortion, sustain, and thick tone of blues-rock when Eric Clapton mated it to his Les Paul at the historic John Mayall sessions.

The solid-state Roland JC-120 is a workhorse clean-tone amp with built-in chorus effects. Funk, jazz, and studio players consider it indispensable, but legendary bluesman Albert King also played one in later years. Jazz guitarists Joe Pass and Herb Ellis began playing small, lightweight, solid-state combo amps made by Polytone. The Mini-Brute, a mainstay of the Polytone line, has led to the current variants made by AER, Acoustic Image, Evans, and Jazz Kat.

Blackface Fender Twin-Reverb

Tweed Fender 4x10 Bassman

Vox AC-30

Marshall "Blues Breaker"

Jazz Kat

Roland JC-120

COMPING

General stuff: Comping is musical parlance for *accompaniment*. Comping in its broadest generic sense can occur in a wide range of styles, from jazz and western swing to rock 'n' roll and blues. Comping also relates to a particular approach and style in jazz accompaniment. Expert compers like Herb Ellis, Wes Montgomery, John Pisano, and Kenny Burrell have developed strategies for interacting with members of the rhythm section and ensembles.

Sonic stuff: Many players "lay out" (i.e., rest) or play straight four-to-the-bar rhythm guitar if the pianist is comping; others work out specific riffs or figures to be played in tandem with the keyboardist. Sometimes the pianist lays out and allows the guitarist to be the comping instrument. While other times the pianist plays a single-note line while the guitarist comps.

> *"Keep it simple. It's better to play too little than too much. Many players turn up the volume and play big, syrupy-sounding chords which get in everybody's way and make the whole rhythm section sound logy and dull. The modern player should turn down his volume and strive for a live sound and long sound that blends with the drummer's top cymbal and long sound of the bass player."*

> —Herb Ellis, *The Herb Ellis Jazz Guitar Style*, 1963

Playing stuff: Comping in jazz is an art form. When playing in organ groups or substituting for the piano in large ensembles, the comping of the guitarist is fundamental, supplying harmony, rhythmic variety, and support for a soloist. The notion of balanced textures, smooth voice leading, interesting chord types, rhythmic punctuation and phraseology, and passing chords are paramount concerns. The following phrase contains all of the above and is based on the daunting progression of John Coltrane's "Giant Steps." Note the use of small, compact chords, which were chosen to avoid clashes with the bass and common tones in progressions like B6/9–D7–Gmaj7 and Am11–D9–Gmaj9–B♭13. Passing chords are used to connect E♭maj7 and Am11 in measure 3.

TRACK 12

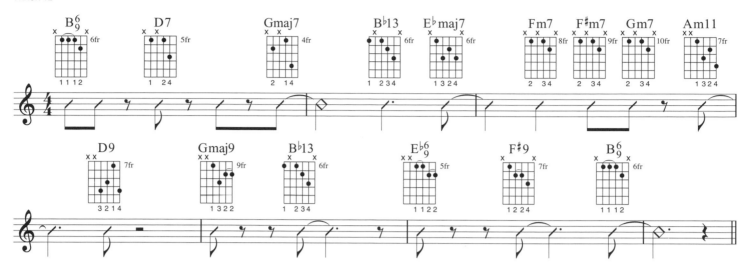

Comping in blues and classic rock 'n' roll is readily expressed by this absolutely emblematic rhythm figure. In this phrase, the guitar assumes a steady eighth-note pattern and alternates between root–5th and root–6th dyads.

TRACK 12
(0:15)

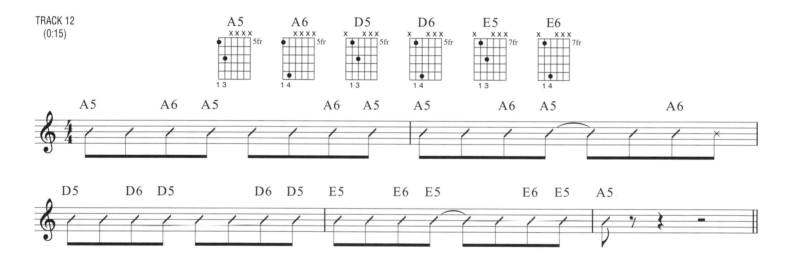

COUNTRY

Historic stuff: Country music, also called country & western, is a uniquely American art form. The origins of country go back to the twenties and old-time bluegrass, Anglo-American folk songs, string-band music, fiddle-tunes, and the hillbilly subgenre. In the forties, two camps of country formed; one side retained its folksy acoustic-based bluegrass and hillbilly roots, while the other looked to the future, with amplified instruments, western swing, honky tonk, pop, and rockabilly. In due course, eighties pop values affected country music and its production values. The glossy Nashville sound dominated for a number of years until a crop of young, latter-day country players like Brad Paisley and Dwight Yoakam led the return to its roots.

General stuff: What is country? Country music to the trained ear is remarkably diverse. It can mean Johnny Cash, Roy Rogers, Bob Wills and the Texas Playboys, Dolly Parton, George Jones, Buck Owens, Jimmie Rodgers, Garth Brooks, Kenny Rogers, Asleep at the Wheel, Patsy Cline, Merle Haggard, the Judds, Tennessee Ernie Ford, Emmylou Harris, Ricky Skaggs, or Travis Tritt. Similarly, country guitar can mean Merle Travis, Chet Atkins, Hank Garland, Don Rich, Tony Rice,

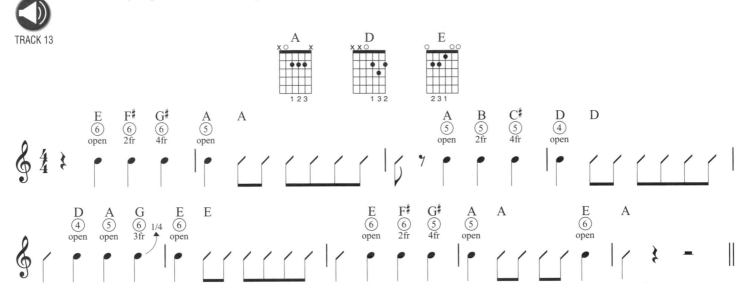

Phil Baugh, Willie Nelson, Roy Clark, Jerry Reed, Albert Lee, Jimmy Bryant, Doc Watson, Keith Urban, Doyle Dykes, or Scotty Anderson—and, at times, James Burton, Buffalo Springfield, George Harrison, and Scotty Moore.

Playing stuff: Traditional country strumming is exemplified by this driving rhythm phrase. Way back before country and bluegrass parted ways (sometime in the forties), acoustic patterns with simple, open-position "cowboy chords" were the norm and the lingua franca of the genre. Note the use of steady eighth-note strum rhythms, which are alternated with bass-register pickup melodies.

TRACK 13

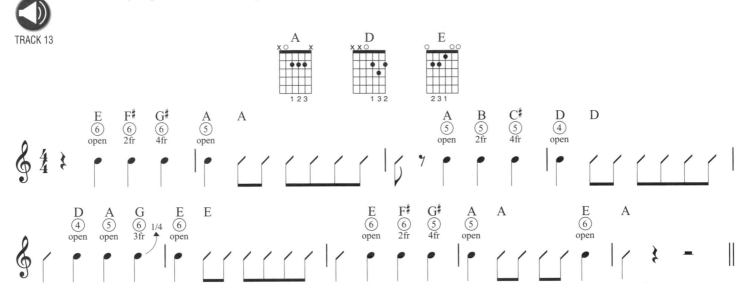

Modern country picking owes a tremendous debt to Appalachian melodies and string-band origins. This lick is played on electric guitar, with a twangy country tone, but sports an undeniable connection with the fiddle tune via its winding scalar lines, two-beat groove, and propulsive rhythm feel.

TRACK 13
(0:14)

DADGAD TUNING

General stuff: "Dad-Gad" (DADGAD) is a popular alternate tuning used in Celtic, New Age, pop, rock, and folk styles. DADGAD is the most well-known modal tuning and can be seen as an open Dsus4 (suspended 4th) chord. The resultant open, unresolved sound is a big part of its charm. DADGAD is particularly well-suited for playing modal melodies with droning open strings.

Historic stuff: DADGAD reached the mainstream through a circuitous route. Celtic folk singers and U.K. guitarists like John Renbourne and Bert Jansch caught the ear of future rock god Jimmy Page, who began using the modal tuning in a rock setting—first, with the Yardbirds, and, later, in Led Zeppelin.

Since the sixties, DADGAD has flourished across genres and has found a particular niche within the New Age movement, where it is especially prized for its otherworldly modal quality. DADGAD is the sound of the Yardbirds' "White Summer," Led Zeppelin's "Black Mountainside" and "Kashmir," Michael Hedges' "Ragamuffin," Phil Keaggy's "Country Down," Adrian Legg's "Coging's Glory," Bert Jansch's "St. Fiacre," and many pieces by Pierre Bensusan.

Technical stuff: DADGAD is accomplished by lowering the sixth, second, and first strings in standard tuning a whole step, to D, A, and D, respectively.

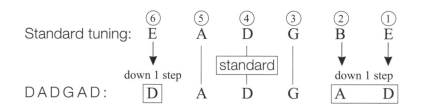

Playing stuff: This phrase conveys the unusual, vaguely ethnic quality associated with DADGAD tuning. There are allusions to Celtic and Eastern modal sounds throughout the folksy figure, and the parallel octave passage, with droning open strings at the phrase ending, is absolutely definitive.

TRACK 14

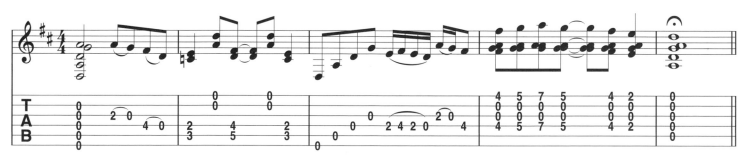

The rock and pop side of DADGAD is presented in this chordal figure. Ringing open strings are a prominent part of every chord in the phrase, which is the essence of the drone. Note the uncommon fingerings of typical suspended chords and triads, as well as the D5 power chord.

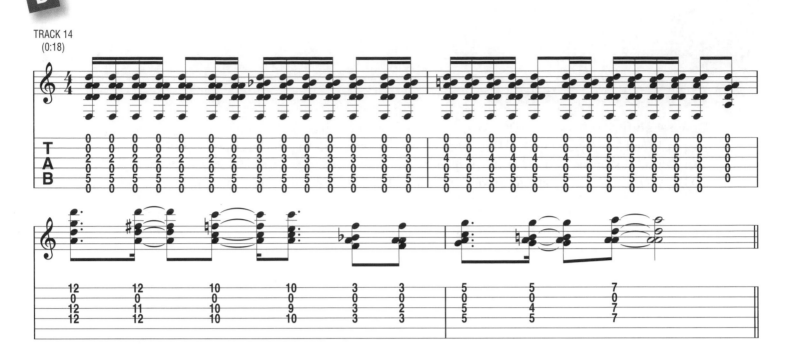

DISTORTION

General stuff: It's hard to believe that distortion used to be considered an undesirable aspect of amplified guitar music. At one time, many amp manufacturers promised loud, distortion-free sound. Indeed, in 1961, Fender yanked its flagship tweed 4x10 Bassman of the fifties from the production line because it was deemed to be too distorted. Appropriately, this particular model was the template for early Marshall amplifiers, which turned distortion into a requisite tonal color for electric guitarists.

Technical stuff: Distortion occurs when the electric-guitar output signal *overdrives* an amplifier. The guitar's full output produces enough level to overdrive most tube amps by simply raising the volume to an input beyond its power-handling capabilities. At this point, the signal flattens out or clips because the voltage peaks of the signal are trying to go higher than the amp permits. This is the principle and strategy behind the use of small low-wattage amps for distorted sounds in recording studios. In many classic tube amps, like old Fenders, Marshalls, Voxes, and Gibsons, the natural distorted sound is a much-desired timbre, as in the case of the vintage Bassman.

Sonic stuff: Guitar-amp combinations are often chosen for their ability to deliver desirable distortion. Consider the combination of a humbucker-equipped Les Paul and a Marshall amp, or a Fender Strat paired with a Vox AC-30 amp. The humbucker/Marshall sound is the basis of hard rock and metal tone, while the Strat/Vox sound has its own unique semi-distortion tonality that is ideal for pop rock, electric blues, roots-rock music, and contemporary country.

Many rock players require additional distortion and thus have increased the level of the guitar output with various boosters, preamps, and overdrive boxes. Single-coil pickups have less output than humbuckers, prompting innumerable Strat players to add gain boosters or fuzz boxes to the signal path. Jimi Hendrix used a Fuzz-Face distortion unit with his Marshall stacks, while Stevie Ray Vaughan applied a Tube Screamer to his Fender combo amps. Some amp manufacturers addressed this need during the seventies, building amps with master-volume and channel-volume controls, which allowed the player to crank the preamp for distortion and adjust the output level with a second control. Others players, like Tom Scholz, Steve Lukather, and Steve Vai, have used a power attenuator or load resistor to lower the level of the entire amp—preamp and power amp— allowing both sections to be overdriven and fed into a second power amp and speakers or a speaker emulator and a mixer.

The distortion of a standard tube amp is readily accessed by simply raising its volume and tone controls (as desired) and using the guitar's volume control or a volume pedal to determine gain. This type of distortion increases incrementally with the signal's level. Unless you're playing large venues, this procedure is usually inadequate for high-gain results with large, high-wattage rigs. Smaller amps are often used in clubs and miked. With an amp that is rated between 15 to 50 watts, overdrive and distortion can be achieved at lower volume levels. That's why amps like Fender Champs, Princetons, Pro Juniors, Deluxes, Vox AC-15s, and Gibson EH-150s present a viable solution in smaller venues and recording studios.

Another solution is the solid-state distortion effects unit, which can produce outboard distortion with any amp. These units are often placed early in the signal path, feeding a distorted sound to subsequent pitch shifter, wah-wah, chorus, phaser, and echo pedals, and then the amp input.

Distortion effects units generally fall into two categories: Overdrive and Distortion. The former seek to emulate the milder, warmer tone of an overdriven tube amp, while the latter create harder, more aggressive fuzz sounds. The Ibanez Tube Screamer and the Boss Blues Driver are examples of overdrive boxes. Distortion pedals are exemplified by the MXR Distortion Plus, Boss DS-1, and Boss Heavy Metal. Related to distortion units are the true fuzz boxes, which include the Maestro Fuzz-Tone, Dallas-Arbiter Fuzz Face, Electro-Harmonix Big Muff, and Sola Sound Tone Bender. These units have an unmistakable gritty, hard-clipped sound.

Playing stuff: When using a distortion unit, follow these basic guidelines: Turn your guitar volume all the way up. Use the effect's volume to adjust the difference in level when the unit is on or off. The overall volume is set on the amp.

DOUBLE STOP

General stuff: A double stop, also called a dyad, is two notes played simultaneously. On the guitar, a double stop can be played on adjacent strings or with one or more strings in between. Depending on the desired texture and musical effect, double stops can be articulated with a pick, with hybrid picking, or fingerstyle.

In the broadest sense, any interval can be a double stop, including the shapes in a Chuck Berry lead/rhythm break or the fingerpicked walking 10th intervals in classical guitar and the Beatles' "Blackbird." Moreover, double stops can mean the sweet parallel 3rds in pop music, the hard-rock 4ths in "Smoke on the Water," the honky-tonk claw-picking style of Jerry Reed, the parallel 6ths of country music, the slurred two-note figures in R&B, and numerous piano-inspired jazz and blues licks.

Sonic stuff: In a more specific idiomatic sense, the term double stop is commonly used to describe shapes on adjacent strings and stylistic usage. This is how Chuck Berry applies double stops to his solos and riffs, forming the basis for the dyad in rock 'n' roll improvisation. Countless players have accessed this sound, from Scotty Moore, Jimmy Page, Hank Garland, Jimi Hendrix, Stevie Ray Vaughan, and Kenny Burrell to John Lennon, James Burton, Eddie Van Halen, and Howard Roberts—virtually every guitar player with a blues base.

Playing stuff: Double stops are exemplified in this ode to Chuck Berry, who practically invented the style we call rock 'n' roll lead guitar. This telling lead/rhythm phrase combines several idiomatic moves, from straight-barred solo shapes to parallel 3rds.

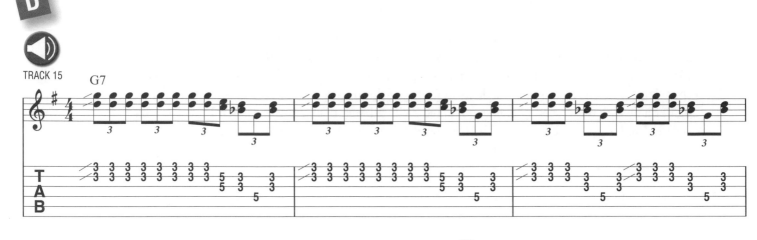

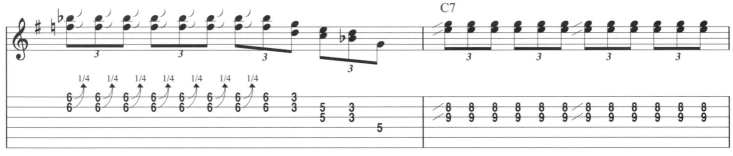

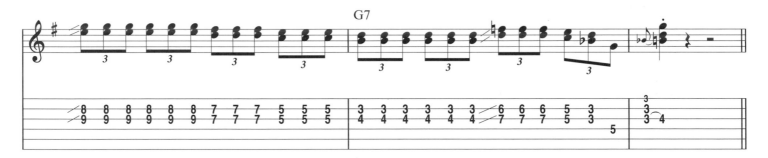

Double stops are often found in jazz, swing, and blues styles. Below is the sort of double-stop figure that is used by Howard Roberts, Joe Pass, Kenny Burrell, and George Benson. Note the use of keyboard-like pedal points throughout the passage.

DROP-D TUNING:

General stuff: Drop-D tuning is the most popular and most common alternate tuning—and argu-ably the simplest. Drop-D tuning is accomplished by dropping (lowering in pitch) the low E string a whole step to D. In Drop-D tuning, the guitar is tuned, from low to high: D–A–D–G–B–E. Why is Drop-D tuning used? The short and logical answer is that it increases the guitar's range, making possible chords and bass lines unavailable in standard tuning.

Found in jazz, blues, country, classical, hard rock, and heavy metal, Drop-D tuning is both ubiq-uitous and stylistically diverse. Johnny Smith, Andres Segovia, Chet Atkins, Edddie Van Halen, George Benson, and Adam Jones of Tool have made divergent and uniformly shrewd use of this simple maneuver.

Playing stuff: This phrase is based on the use of natural harmonics, open strings, and Drop-D tuning. The chiming music-box pattern culminates with two unique voicings made accessible by Drop-D tuning, D7sus4 and G. D7sus4 includes the D natural harmonic, as well as low D on the dropped sixth string. The G chord is a widely spaced open voicing with a spread fingering that is facilitated by Drop-D tuning.

TRACK 16

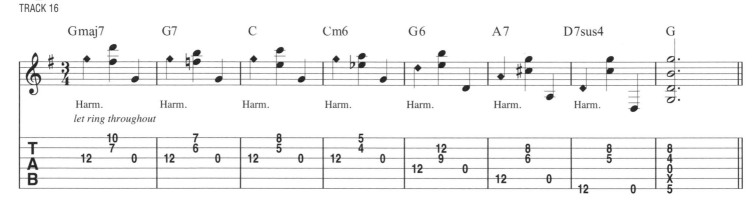

The hard-rock face of Drop-D tuning is presented in this colorful Soundgarden-style riff. Here, unique arpeggiated suspended chords and 5th-based sonorities can be generated with simple, largely barred fingering shapes that are not possible (or impractical, at the least) in standard tuning.

TRACK 16
(0:20)

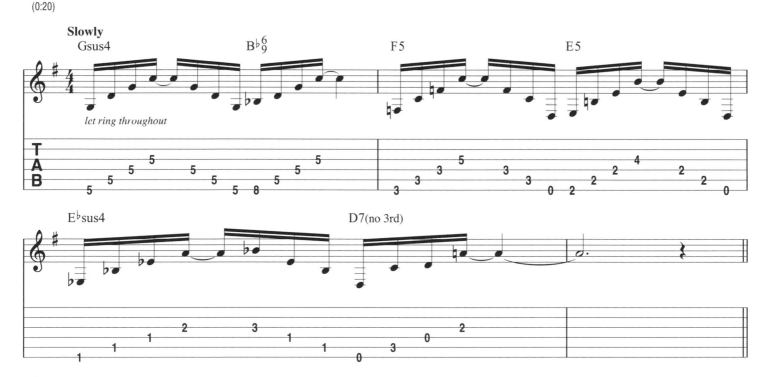

EFFECTS

General stuff: Effects processors are as numerous and diverse as the players who use them. Effects for the electric guitar are the most common, though, these days, acoustic guitars are often amplified with dedicated amps that contain processing like chorus, reverb, and delay. Effects vary considerably in type and tone, from physical machines with moving parts, like the tape-echo units and Leslie rotating-speaker cabinets, to vintage analog effects with germanium transistors, to modern digital-effects units.

Sonic stuff: Guitar effects processors range from simple reverb to time-based sounds like echo, chorus, and flanging, modulation effects like vibrato, tremolo and phasing, and tone-altering devices such as fuzz boxes, envelope followers (also called auto-wah), octave dividers, harmonizers, and ring modulators.

Of these effects, fuzz has become a separate, much-debated sub-category for guitarists. Desire for different degrees and qualities of distortion, analog and true tube overdrive, and classic fuzz tone have resulted in a virtual cavalcade of effects units, from the vintage Maestro Fuzz-Tone (remember the Stones' "Satisfaction"?), the Dallas-Arbiter Fuzz Face (Jimi Hendrix's favorite), and the Colorsound Tone Bender (used by Jeff Beck), to the MXR Distortion Plus (preferred by Randy Rhoads), the Boss Distortion DS-1 box (think Gary Moore and Joe Satriani), and the Ibanez Tube Screamer (a perennial choice of Stevie Ray Vaughan). These units are plugged in between the guitar and a conventional amplifier. Other guitarists, like Carlos Santana, Eddie Van Halen, Steve Lukather, Robben Ford, and Allan Holdsworth, prefer to get their distortion from overdriven amplifiers that function as glorified, overfed fuzz boxes. Each has its own sound and response.

Multi-effects units were developed in the late seventies and were the norm by the early eighties. Multi-effects units combined numerous effects in one box, some of which were of the pro-level rack type, like the Lexicon, Ibanez, and Yamaha units, while others are represented by floor stomp-box types, such as those currently made by Roland and Digitech.

Nowadays, many amplifiers come with built-in, programmable effects, often of the high-quality digital variety. Some, like the Fender Cyber Twin, have included actual tube preamps to simulate the sound of overdriven tube amps, as well as the standard effects sounds favored by many rock, pop, and metal guitarists.

Playing stuff: What are those effects, and what do they sound like? It is instructive and illuminating to play a similar lick through some basic types of processors to hear what they do. Let's put a pentatonic blues lick to the test.

TRACK 17 Echo is at the extreme end of time-based processing. This example exploits longer and easily perceived delays of the input signal. Here, the delay is set for 350 milliseconds with a fair amount of feedback to keep the echo repeats going. Note: Low feedback settings produce smaller amounts of regeneration, like the single, tight slap back echo commonly heard in rockabilly.

TRACK 17
(0:09) Chorus and flanging are at the short end of time-based effects. Very short delay settings of 40 to 80 milliseconds color and enlarge the guitar sound. This effect is a favorite of Andy Summers, Pat Metheny, Alex Lifeson, and countless studio guitarists.

TRACK 17
(0:15) Distortion is a mixed bag, as previously noted. This example presents classic fuzz tone as popularized in the sixties. In contrast to smooth amp distortion, the idea here is to produce a sharp, buzzy, square-wave effect.

TRACK 17
(0:20) Pitch-shifters, harmonizers, and octave-dividers are members of the same sonic family. Here, the pitch-shifter is set to generate a second note that is a 5th higher than the first.

EIGHTH NOTES

General stuff: Eighth notes are a common subdivision of rhythm. Consider a measure of 4/4 meter as having four equal beats (i.e., quarter notes) to the bar. The quarter notes are counted "1–2–3–4," and the basic pulse is on beats 1 and 3. Within this structure, a measure of music can be subdivided into eight equal notes, appropriately called eighth notes. A measure of eighth notes is counted "1–and, 2–and, 3–and, 4–and."

Many rhythmic phrases are based on eighth-note beats. Moreover, many styles of music are characterized by their treatment of eighth-note rhythms. Among these are rock 'n' roll, techno pop, heavy metal, swing jazz, blues, Baroque classical music, Latin and Bossa Nova, and African and Afro-Cuban music.

Technical stuff: It is useful to visualize eighth-note rhythms on a grid. If we create a chart of boxes to represent a one-measure time line with its counts, we can create a representation of a measure of eighth notes. In this diagram, the basic pulse is indicated by accents over beats 1 and 3. A string of eighth notes are shown in the bottom line, under the boxes and count.

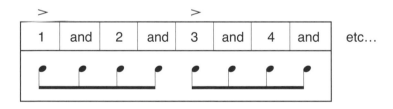

Playing stuff: Beyond math and theory is the real world of feel, where your perception of eighth-note rhythms must be put to the test. Where to start? It is helpful in the beginning to put on your favorite music and purposely count eighth notes along with a track. This exercise is particularly easy when you relate straight eighth-note rhythms to rock songs like the Beatles' "Get Back," Deep Purple's "Smoke on the Water," Van Halen's "Unchained," and Ozzy Osbourne's "I Don't Know." Similarly useful results can be obtained with J.S. Bach's "Bourrée in E Minor" and several keyboard inventions.

In these examples, eighth-note rhythms are presented in three common musical contexts.

TRACK 18

Eighth-note rock rhythms are among the most accessible to the listener. This exemplary rock phrase is made of three chords and steady eighth-note strums, yet is absolutely transcendent.

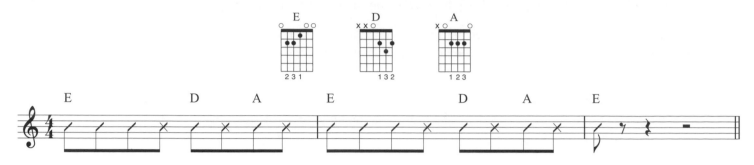

TRACK 18
(0:07)

Eighth-notes are the most common and prevalent rhythms in swing jazz. This lick features swung eighth notes and is based on the solo style of Charlie Christian, the founding father of modern jazz guitar. His improvisations regularly exploited strings of eighth notes.

TRACK 18
(0:15)

Eighth-note arpeggiation is frequently found in the metronomic riffs and rhythm figures of textural pop and alternative-rock songs. This phrase is palm-muted, which adds to its percussive, rhythmic feeling.

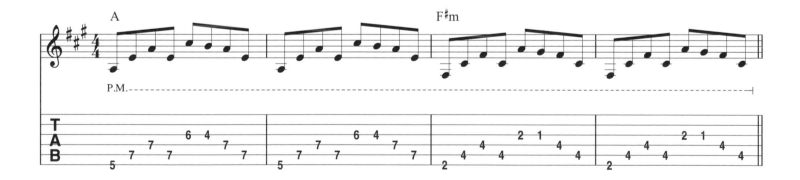

FEEDBACK

General stuff: Feedback is the term used to describe a common phenomenon of amplified music. Feedback occurs when an electric guitar or microphone picks up its own amplified signal and feeds it back through the amplifier.

It is crucial to distinguish between harmonic and microphonic feedback. *Microphonic feedback* is generally undesirable, unpredictable, and sounds like an uncontrollable squeal or low rumble with no viable musical relation to the notes an instrument is producing. It is similar to the high-pitched noise a microphone makes when placed too close to a PA speaker. A faulty guitar pickup or amplifier tube that has become "microphonic" can yield a comparable result.

By contrast, *harmonic feedback* is musically related to what an electric guitarist is playing and is a member of the note's harmonic-overtone series. This means that the feedback has musical merit, can be anticipated and controlled, and is employed by the musician as a coloristic and expressive resource.

Sonic stuff: Controlled harmonic feedback began with the rock styles of the sixties. This type of feedback has been used by and associated with Jeff Beck, Eric Clapton, the Beatles, Jimi Hendrix, Carlos Santana, Ted Nugent, and practically every electric guitarist to follow. Many players, like Clapton and Santana, regularly use feedback to produce infinite sustain and lend a vocal quality to their music. Harmonic feedback is now a standard sound in rock, pop, and metal.

There are numerous factors to consider when attempting to create and control harmonic feedback with an electric guitar. These include the player's location relative to his or her amplifier (physical proximity and position), the susceptibility of the guitar to feed back, the output strength of the pickups, and the amount of gain in the amp. Some players use a fuzz unit, treble booster, compressor, or volume booster to coax harmonic feedback from the guitar/amp combination. Others prefer to create feedback with just a high-gain amplifier, like a cranked Marshall or Mesa Boogie, and the guitar. Additionally, players like Ted Nugent and Trey Anastasio up the ante by using a hollowbody guitar, which is inherently more prone to feed back.

> *"It feels really good to hold a note for days, to control the feedback on just one beam of power. Sometimes the way you can hold a note depends on how you set the tone and volume controls on the guitar and amp.*
>
> —Carlos Santana, *Guitar Player*, 1970

> *"I never use sustain devices at all. I just do it the old fashioned way—just get close to the amplifier. I still have to move back and forth until I can find just the right kind of sustain."*
>
> —Carlos Santana, *Guitar Player*, 1974

> *"When one note feeds back in a certain spot it will occupy all the acoustic area of that note and no other note will be able to get in edgewise. I can catch an A-note feedback, step to the side two inches, and another note will kick in. I used to put tape on the stage to mark the spots."*
>
> —Ted Nugent, *Guitar Player*, 1976

Playing stuff: This simple rock melody demonstrates the sound of harmonic feedback that is produced by a guitar with a humbucking bridge pickup played through a high-gain amplifier.

FENDER TONE

General stuff: Fender tone is a catch-all term used to describe the (now generic) sound that is produced by Fender solidbody electric guitars, most notably the two-pickup Telecaster and three-pickup Stratocaster. Fender guitars are reknowned for their twang. Happenstance has it that the Tele and Strat were originally designed with country pickers and western-swing players in mind, and twang is synonymous with those genres. This quality prevails and distinguishes Fender tone from that of other instruments.

Historic stuff: The earliest advocates of the Tele, Fender's first solidbody electric, introduced in 1950, were slick pickers like Jimmy Wyble (of Spade Cooley's western band), cowboy acts like the Silver Spur Boys, and virtuoso country guitarist Jimmy Bryant. But that didn't stop Gatemouth Brown, B.B. King, Carl Perkins, Paul Burlison (Johnny Burnette's Rock 'n' Roll Trio), Gene Vincent, and Steve Cropper from picking up Teles in the fifties. Tele twang was epitomized by the Bakersfield brand of country rock in the sixties and performers such as James Burton, Buck Owens, and Don Rich, but it was also harnessed by Muddy Waters, Albert Collins, Joe Messina (Motown), Jeff Beck, George Harrison, Jimmy Page, Roy Buchanan, and jazz-oriented session players like Howard Roberts and Bob Bain.

Nowadays, the Telecaster family tree includes all of the aforementioned players, as well as disparate guitarists such as Keith Richards, Bruce Springsteen, Ed Bickert, Albert Lee, Andy Summers, Al McKay, Merle Haggard, Bill Frisell, Danny Gatton, Robben Ford, Roy Nichols, Jerry Donahue, Ted Greene, and Scotty Anderson.

Sonic stuff: The classic Tele tone is epitomized by the sharp treble bite of the slanted single-coil bridge pickup, which is ideal for country picking and rock 'n' roll. This remains the definitive sound of the instrument, unmatched by any other. But the Tele is capable of soft rhythm tones with no treble as in its original early-fifties incarnation, a unique neck-pickup sound.

In search of further tone expansion, Tele master James Burton designed a signature model with three single-coil pickups. Moreover, some players, like Albert Collins, Andy Summers, Jeff Beck, Mike Stern, and Keith Richards, have installed neck humbuckers in their Teles to broaden the guitar's sonic palette.

Historic stuff: Today, the Stratocaster is synonymous with rock-guitar heroics, but it wasn't always so. Like the Tele, the Strat was the brainchild of Leo Fender and originally developed in collaboration with West Coast country players like Bill Carson. Introduced in 1954, the Strat upped the ante with three single-coil pickups, a contoured double-cutaway body, and, most important, a hand vibrato tailpiece that was intended to emulate Hawaiian guitar and country pedal-steel sounds. Appropriately, western-swing legend Eldon Shamblin (Bob Wills' Texas Playboys) became one of the first Strat artists.

The Strat soon found advocates across genres. In the fifties, pop players like Buddy Merrill (Lawrence Welk) and Mary Kaye, as well as bluesmen Buddy Guy and Otis Rush, used Strats. Buddy Holly, Ritchie Valens, Ike Turner, the Ventures, Dick Dale, the Surfaris, Beach Boys, Curtis Mayfield, and Hank Marvin made Strats a vital part of classic rock 'n' roll.

The Strat fell out of favor briefly with rockers during the mid-sixties British Invasion but was dramatically brought out of its decline by the ultimate Strat cat, Jimi Hendrix, in 1967. Jimi's groundbreaking efforts launched a post-sixties school of Strat players, beginning with the conversions of Jeff Beck, Eric Clapton, Ritchie Blackmore, and Robin Trower. Even Larry Carlton opted for a Strat-style guitar in the mid-eighties. Other significant Strat cats include David Gilmour, Rory Gallagher, Mark Knopfler, Stevie Ray and Jimmie Vaughan, Yngwie Malmsteen, Eric Johnson, Robert Cray, Henry Garza, and John Mayer.

Sonic stuff: The Strat's definitive tones are closely associated with its unique electronic circuit. Fender's three single-coil pickups were originally selected with a three-way switch for separate neck, middle, or bridge tones. Savvy players soon discovered unique sounds lurking in the "in-between positions" and wedged their switches accordingly to select those additional distinctive tones. Hendrix, Clapton, and Knopfler created unforgettable quacking timbres with the bridge and middle pickups engaged simultaneously. The neck and middle pickups offered a similar but mellower option. By the late seventies, demand for all five Strat sounds prompted the invention of a stock five-position switch, now standard.

In the eighties, the Strat was modified by many leading hard-rock and metal players to sport two single-coil pickups (neck and middle) and a bridge humbucker. This layout, favored by Steve Vai, Steve Lukather, Dave Murray, Brad Gillis, Kirk Hammett, Jake E. Lee, Reb Beach, and Vernon Reid, allowed players to go from thinner Fender single-coil sounds for textural parts and funky rhythm to fat humbucker tone for shred solos.

Fender 1952 Telecaster

Fender James Burton Tele

Fender Stratocaster

FINGERPICKING

General stuff: Fingerpicking is one of the most prevalent and important techniques on the guitar. It is used in every form of music in which the guitar has a presence. Fingerpicking ranges from the finesse of classical artists Andres Segovia and John Williams and the jazz chord-melody work of Joe Pass, George Van Eps, and Ted Greene to the country polyphony of Chet Atkins and the blues solos of Otis Rush and Hubert Sumlin. Moreover, major rock guitarists like Jeff Beck, Mark Knopfler, and Robby Krieger have long discarded their flat picks in favor of playing exclusively with their fingers, while others employ some form of fingerpicking for alternative textures and articulations.

Technical stuff: Fingerpicking generally means plucking the guitar strings with the thumb and finger tips. Classical guitar literature names these digits *p–i–m–a* from the Spanish tradition: Pulgar=thumb (*p*), Indicio=index (*i*), Medio=middle (*m*), and Anular=ring (*a*). The pinky is not used in classical traditionally, although it is ocassionally employed in jazz or country styles.

Classical fingerpicking has a formalized set of rules and principles with respect to how the thumb, index, middle, and ring fingers are to be placed and used to play chords, single notes, and arpeggios.

> *"The right hand should not touch the face of the guitar—when you play, it will be raised about 3 ½ inches. An inverted 'V' [from the player's perspective] is formed by the thumb and first finger. This ensures independent movement by each, without crowding when you play."*
>
> —Frederick Noad, *Solo Guitar Playing*, 1968

Classical fingerpicking breaks down into two types of strokes: rest stroke and free stroke. The rest stroke is generally used for playing single-note melody lines and is played in a two-part alternating pattern with the index and middle fingers. For example, the index-finger tip attacks the string in a downward motion and comes to rest on the adjacent string, dampening it. Then, in a similar motion, the middle finger picks a different note and comes to rest. The two alternate in a continuous pattern.

The *free stroke* is used for chords and arpeggios. The technique calls for the hand to be arched over the strings, away from the face of the guitar. The thumb, or *p*, plucks bass strings, while *i–m–a* fingers generally attack the top three strings. The thumb and fingers pluck the strings in a small, semi-circular "gripping" motion and remain floating over the strings. The fingers do not rest on adjacent strings. Chords are plucked together in a synchronized motion that is similar to a keyboard attack. In arpeggios, chord tones are plucked one by one with the thumb and fingers.

Sonic stuff: Country, blues, jazz, folk, and rock players often deviate from the strict rules of classical fingerpicking. It is common to see the plucking-hand fingers rest on the guitar face in folk and rock styles. Country pickers Chet Atkins and Merle Travis play with a collapsed wrist to mute bass strings. Jazz guitarists Joe Pass, John Pisano, and George Van Eps often use the pinky to pluck larger chords. Moreover, Chet Atkins, Merle Travis, Scotty Moore, James Burton, Ed Bickert, and Eric Johnson use various combinations of thumb pick, finger picks, and flat pick in conjunction with standard fingerpicking.

Playing stuff: Classical fingerpicking of broken chords is exemplified by this haunting Spanish theme. Use the free-stroke technique and *p–i–m–a* fingers exclusively. The thumb plays the sixth string, while ring finger plays the first, middle plays the second, and index plays the third.

TRACK 20

Blues players frequently apply fingerpicking to Delta-style figures. This turnaround employs a variant of classical free-stroke technique.

TRACK 20
(0:12)

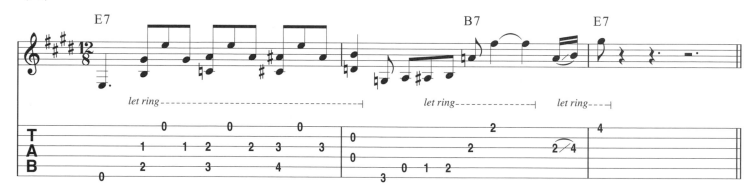

Country and rockabilly players have found the "banjo roll" style of articulation valuable for arpeggio figures. This phrase also contains a fingerpicked string bend and plucked chord.

TRACK 20
(0:21)

Fingerpicking is put to good use in walking bass lines. This Dm7–G7 jazz intro figure employs the technique to create a contrapuntal feeling of an independent upright bass player walking in quarter notes while a piano is comping.

TRACK 20
(0:32)

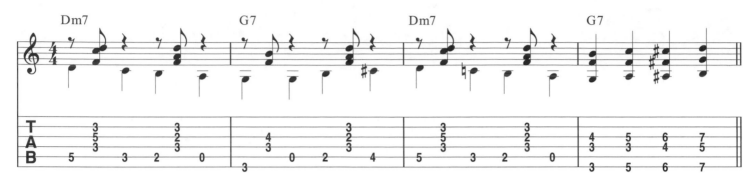

FUNK

General stuff: Funk is a musical style that grew out of the R&B of the sixties. The roots of funk reach back to a variety of sources, including blues, classic "race records" of the forties and fifties, gospel, rock 'n' roll, soul jazz, and Motown. Mature funk is characterized by a looping, repetitive quality that exploits an ensemble groove in which different interlocking instruments take on a minimal but integral role. Funk is a classic case of "less is more."

Historic stuff: James Brown is globally acclaimed as the founding father of funk. His music of the fifties had a traditional R&B bent but, by the mid-sixties, he had developed a unique style and sound that was based on extended vamps, minimal but kinetic arrangements, and the scratchy guitar of Jimmy Nolen.

Sonic stuff: Jimmy "Chank" Nolen is the personification of funk guitar. If James Brown is the founding father of funk, then Nolen is the founder of funk guitar. His pioneering style emphasized tight, looping single-note riffs, jazz-oriented chords, and percussive, scratchy strumming. The latter is arguably the most readily recognizable sonic aspect of funk guitar.

Many of Nolen's riffs are based on sixteenth-note strum patterns and jazz chord voicings, as in the famous break of "Papa's Got a Brand New Bag." Other definitive Nolen funk figures exploit minimal pulse-oriented, on-the-beat strums and single-note ensemble licks, as in "I Got You (I Feel Good)." In yet others, stylistic muted-string scratches and extended jazz chords are at the center of the music. Consider the JB classic "Get Up."

Funk has since crossed over to affect a wide variety of modern music. Rockers like Joe Walsh, Jeff Beck, Jimi Hendrix, and Robin Trower got the message early on and frequently incorporated funk-guitar elements into their playing.

The very nature and MO of soul and R&B music in the seventies was changed by second-generation funk acts like Parliament/Funkadelic, the Isley Brothers, Sly and the Family Stone, Kool and the Gang, Earth, Wind and Fire, and George Clinton, who expounded on the style built by the James Brown band.

Funk affected many jazz, pop, disco, and rock acts to follow, including the Bee Gees, Commodores, Red Hot Chili Peppers, Living Colour, Stevie Wonder, Herbie Hancock, George Benson, Nile Rodgers, Lenny Kravitz, Spin Doctors, and Rage Against the Machine. It goes without saying that funk is a must-know dialect of contemporary music.

Playing stuff: Funk guitar is characterized by the cycling vamp riff. Here, the Jimmy Nolen influence is undeniable with the use of 9th and 13th chords, chromatic motion, sixteenth-note rhythms, and those indispensable scratchy strum figures.

TRACK 21

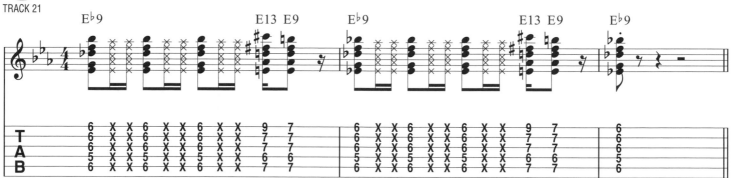

Funk guitar is also famous for its single-note loop riffs. This emblematic lick makes use of a repetitive single-note riff, which is played in sixteenth notes and made even more percussive by the stylistic palm muting.

TRACK 21
(0:08)

GIBSON TONE

General stuff: Gibson tone is inextricably bound to the advent of the electric guitar itself. The first commercially marketed Electric Spanish guitar (bearing the prefix "ES") was a Gibson, the ES-150. Practically every major electric guitar player in the thirties, forties, and early fifties played a Gibson—or strived to— whether in jazz, blues, country, or rock 'n' roll. The Gibson electric sound is synonymous with rich tones, resonance, and sustain. And Gibson designs and innovations have influenced countless manufacturers and luthiers.

Historic stuff: During the heyday of swing music, Charlie Christian established the classic jazz-guitar tone, which remains nearly unchanged to the present day. He achieved his tone with the first Gibson archtop electric guitar and a small Gibson amplifier. At about the same time, Christian's colleague, T-Bone Walker, laid the cornerstone of electric blues tone with a similar rig. When rock 'n' roll guitar was invented by Chuck Berry and Scotty Moore (Elvis Presley), it was delivered on Gibson archtop electrics, ensuring the Gibson tonal legacy in the first stages of rock and pop. Moreover, virtuoso pickers Merle Travis and Hank Garland exemplified the Gibson archtop tone in country music.

Gibson solidbody guitars have a similarly impressive legacy. The legendary guitarist/inventor Les Paul is credited with building the first solidbody electric guitar in the forties, but the Gibson company wasn't ready for it—yet. Ten years later, a line of Les Paul guitars was marketed under the Gibson banner. These instruments found their way into the hands of Muddy Waters, John Lee Hooker, Hubert Sumlin, Freddie King, and Link Wray. Future Gibson solidbody guitars, such as the Flying V, Explorer, SG, and Firebird, were added to the line in the late fifties and early sixties. These instruments are associated with Albert King, Lonnie Mack, Eric Clapton (in Cream), Tony Iommi, Michael Schenker, Angus Young, Johnny Winter, and Robby Krieger.

When British blues music invaded the world, it was played on Gibson Les Pauls, in the hands of Keith Richards, Eric Clapton, Peter Green, Mick Taylor, Jeff Beck, and Jimmy Page. American counterparts like Mike Bloomfield and Carlos Santana reinforced the connection of Les Pauls and blues-rock sound in the States. Subsequent blues-rock sounds that were developed in the sixties led to the development of hard rock and heavy metal, particularly with respect to guitar tone.

Another branch of the Gibson tone family stems from the semi-hollow thin-line electric guitar. The ES-335, 345, and 355 of the late fifties were the first entries and remain industry workhorses. A number of notable players are now identified with these instruments, including B.B. King, Chuck Berry, Freddie King, Larry Carlton ("Mr. 335"), Alvin Lee, Lee Ritenour, and John Lee Hooker.

Sonic stuff: Since the thirties, Gibson tone has been the de facto standard for jazz guitar. This is essentially a neck-pickup sound on an archtop guitar. That holds true if the neck pickup is an original bar pickup (classic Charlie Christian, Oscar Moore, Barney Kessel, Tal Farlow, and Hank Garland), a single-coil P-90 (Jim Hall, Howard Roberts, Herb Ellis, Grant Green, and Emily Remler), or a humbucker (Wes Montgomery, Kenny Burrell, Joe Pass, Pat Martino, and Pat Metheny). The floating-pickup Gibson tone is stringier, with more acoustic qualities. This is the tone of Johnny Smith, Pat Martino on *El Hombre*, George Benson on *Breezin'*, and Stevie Ray Vaughan on "Stang's Swang."

In any case, the stereotypical Gibson jazz tone is a clean, mellow sound with slight amp overdrive, just enough for warmth. Many players find the elusive "sweet spot" by setting the guitar's volume between 6 and 8, thereby engaging the capacitor in the electronic circuit and creating a damping effect. The tone control is usually set between 4 and 7, depending on the player's pick attack and playing style, to avoid the brightness of full-treble response. These settings are similar to those used by pop and studio players for a generic jazz tone. On the other side of the coin, blues and rock players like T-Bone Walker (ES-5), Chuck Berry (ES-350), Robben Ford (Super 400), Scotty Moore (L-5), Steve Howe (ES-175), and Ted Nugent (Byrdland) sought brighter, higher-output sounds from their "jazz guitars."

Blues players such as B.B. King, Albert King, Freddie King, and John Lee Hooker set their humbucker-equipped guitars with both bridge and neck pickups selected (the switch set to the middle position) and use the volume controls to adjust the mix of the pickups on the fly. The tone controls are generally higher, especially treble on the bridge pickup setting.

Modern rock guitar is dependent on the Gibson tone. The sound established by Clapton, Beck, and Page playing Les Pauls with overdriven amps remains the preferred tone for solos, power chords, and heavy riffs. This is essentially a bridge-humbucker tone with the volume and tone controls set high enough to produce the desired timbre and amp response (or distortion-box response). Shred solos require a greater range of upper-partial harmonics and are often "full tilt" (i.e., both controls on 10). A variation of the Gibson rock sound is the so-called "woman tone" of Cream-era Clapton, which was also employed by Slash on "Sweet Child O' Mine." This is a neck-pickup setting with the tone control rolled down to 0 or 1. The effect is an extremely bassy, thick sound with an exaggerated emphasis on the fundamental.

The rock tone created by Gibson's first solidbodies started an avalanche. There is virtually no end to the variants of the bridge-humbucker/solidbody configuration in the hard-rock and heavy-metal genres. Consider the use of the Les Paul itself by the likes of Paul Kossoff, Billy Gibbons, Carlos Santana, Duane Allman, Ace Frehley, John McLaughlin, Peter Frampton, Randy Rhoads, John Sykes, Gary Moore, Slash, and Zakk Wylde. And no matter how pointy the guitar gets, who the manufacturer is, or what amp is used, the basic metal sound still comes down to a powerful bridge humbucker fitted to a solidbody instrument. That's what Eddie Van Halen did when he mounted a vintage PAF on a Strat-style body. And that's also the lead sound of Steve Vai, Mick Mars, Tom Morello, Joe Satriani, Dimebag Darrell, Kirk Hammett, and John Petrucci. The sonic trend has continued through virtually every phase of hard rock and metal to the present day.

Gibson ES-150

ES-175 with P-90 pickups

Les Paul Standard with humbuckers

ES-335

GUITAR SYNTHESIZER

General stuff: A synthesizer is an electronic instrument that creates and shapes a tone by varied levels of voltage. In the golden days of the fifties, synthesizers were controlled by physically changing patches (wiring together oscillators, filters, and amplifiers). The first production synthesizer to use a keyboard controller was designed by Robert Moog and was marketed in 1964. Moog synthesizers are heard in avant-garde music, as well as the Beatles' "Here Comes the Sun." The idea of merging the electric guitar with tone-generating synthesizers goes back to the seventies. The guitar synthesizer, or "guitar synth," is an instrument that combines electric guitar and synthesizer technology, using the guitar as a controller. This is done through the process called *pitch-to-voltage conversion*, whereby a hexaphonic (six-sound) pickup is mounted under the strings, where it picks up the string vibration and converts it to voltage, which is then fed to a synth unit, where patches are selected. The hex pickup enables each string to act as a switch, making it possible to select a separate synth sound for each string.

Sonic stuff: Early guitar synths were monophonic (one note at a time) and had tracking problems, especially for guitarists with less-than-impeccable technique. Current guitar synths are polyphonic, allowing any number of fingered notes to create synth sounds. The Roland systems that were developed in the eighties were the first commercially viable guitar synths. Nowadays, Roland hex pickups are routinely mounted on many common electric guitars, including a Fender "Roland-ready" Strat.

Guitarists who have successfully incorporated guitar synthesizers into their music include John McLaughlin, Lee Ritenour, Andy Summers, Pat Metheny, Steve Morse, Robert Fripp, Al Di Meola, Frank Zappa, and Allan Holdsworth. Some players choose to emulate traditional keyboard synth sounds or imitate instruments like the saxophone, trumpet, vibraphone, or a horn section on the guitar, while others create unique, unprecedented electronic soundscapes. The guitar synth is still very much a work in progress and leaves a wide-open field of experimentation for imaginative players. One wonders what Jimi Hendrix would have done with it.

Hex pickup on a Strat

Playing stuff: The modern guitar synth works with some very convincing sampled sounds. Many of these are "digital snapshots" of an actual sound: a muted trumpet, tenor sax, acoustic piano, pipe organ, string quartet, or even a vocal choir, complete with breathy nuances. It is incumbent upon an aspiring guitar-synth player to become familiar with the idiomatic language of an instrument. It is much more interesting and gratifying to hear the guitar synth emulate a real sax or trumpet lick than to just run your favorite pentatonic guitar lick in the blues box. This demonstrative phrase is a jazz-sax melody played on a Strat with a Roland GR-30 synth system and a stock Roland patch.

TRACK 22

Here's what the same melody sounds like with a harmonic patch.

TRACK 22
(0:10)

In this example, a string patch is used with a haramonizer set to a 5th above, creating a thick, dense chord.

Strings

And here's a string patch (without the harmonizer) in a more contrapuntal setting.

Strings

Les Paul with Roland guitar synth pickup

Roland GR-20 guitar synth

HARMONICS

General stuff: Harmonics are inherent in all vibrating physical structures, whether it's a tolling church bell, a tapped water glass, or a plucked guitar string. Harmonics are based on the overtone series. Therefore, a passing knowledge of the science of acoustics is helpful to understand how harmonics work and can be used musically.

Technical stuff: The overtone series is a mathematical calculation of the frequencies in a vibrating object. It's based on slow versus fast vibrations (i.e., patterns of energy). Both types are present in a single vibrating object—for example, a guitar string. The slowest frequency is the lowest note, called the *fundamental*. Above this are the overtones; in theory, arranged as the following pitches (upper-partials): octave (first harmonic), octave and a 5th (second harmonic, 12th interval), two octaves (third harmonic), two octaves and a major 3rd (fourth harmonic), and two octaves and a 5th (fifth harmonic). We can translate this information from math to sound and demonstrate it by applying it to an open guitar string.

Sonic stuff: On a guitar, overtones are accessed as harmonics by fingering the places where they occur on the string length. These points are called *nodes* and align with the peaks and valleys of a vibrating string's wave forms. Let's choose the A (fifth) string and create harmonics that spell the overtone series. The fundamental is the open string. All the harmonics are present in this sound, but the fundamental tone predominates. In high-gain rock distortion settings, it is easier to hear the upper-partials with the fundamental, as the higher-pitched harmonic content is often boosted.

Harmonics are generated by lightly touching a vibrating string at certain points along the string length. Pluck the open string (fundamental), and then touch the string over the twelfth fret (octave, first harmonic) with the fret hand. This is the mid-way point; here the node divides the string in half. Next, touch the string over the seventh fret (octave and a 5th, second harmonic), fifth fret (two octaves), fourth fret (two octaves and a major 3rd), and, finally, between the third and fourth frets (two octaves and a 5th). Again, with higher gain settings, harmonics are boosted and even higher overtones are perceptible between the third and second frets. These overtones sound like two-octaves-and-a-minor-7th and three-octaves-and-a-9th, respectively. This entire array of upper-partial tones belongs to a family of sounds called *open harmonics* (or *natural harmonics*).

Natural harmonic

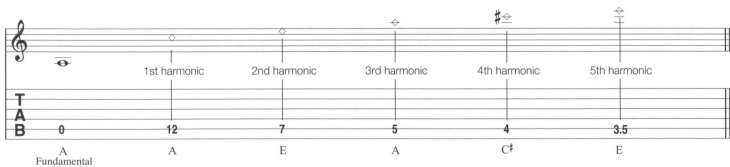

On the guitar, harmonics generally fall into two categories: natural harmonics and artificial harmonics. *Natural harmonics* are created by touching node points along an open string, as illustrated above. *Artificial harmonics* are produced by touching the node point with a pick-hand finger tip above a fretted note. The most common type of artificial harmonic generates an octave above a fretted note and has often been used by classical guitarists, as well as Larry Carlton, Andy Summers, Lenny Breau, Allan Holdsworth, Chet Atkins, and Ted Greene.

To create an artificial harmonic, fret a note and then pluck the string with the pick hand twelve frets higher. For example, fret the note C on the G string (third string/fifth fret) and simultaneously pluck the string over the seventeenth fret. There are two typical pick techniques: the classical approach and the plectrum approach. The classical technique uses the index finger to touch the string at the node. The piacking hand then plucks behind it with either the ring or pinky finger. The *plectrum technique* also employs the index finger to touch the node but uses the pick, held by thumb and middle finger, to pluck the string.

Artificial (harp) harmonic

Another form of artificial harmonic is the *pinch harmonic*. This is a common rock technique used by players like Eddie Van Halen, Steve Vai, Joe Satriani, Billy Gibbons, and Zakk Wylde. Pinch harmonics are produced by attacking the string (fretted notes are most typical but open strings are possible) with the pick and the edge of the fret-hand thumb. At first, most uninitiated guitarists generate random harmonics with this approach. However, with practice and repetition, skilled players can establish pick-hand positions that guarantee that the desired harmonic is created.

Playing stuff: Natural harmonics are indigenous to the classical-guitar repertory, exemplified by pieces like Villa Lobos Prelude No.4. Natural harmonics are also exploited by rock guitarists such as Steve Howe, The Edge (U2), Eric Johnson, and Eddie Van Halen. This phrase presents a melody in E minor. Note the use of natural harmonics over the twelfth and seventh frets to play the descending E minor pentatonic scale and the use of harmonics over the seventh, fifth, and twelfth frets to complete the line.

TRACK 23

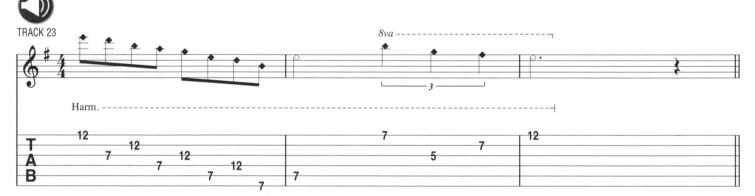

Artificial (plucked) harmonics are also common across genres. Barney Kessel, Johnny Smith, Tal Farlow, and Larry Carlton are a few of the modern electric players who have harnessed the sound. This phrase, over a ii–V progression in the key of D, exploits artificial plectrum harmonics by applying them to an Em7 melody, and includes a sweep of the A13♭9 chord. Here the pick hand quickly brushes the fretted shape to produce a series of artificial harmonics that are related to the chord.

TRACK 23
(0:08)

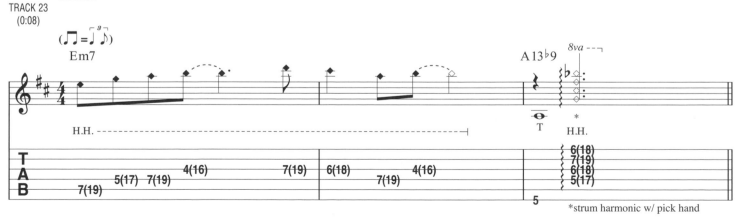

*strum harmonic w/ pick hand

Lenny Breau, Andy Summers, Ted Greene, and Chet Atkins employ(ed) a combination of artificial harmonics and natural fretted notes, generally alternated in specific patterns. The ringing chord-based effect has prompted listeners and players to name it *harp harmonics*. This phrase illustrates the idea with a barred Am11 and Gm11 chord form, and has a sustained harp-like quality. Let the notes ring throughout.

TRACK 23
(0:19)

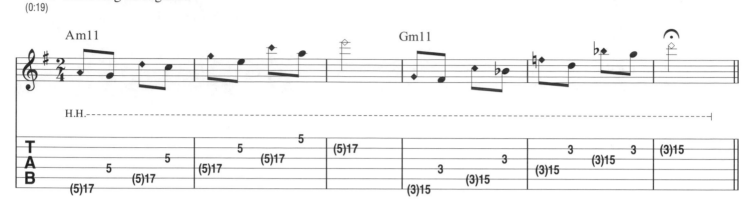

Eddie Van Halen and Billy Gibbons of ZZ Top are well-known practitioners of the pinch harmonic. The unique squealing effect is demonstrated in several forms in this characteristic phrase. Note the use of bent pinch harmonics and regular fretted notes, as well as a held bend with wide whammy-bar vibrato.

TRACK 23
(0:26)

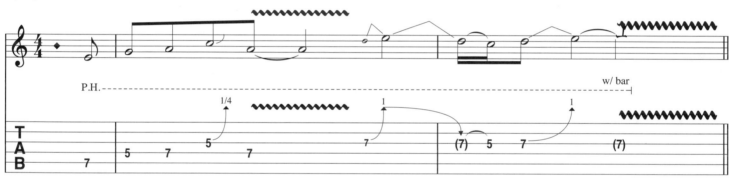

HARMONIC MINOR SCALE

General stuff: The harmonic-minor scale is a seven-note diatonic pattern with an augmented 2nd interval between the sixth and seventh steps. The harmonic-minor scale is heard prominently in European classical and Near Eastern music, bebop jazz, neoclassical heavy metal, jazz-rock fusion, flamenco, and some quirky alternative-rock songs. If this question arises: What unites Charlie Parker, Yngwie Malmsteen, J.S. Bach, and Al Di Meola? The answer is: The harmonic-minor scale.

Technical stuff: In the key of A, the harmonic-minor scale is spelled: A–B–C–D–E–**F–G♯** (augmented 2nd interval in bold). This interval changes the diatonic natural-minor scale (or Aeolian mode; the same scale, both of which are spelled with a G note) into a unique structure with strong harmonic connotations. The G♯ tone makes possible an indigenous *dominant-seventh chord*, E7 (the V7 of A minor), as well four diminished-seventh chords built upon on the B, D, G♯, and D tones of the scale. Moreover, the altered chords E7♭9 and E7♭9♯5 are also found in this scale.

Playing stuff: The harmonic-minor scale has several common guitar fingerings. Two of the most familiar are of contrasting types: positional and linear. The positional type is played in and around a central position on the fingerboard. This example is a typical "box-based" A minor example that is centered at the fifth position.

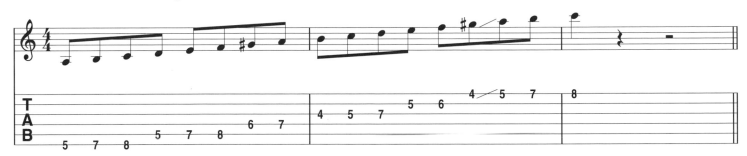

Many players have utilized the linear form of the harmonic-minor scale. This example moves through three octaves, using an almost identical fingering shape.

TRACK 24

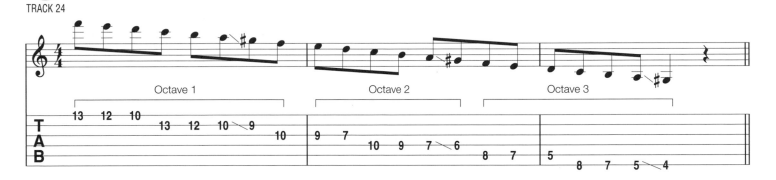

Bebop and modern jazz players have, for decades, used the harmonic-minor scale to define the minor mode or movement to a relative-minor key center via its ii–V–i progression. This bop phrase in C minor, translated to the guitar, has moves associated with Charlie Parker and John Coltrane.

TRACK 24
(0:07)

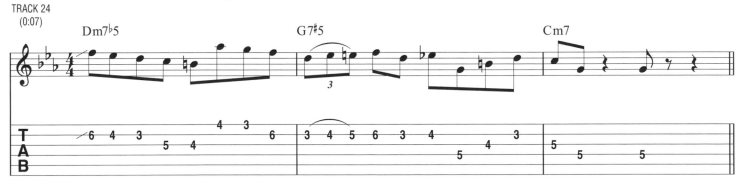

Rock guitarists, particularly those with a neoclassical bent, have found compelling qualities in the harmonic-minor scale. This next lick demonstrates a characteristic scalar line with interval leaps and a trilled arpeggio melody.

HUMBUCKING PICKUP

General stuff: The *humbucking pickup* was developed in the late fifties and began to appear on many Gibson, Epiphone, Gretsch, and Guild guitars by the early sixties. The idea is to "buck hum" (reduce 60-cycle hum) through the use of two coils in the pickup circuit. Where earlier pickups, like Gibson's P-90, the Gretsch DeArmond units, and Fender's Strat and Tele pickups, had only one coil, humbucking pickups have two separate coils wired electrically out-of-phase, as well as opposite magnetic polarity. In this configuration of two magnets, one is reverse-wound, which cancels or lessens hum. Another attribute is a darker, thicker tone with louder output and more sustain, which is preferred by many players over the brighter, thinner sound of single-coil pickups.

Gibson guitars made in the late fifties—like the Les Paul Standard, ES-335, 345, and 355, and signature archtops such as the ES-175, ES-350T, Byrdland, L-5CES, and Super 400CES—bear the early PAF (Patent Applied For) humbuckers. PAFs are the most coveted of the humbucking pickup family.

Sonic stuff: The humbucking pickup produces a fatter, louder sound that is preferred by jazz players like Wes Montgomery, Kenny Burrell, Joe Pass, Pat Martino, and Pat Metheny, as well as blues guitarists B.B. King, Albert King, Freddie King, and John Lee Hooker. Moreover, Larry Carlton and Lee Ritenour exploited humbuckers in the late seventies, as did Eric Clapton, Jeff Beck, and Jimmy Page during the British-blues boom a decade earlier.

Many rock guitarists, like Allan Holdsworth, Eddie Van Halen, Steve Vai, and Steve Lukather, have installed bridge humbuckers in Strat-style guitars, a trend that prompted leading manufacturers to offer the two single-coil/humbucker rock-lead setup on stock instruments. Similarly, Keith Richards, Andy Summers, Mike Stern, and Albert Collins prefer neck humbucking pickups on their Fender Telecasters.

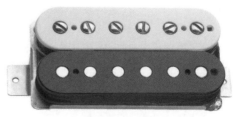

Humbucking pickup without cover,
showing two coils

INTERVAL

General stuff: An interval is the distance between two notes. Intervals are of two types: harmonic (two notes sounded together) and melodic (two notes sounded in succession). The quality of an interval is determined by its size and by its position relative to a keynote (or root of a chord). Intervals define scales and melodies, as well as chords and arpeggios.

Technical stuff: An interval is named for the number of steps it spans and is counted by starting with "1" on the first note. The interval of a 4th (for example, from C up to F) encompasses the following steps: C(1)–D(2)–E(3)–F(4). Intervals can be reckoned in descending or ascending direction.

It is useful to be familiar with intervals spanning two octaves. Let's begin by considering the first octave. With C as the keynote, this chart illustrates the diatonic intervals and their names in the first octave of a major scale. The unison, 4th, 5th, and octave intervals are called perfect intervals. The 2nd, 3rd, 6th, and 7th are called *major intervals*.

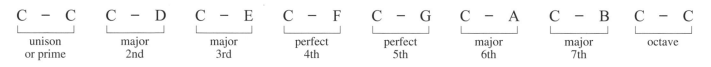

C – C	C – D	C – E	C – F	C – G	C – A	C – B	C – C
unison or prime	major 2nd	major 3rd	perfect 4th	perfect 5th	major 6th	major 7th	octave

There are other intervals besides those in a major scale. This chart presents the remaining intervals in the first octave for chromatic tones outside the scale. Here we find the minor intervals: 2nd, 3rd, 6th, and 7th, as well as the *augmented 4th*.

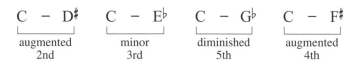

C – D♭	C – E♭	C – F♯	C – A♭	C – B♭
minor 2nd	minor 3rd	augmented 4th	minor 6th	minor 7th

Enharmonic intervals are those which sound the same but are spelled and named differently. For example, C–D♯ sounds the same as a minor 3rd (C–E♭), but is called an augmented 2nd because the note names (C and D) are a 2nd apart. Similarly, the diminished 5th interval (C–G♭) sounds the same as the augmented 4th (C–F♯), but is reckoned by a five-step spelling.

C – D♯	C – E♭	C – G♭	C – F♯
augmented 2nd	minor 3rd	diminished 5th	augmented 4th

General rules: A major interval that is contracted by a half step becomes a minor interval. A perfect interval that is expanded by a half step becomes augmented, whereas a perfect interval that is contracted by a half step becomes diminished.

Intervals that are larger than an octave are called *compound intervals*. Above the octave, the following names are commonly used within seventh-chord voicings: 9th (C–D), 10th (C–E), 11th (C–F), and 13th (C–A). For example, in a C13 chord, the C–A interval is relevant to the chord structure (root and 13th). Otherwise, the spelling retains its first-octave names.

C – C	C – D	C – E	C – F	C – G	C – A	C – B
octave	major 9th	major 10th	perfect 11th	*perfect 12th	major 13th	*major 14th

*theoretical; rarely used

Intervals are divided into two qualities: *consonant* and *dissonant*. Consonant intervals sound stable and don't require resolution. These include unisons, octaves, 5ths (perfect consonances), and 3rds and 6ths (imperfect consonances). Dissonant intervals sound unstable and have an urgency to resolve to a consonant interval. These include augmented and diminished intervals, major and minor 2nds and 7ths, and the perfect 4th. These are potential components for common dissonant major, minor, and dominant-seventh chords like C7#11 (or C7♭5), C7#5, C11, C9, C7♭9, C7#9, and others.

Consonant intervals

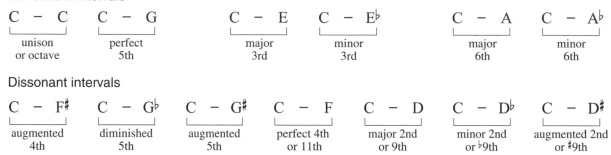

C – C	C – G	C – E	C – E♭	C – A	C – A♭
unison or octave	perfect 5th	major 3rd	minor 3rd	major 6th	minor 6th

Dissonant intervals

C – F#	C – G♭	C – G#	C – F	C – D	C – D♭	C – D#
augmented 4th	diminished 5th	augmented 5th	perfect 4th or 11th	major 2nd or 9th	minor 2nd or ♭9th	augmented 2nd or #9th

Intervals can be inverted in two ways: harmonically and melodically. *Harmonic inversion* occurs when an interval's lower note is transferred into a higher octave, or visa versa. With harmonic inversion, a C5 power chord (C–G) becomes a 4th dyad (G–C), as used by Ritchie Blackmore (can you say "Smoke on the Water"?) and others. Play the first example and realize that many rock and blues riffs have used this device.

Harmonic inversion

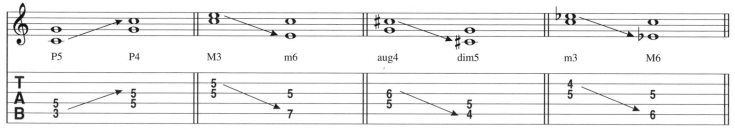

Melodic inversion occurs when a melody's intervallic contour is mirrored in the same exact number of steps. If the first three notes of a melody are C–D–E, a simple ascending stepwise line, then its melodic inversion is the mirror image: C–B♭–A♭, the same intervals but in a descending stepwise line. The same holds true for arpeggio melodies. Interestingly, applying melodic inversion to a C6 arpeggio melody creates an Fm7 arpeggio. Melodic inversion is a favorite device and valuable tool of countless composers, from J.S. Bach to Arnold Schoenberg.

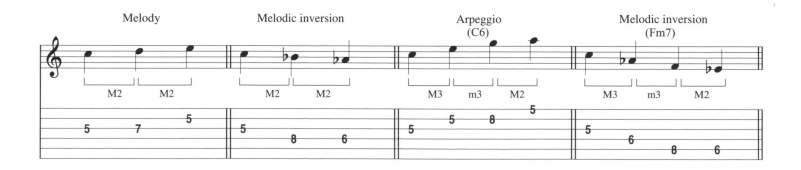

INTONATION

General stuff: Intonation is the capability of the guitar to be in tune with itself throughout its entire range. It's is the result of several factors: placement and adjustment of the bridge, proper placement of frets, action, age, condition of the strings, and the attitude of the neck. Distortion or twisting of the neck and placement of frets are situations best corrected by experts. Adjustments of the bridge and action or changing strings can be easily remedied by a player with knowledge of the basics and a little practical experience.

Technical stuff: The bridge on many guitars can be set for optimal string-length intonation by adjusting movable saddles. These are found on instruments like a Strat, Tele, Les Paul, SG, 335, or an archtop with a Tune-O-Matic bridge. Assuming that the neck is not twisted, the strings are in good condition, the action is not too high, and the frets are properly seated, adjusting the intonation can be accomplished with a simple step: moving the saddles' screws with a screwdriver.

The basic principle is as follows: The string is too short if it sounds sharp when tuned and fretted. It is too long if it sounds flat. Increasing the string-length distance from bridge to nut makes the intonation go in the flat direction. Conversely, decreasing the distance causes the intonation to go in the sharp direction.

Quick formula: To go sharp, make the string shorter (move the bridge saddle closer to the nut). To go flat, make the string longer (move the bridge saddle away from the nut).

To set intonation at the bridge, follow this simple procedure:

1. Tune the guitar with a tuner. It is ideal if the tuner has a meter that shows the relation of a note to a fixed reference point with a needle or an LCD display, a common feature on chromatic tuners. Depending on the guitar, I use an Intelli-Touch tuner that mounts to the headstock, or a Roland chromatic tuner that requires a cable connection.

2. Using the tuner, test the current intonation by playing an open string and then fretting the same string at the twelfth fret. I also compare the natural harmonic at the twelfth fret with the fingered note. The two notes should be close. Absolute mathematical perfection is rare. Bear in mind that almost all intonation on the guitar is a relative phenomenon that almost always involves a compromise.

3. If the fingered note is sharp, use the screwdriver to move the saddle away from the nut, increasing string length. If the fingered note is flat, move it in the opposite direction, decreasing string length. Keep comparing fretted notes with harmonics throughout the process. Oftentimes, the harmonic will reveal that, while moving the bridge saddle, the string has gone sharp or flat. Retune before making further intonation adjustments.

Setting the intonation on a guitar with a floating bridge is bit more problematic, as it requires moving the bridge itself until it is in the correct position and in tune. Loosen the strings until the bridge can be moved slightly. Check intonation with a tuner again; this time beginning with the high E string, and then line up the rest of the bridge until the proper intonation is achieved. Most modern bridges of this type have a *compensated saddle*, whereby the wood has been cut in a pattern of different, presumably correct, resting points.

The typical pattern of intonation for most guitar bridges forms a characteristic visual shape. Note the graduated direction for the bass strings, which, when fretted, generally need longer string length for the best intonation. The dip down occurs at the transition to the unwound third string. The same holds true for guitars with a wound third string, except that the dip occurs at the transition to the unwound second string.

With unwound 3rd string:

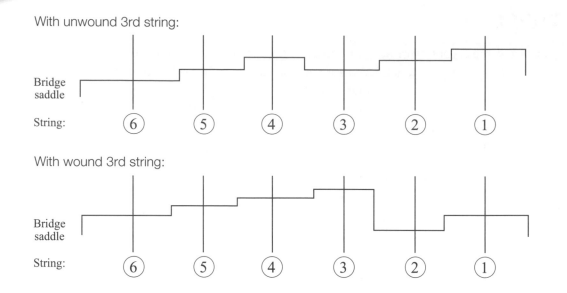

With wound 3rd string:

Bridge saddle

String: 6 5 4 3 2 1

INVERSIONS (CHORD INVERSIONS)

General stuff: Intervals, melodies, and chords can all be inverted. (Harmonic and melodic inversion of intervals and melodies are covered in the section on *Intervals*.) The process involves exchanging the position of notes in an interval in an ascending or descending direction. Chord inversions involve more than two notes and require a deeper explanation. Truth be told, knowledge of chord voicings and inversions is an invaluable asset for any guitarist.

Technical stuff: Knowledge of chord inversions is easily understood by defining the process with triads, which are three-note chords. In this example, a first-position C major chord is broken down into triads on adjacent string sets. The inversion takes place with a set of three differently voiced triads (one for each note in a three-note chord), beginning in open position and then proceeding up the fingerboard in a linear manner. Note that the chords are labeled to reflect the inversion; the root-position form is named C (C in the bass, the lowest note of the chord), the first inversion is C/E (C with E in the bass), and the second inversion is C/G (C with G in the bass).

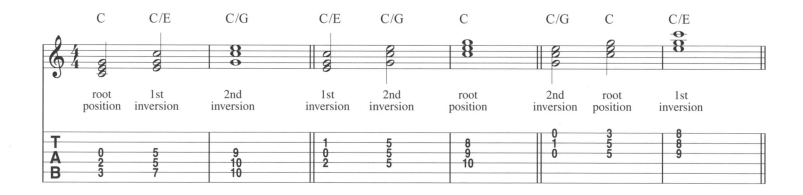

A four-note seventh chord, such as a minor-seventh chord, has four positions in its sequence of inversions. This example presents two different common voicings for Cm7 and Gm7. Each is constructed of four notes. The first voicing is on consecutive strings; the second is a divided voicing, with notes on the sixth, fourth, third, and second strings.

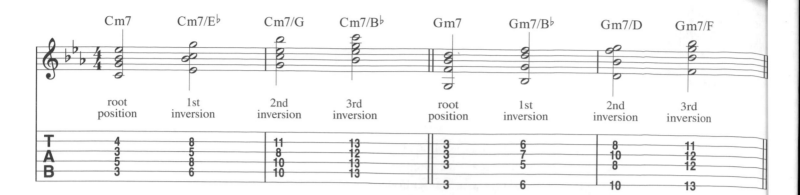

When inverted, certain chords are *symmetrical*; that is, the same chord form can be maintained in a fixed shape as the voicing is moved up or down the fingerboard. The intervals within the chord are *equidistant*, thus yielding identical shapes at different positions on a particular string set. Players like Wes Montgomery, Joe Pass, Johnny Smith, and Yngwie Malmsteen have gotten considerable mileage out of applying this device to their music. This example depicts the idea and motion with inversions of augmented and diminished chords.

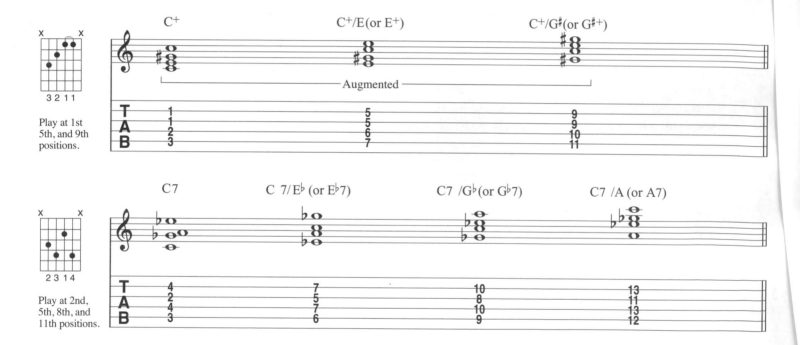

JACK

General stuff: The humble output jack is arguably the most neglected part of the electric guitar. In the words of Rodney Dangerfield, it simply gets "no respect." As guitarists, we focus on the right pickups, the tuning keys, the tone and volume pots, the switching, the strings, the bridge, the vibrato bar, the nut… You get the idea—we often exclude the output jack. But there is nothing that can spoil the attention lavished on the aforementioned components or an important gig like a faulty jack.

The output jack is where the signal leaves the guitar and is fed to the effects processors or the amplifier. A jack needs minimal but regular examination. Listen for undue noise, buzz, crackling, intermittent operation, or decreased signal strength when you first plug into the amp. A jack can suffer from corrosion, physical damage, or loose wiring, and these conditions can cause problems.

Technical stuff: Maintenance is simple. Occasionally clean the jack's internal contact points with a Q-Tip and solvent, like WD-40. You'll be surprised at the buildup of gunk at the vital juncture of cord and jack. If you hear intermittent sound, it might be metal fatigue. Test the jack by slightly moving the cord to see if better contact can be made with repositioning. This can be remedied by carefully removing the jack (keep the wiring intact if possible) and gently bending the metal contacts back into place. On some guitars, this can be accessed via a back panel. In extreme cases, the jack will have to be replaced. This is a simple job for any repair shop and can also be done by someone with basic soldering skills and tools, such as a socket wrench. The same holds true for loosened wires. In most cases, they can be easily re-soldered.

The jack can come loose with regular use. Check the nut that holds the jack to the guitar. If there is any slippage, carefully tighten it. The preferred tool is a socket wrench. Although a pair of pliers will work, they can easily slip and scratch the surface of the instrument. Do not over-tighten the nut, as this can cause the wood or plastic around the jack to crack. Strats, Teles, and modern Les Pauls have metal mounting hardware and are less susceptible to damage through over-tightening, but exercise similar care just the same.

Playing stuff: Many players like to loop their cords over the strap button, allowing the strap to hold the cord snugly in place and out of the way of foot traffic. For an example, check out the historic photos of the Beatles' first U.S. concerts. This simple procedure will assure that the cord is not accidentally pulled out of the jack during a spirited performance.

KEY SIGNATURE

General stuff: A key signature designates the key, or tonal center, of a piece of music via a deliberate grouping of sharps or flats. The key signature is written at the beginning of the musical staff, following the clef sign, and makes the scale that is established by the keynote conform to a specific pattern of diatonic steps, as in the major scale.

Technical stuff: The purpose of a key signature is to eliminate the tedious process of writing every raised or lowered note as an accidental. In some modern music, like atonal music or free jazz, a key signature is often not used. The key of C major contains no sharps or flats, thus no sharps or flats are in its signature.

Sharps and flats are written as a vertical/horizontal arrangement, occupying a specific line or space on the staff. In sharp keys, the *leading tone* (*major-seventh step* of a scale) is the farthest right-hand sharp in the grouping. For example, F♯ is the leading tone of G major, C♯ is the leading tone of D major, etc. This line illustrates the six sharp keys:

In flat keys, the right-hand flat is the fourth step of the scale. For example, in F major, the fourth step is B♭, the right-hand flat (in this case, the only flat). With two or more flats, it's easy to distinguish the key; it's the flat next to the right-hand flat. For example, in E♭ major the second right-hand flat is E♭, the keynote. This line illustrates the six flat keys:

Key signatures save the composer from having to rewrite sharp or flat symbols repeatedly when writing music in keys other than C major. In this example, since the key signature is D major, all the F and C notes are automatically assumed to be played as F♯ and C♯.

In the event that the composer desires an F natural or C natural note, a *natural* sign is used to show the temporary reversion from the sharp (or flat) designated in the key signature. Generally if, for example, C♯ is played again in the following measure (in the same octave), a *courtesy accidental* is used (a sharp in this case) to remind the performer of the key signature.

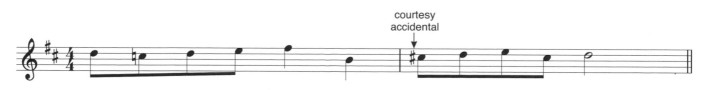

The "chord clock" is a useful visual aid for depicting the position of sharp and flat keys and the number of sharps or flats in a key. This diagram of the chord clock presents the sequence of keys. It places the sharp keys on the right-hand side (clockwise from 1:00 to 6:00) and the flat keys on the left-hand side (counter-clockwise from 11:00 to 6:00). The clockwise direction is known as the cycle of 5ths due to the key-note movement by intervals of a 5th: C–G–D–A–E–B–F♯. The counter-clockwise direction yields the cycle of 4ths, with key-note movement by intervals of a 4th: C–F–B♭–E♭–A♭–D♭–G♭. At 6:00, F♯ and G♭ are one and the same, pitch-wise. These are called *enharmonic keys*.

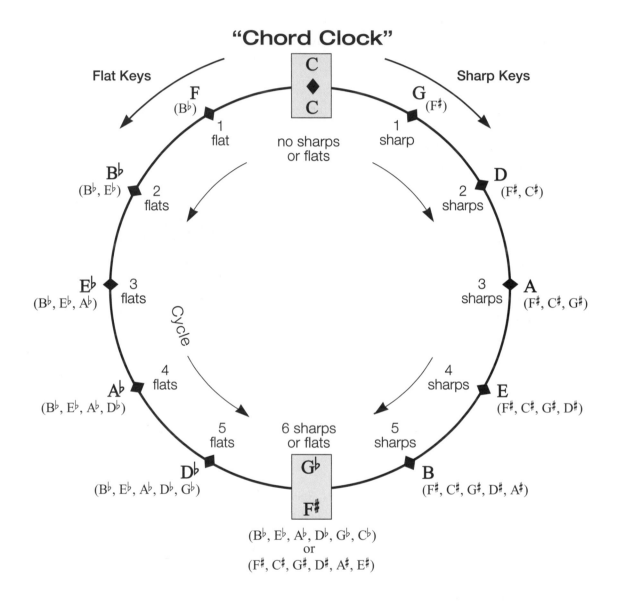

LEAD GUITAR

General stuff: Lead guitar is a generic term that usually designates the role of a guitar soloist as opposed to a background chord or rhythm player. In combos with two (or more) guitarists, players generally assume these roles based on the song and/or the players' musical strengths.

Lead guitarists in rock, blues, and country bands are typically called upon for a distinct set of skills. Among these skills are the ability to create genre-specific improvised solos, double and/or enhance the basic rhythm parts, generate arpeggio extensions of a rhythm guitarist's chord patterns, and add fills and decorative nuances to the arrangements.

Historic stuff: When you listen to a typical two-guitar rock combo, you will no doubt be able to discern the separation of lead and rhythm roles. Check out Scotty Moore and Cliff Gallup with Elvis Presley or Gene Vincent, Hubert Sumlin with Howlin' Wolf, George Harrison in the early Beatles, Jeff Beck in the Yardbirds, Ace Frehley in KISS, Gary Moore in Thin Lizzy, Uli Roth in the Scorpions, Slash in Guns N' Roses, and Kirk Hammett in Metallica. The distinction is even more profound when the rhythm is played on acoustic guitar and the lead guitarist is playing an electric guitar, as is the case with much of country music.

Lead and rhythm roles are assigned in jazz as well. Two of the most celebrated jazz-guitar albums, Joe Pass' *For Django* and Pat Martino's *The Visit (Footprints)*, are clearly divided along lead- and rhythm-guitar roles. In these settings, chordal guitarists John Pisano and Bobby Rose, respectively, comp like a piano or keyboard instrument, adopting a freer, more responsive role in relation to the soloist, one quite different than the strict four-to-the-bar strumming rhythm style of Freddie Green.

LEGATO PHRASING

General stuff: Legato is an Italian word that literally means *connected*. In music, legato is a common term that refers to a smooth connection of tones without breaks between successive notes. On the guitar, this technique is generally executed with hammer-ons, pull-offs, and slides.

Historic stuff: Legato phrasing itself has many different expressions across numerous genres. Some well-known players have elevated legato phrasing to a high art form, including Les Paul, Chet Atkins, Jeff Beck, Allan Holdsworth, Eddie Van Halen, Randy Rhoads, Joe Satriani, and Steve Vai. These guitarists use an abundance of legato patterns to produce long lines that have a smooth, seamless quality. Players like Holdsworth have used legato technique to connote breathy, sax-like impressions in jazz-rock fusion music. Others, like Rhoads, Van Halen, and Satriani, apply legato to long scalar lines in hard rock and metal.

Playing stuff: This classic legato lick is based on a series of repeated pull offs. In this phrase three-note legato patterns are grouped in riff-like descending figures. Note the use of pull offs to open strings. Les Paul and Chet Atkins inspired a host of rock 'n' roll and rockabilly players to add this smooth sound to their licks, including Jeff Beck in the namesake instrumental "Jeff's Boogie."

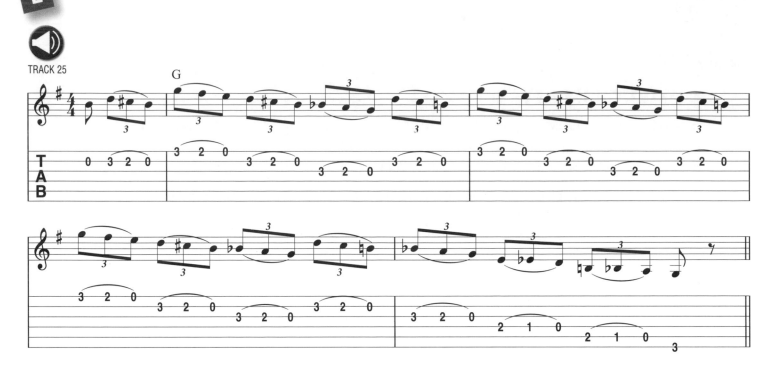

A more modern hard-rock form of legato phrasing is presented in this characteristic phrase. This form of legato turned many rock guitarists on their ears and resulted in countless variants in rock and metal. Van Halen turned to this sort of sound as an emulation of the Holdsworth approach, transferring it to hard rock. In pursuit of a classical-influenced violinistic effect, Rhoads played similar lines in metal. Here, hammer-ons dominate the melody, although a combination of hammer-ons and pull-offs are found at the phrase's ending. Note the use of similar fingering shapes. This is typical of the approach in rock, metal, and fusion.

TRACK 25
(0:08)

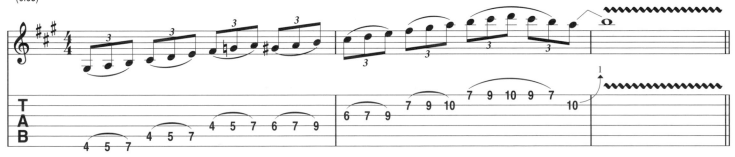

LOCKING NUT

General stuff: Standard vibrato bridge systems are notorious for their tuning problems. Back in the day, the use of a stock Fender-style vibrato bar had to be confined to select moments in the music and was rarely accompanied with the sort of radical string bending that emerged with the hard-rock style. Subsequent players like Jeff Beck, Jimi Hendrix, and Eddie Van Halen had to make all manners of compromises to ensure basic tuning stability.

Historic stuff: In the early eighties, the double-locking tremolo system was developed by Floyd Rose to address the problems associated with aggressive vibrato-bar use. This system employed locking mechanisms at the nut and at the bridge, eliminating the two points where tuning is most affected by the bar. After they were stretched properly, the strings were clamped at the nut and at the bridge with metal pieces and hex-head fasteners. The apparatus quickly found favor with hard-rock and metal players. Eddie Van Halen, Neal Schon, and Pat Thrall were among the first players to use and popularize the Floyd Rose system in the early eighties.

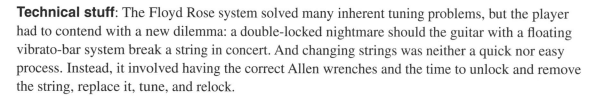

Technical stuff: The Floyd Rose system solved many inherent tuning problems, but the player had to contend with a new dilemma: a double-locked nightmare should the guitar with a floating vibrato-bar system break a string in concert. And changing strings was neither a quick nor easy process. Instead, it involved having the correct Allen wrenches and the time to unlock and remove the string, replace it, tune, and relock.

Retuning also presented a problem: If the string was locked but continued to stretch, it was locked in place, out of tune. By the mid-eighties, locking systems were improved with violin-style fine tuners at the bridge. Another problem was having the correct Allen wrench. One manufacturer switched to slotted locking fasteners that could be removed with a quarter. Another built a wrench holder that could be attached to the back of the headstock.

Sonic stuff: As the locking tremolo system caught on, many rock players rethought and refined their styles around the musical possibilities of the expanded pitch dives, vibrato, and bends that the second-generation vibrato bar offered. Brad Gillis, Steve Vai, Joe Satriani, and Tom Morello are among the leading exponents of this new vanguard in the post–Van Halen era.

Floyd Rose locking nut and bridge

Locking nut

MODES

General stuff: The modes are *seven-note scales* that are built on different arrangements of half steps and whole steps in the diatonic family. There are seven in each key, one for each step of the scale. Medieval modes, also called Ecclesiastic or Church modes, were given Greek names by medieval scholars, and six of the seven were used prominently in sacred music of antiquity, the Middle Ages, and the Renaissance. In more recent times, modes were revived by modern composers of the twentieth century and post-bop jazz musicians. Rock musicians also exploited, and continue to exploit, modes in the shred and fusion camps.

Technical stuff: Modes can be viewed two ways: as appendages or extensions of a prevailing major or minor scale, or as individual distinct scales with their own unique melodic qualities.

Consider the basic major scale, also called the Ionian mode. This common diatonic pattern contains the melodic material for all of the Medieval modes. This example is the C Ionian mode, or the C major scale. Note the specific pattern of whole and half steps.

Major scale/Ionian mode

The well-known Dorian mode is created by starting on a *new tonic*, the note D, in the key as C major. Note the different arrangement of whole and half steps. Also notice specifically that the D to F (tonic to 3rd) is a minor-3rd interval, which defines this scale as a minor scale.

Dorian mode

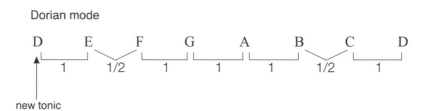

The key to understanding and using the modes effectively lies in recognizing their basic qualities. That comes down to their unique successions of whole and half steps. In the diatonic family, there are three major modes, three minor modes, and one half-diminished mode. In this chart, the three major modes—that is, those having a major 3rd—are placed above the scale and linked to their respective starting tone, or tonic: the Ionian on C, the Lydian on F, and the Mixolydian on G. The minor modes—those with a minor 3rd—are grouped below the scale: the Dorian on D, the Phrygian on E, and the Aeolian on A. The Locrian on B is a mode with a diminished sound, which has a minor 3rd and diminished 5th.

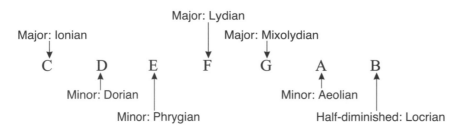

Looking closer, we find that modes have unique harmonic components. Two of the major modes, Ionian and Lydian, have a major-seventh chord quality, while the Mixolydian mode has a major 3rd and lowered 7th, which generates a dominant-seventh sound, G7. That's why the Mixolydian mode has been suitable for blues, rock, and metal. The Lydian mode has an exotic Fmaj7#11 sound, which entices fusion players, as well as modern rock players like Steve Vai, who has described its quality as "Egyptian." The chord associated with the Ionian mode is a straight and pretty Cmaj7. That's one reason why it has found favor in pop, soft rock, R&B ballads, and jazz.

C	Ionian	=	Cmaj7	
F	Lydian	=	Fmaj7	(raised 11th)
G	Mixolydian	=	G7	(dominant 7th)

On the minor side of the modal coin are the three minor modes, all of which have a minor-seventh chord as their tonic seventh chord. So what's the difference? Zooming in, we find there are other subtle distinctions. The D Dorian mode, with its raised 6th (B), has a strong appeal to jazz players as the ii chord in ii–V–I changes. The Phrygian mode, with its lowered 2nd step (E–F), suggests a Spanish flamenco sound. The Aeolian mode, or natural minor scale, connotes a darker classical sound than the Dorian with its natural lowered 6th, F. The Locrian mode, long considered a theoretical mode, has found advocates in the fusion and modern jazz genres. Jazz players use the Locrian mode to define the Bm7♭5 chord in standard changes. Generalizations like these, while somewhat simplistic, can be useful with regard to basic usage and melodic/harmonic quality.

D	Dorian	=	Dm7	(raised 6th)
E	Phrygian	=	Em7	(lowered 2nd)
A	Aeolian	=	Am7	(natural lowered 6th)
B	Locrian	=	Bm7♭5	(half-diminished)

Synthetic (Alternate) modes are an important aspect of modern modal usage. Consider the source scale as being something other than a major scale. For example, the harmonic-minor scale and the melodic-minor scale (ascending form) have different diatonic structures and yield other modes. Two of these are in standard use: the Lydian Dominant and the Phrygian Dominant. The *Lydian Dominant mode* is based on the fourth step (hence the Lydian designation) of the melodic-minor scale. If we spell an A melodic-minor scale, the parent scale, in its ascending form, we then build the Lydian Dominant from its fourth step, D. This mode supports an altered dominant chord with a raised eleventh, like D9#11. Play this chord with the mode and listen for the harmonic connection.

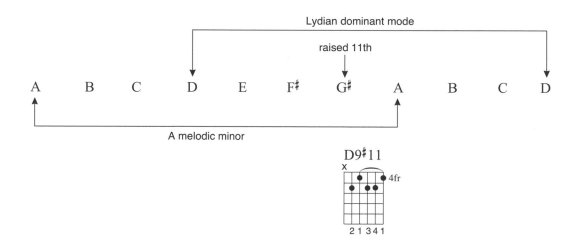

Similarly, the A harmonic-minor scale is the parent scale of the E Phrygian Dominant mode. The *Phrygian Dominant mode* is built on the fifth step of the scale and gets its name from three components: the lowered 2nd step (F, the Phrygian aspect), the major 3rd (G♯), and lowered 7th (D). The notes G♯ and D, along with the new tonic on the fifth step (E), are the dominant elements. The Phrygian Dominant is compatible with an altered chord like E7♭9♯5, as well as the characteristic F–E7 progression of A minor. Those are just a couple of reasons Phrygian Dominant has attracted modern jazz musicians, as well as flamenco guitarists and neo-classical metal players.

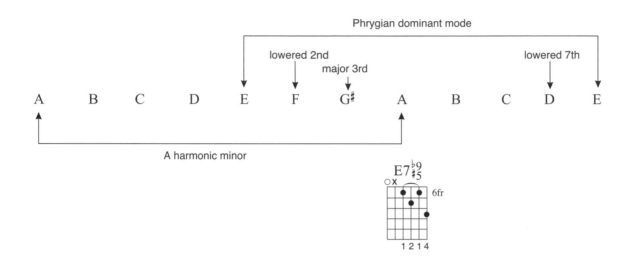

Playing stuff: Modal jazz had a tremendous affect on subsequent free jazz, fusion, pop, R&B, and rock styles. The notion of elaborating on a single tonal center with a combination of modal sounds was brought to the fore by Miles Davis and Bill Evans but was seized by groups like the Doors and the Grateful Dead. This demonstrative phrase in D minor is based on a modal lick from George Benson. Note the use of the D Aeolian mode, the A Phrygian Dominant mode (for A7 sounds), and the D Dorian mode during the unbroken melody.

TRACK 26

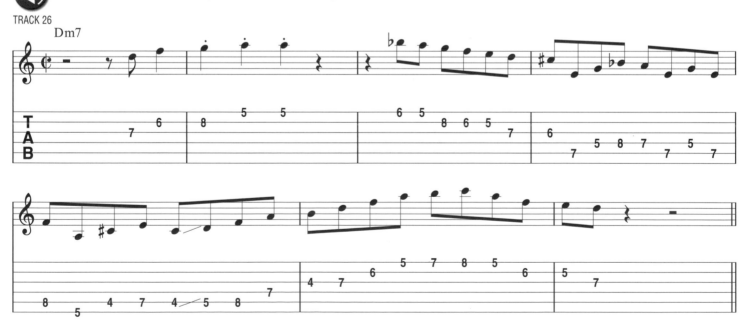

The Phrygian Dominant mode is a striking sound and a favorite resource of neo-classical metal players. This telling phrase contains a characteristic C–B power-chord move, directly related to the B Phrygian Dominant mode, as well as a long flurry of notes taken from the E harmonic-minor scale and posed over the B tonal center.

TRACK 26
(0:09)

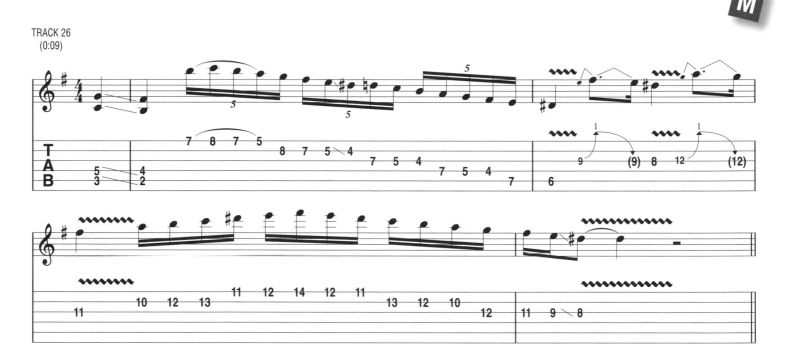

MUTING

General stuff: Muting is the universal guitar technique of left- and/or right-hand damping, used to silence or muffle strings. Classical and flamenco guitar players use muting for occasional pizzicato sound effects. Country pickers mute bass strings for those percussive Travis-picked licks. But electric blues, hard rock, metal, and fusion guitarists use muting as a vital part of general playing technique to control the dynamic timbre of the instrument.

Eric Johnson once commented that he was muting everywhere he wasn't actually fretting a deliberate note. This mindset is essential if you want to play articulate and clean music in a high-volume, high-gain situation. The errant open string or unwanted noise can mar an otherwise great performance, especially at high volumes. Slide-guitar style also necessitates a developed muting technique for judiciously silencing strings that would be inadvertently sounded by the slide bar. Muting is also used to create thicker, more percussive effects on notes and chords in funk, reggae, hard rock, and metal.

> *"I like getting a muffled effect with the side of my hand [on the bridge]. It gets more tone. It's a definite texture you can use in combination with straight picking."*
>
> —Eddie Van Halen, *Guitar Player*

Technical stuff: What is muting and how is it done? Muting is placed in two basic categories, defining which hand is producing the effect: pick-hand palm muting or fret-hand muting. The more obvious, palm muting, is executed by resting the pick-hand palm against the strings. Greater pressure increases the percussive effect. Palm muting is indicated in modern guitar-tab notation with the abbreviation "P.M." A broken line and bracket is used to specify a longer section of music with palm muting.

Fret-hand muting is more subtle. This is generally a preemptive "clean-up" technique, whereby certain fingers do not actually fret notes but, instead, lightly touch strings to neutralize their pitch and cancel their ability to ring out. Two prime examples of fret-hand muting are chords with X's in their grid shape and the parallel octaves of Wes Montgomery. The following diagrams reveal the fret-hand finger muting in action. An Am7 chord and a typical G octave are shown as grids, accompanied by a second grid that depicts the muting finger positions.

Am7 — G octave

Sonic stuff: In the early sixties, palm muting was so prevalent in pop music that several guitar manufacturers were prompted to equip instruments with built-in mutes. These flip-up foam pads (positioned below the strings, before the bridge) were supposed to mechanically facilitate the sound of muting. Fender's Jaguar and Bass VI and Gretsch's White Falcon and Country Gentleman are four of the flagship models that featured built-in mutes circa 1962–64. However, most players preferred to do their muting the old-fashioned way (i.e., with the hand), and these apparatuses proved to be unpopular and short-lived.

Playing stuff: Surf music and instrumental rock make copious use of palm muting. This phrase is typical of the surf genre in its heyday. Here the muting effect is applied to a heavily "reverbed" clean-tone guitar sound for a bubbling, percussive result.

Fender Jaguar with mute

TRACK 27

Rock musicians have long been fond of palm muting the heavy-metal riff. This figure contains a characteristic chugging sixteenths rhythm on the open A string, heavily palm-muted. These pedal-point patterns are alternated with accented power chords. Another aspect of muting is presented in the fret hand–muted X's in the G5 chord.

TRACK 27
(0:09)

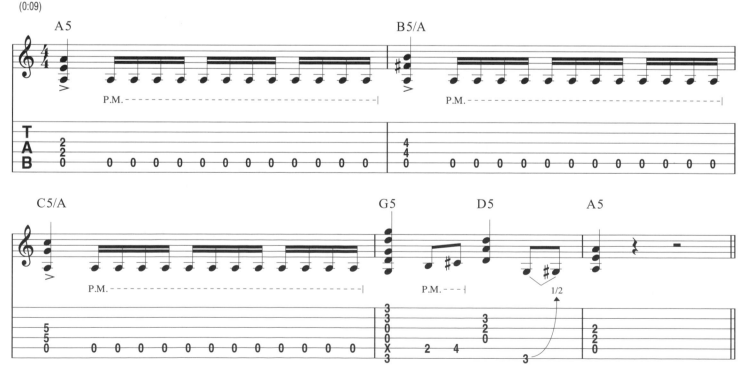

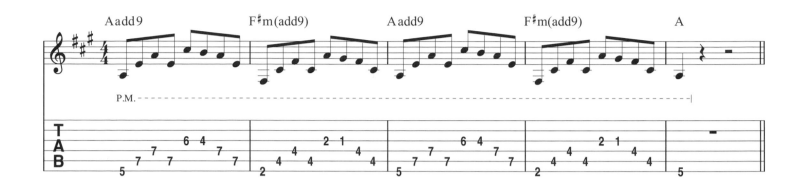

New wave, funk, modern rock, and pop players frequently subject arpeggiated riffs to palm muting. This phrase depicts a classic power-pop arpeggio figure doled out in a steady eighth-note rhythm and fully palm-muted. A little chorus or phasing imparts a lush sheen to such hypnotic metronomic riffs.

TRACK 27
(0:21)

Palm muting technique

NASHVILLE NUMBER SYSTEM

General stuff: The *Nashville Number System*, also called "Nashville Shorthand," was developed and utilized by Nashville session players to facilitate "head arrangements" (done without written notation) in the studio. In studio sessions, time is money, and many gifted players were "ear musicians" who did not sight-read music. The idea of a universal system for "ear players" was appealing—especially one that could create quick, workable arrangements that were based on chords that a player was already using regularly.

Technical stuff: Nashville numbering grew out of the "shape notes" of gospel music. The principle involves assigning a number to each step of the diatonic scale. Unlike the Roman numerals of classic common-practice theory (I, II, III, IV, etc.), the Nashville system uses Arabic numerals: 1–2–3–4, etc. In C major, this would be written as follows: C–D–E–F–G–A–B becomes 1–2–3–4–5–6–7. In arrangements, the numbers are used for chords, allowing for very easy transposition. For example, a 1–4–5 in C major is C–F–G. If the arrangement is transposed to another key, the numbers remain the same but with a new starting, or key note. In F major, 1–4–5 is F–B♭–C. In D major, 1–4–5 is D–G–A. Bottom line: a 1–4–5 progression is notated the same in any key.

More complex chords receive additional designations to specify their quality and color. The relative-minor chord is written as 6m, 6min, or 6- (Am in the key of C). The major-sixth chord is written as 16. Similarly, if the numbers 7, 9, 11, or 13 follow a number, those chords are dominant. A typical C–Am7–Dm7–G7 progression would be written as follows:

$$1 \quad — \quad 6\,m^7 \quad — \quad 2\,m^7 \quad — \quad 5^7$$

> *"The Nashville numbering system provided us the shorthand that we needed so that we could depend on our ears rather than a written arrangement. It took far less time to jot the chords, and once you had the chart written, it applied to any key. The beauty of the system is that we don't have to read. We don't get locked into an arrangement that we may feel is not as good as one we can improvise."*

> —The Jordanaires' Neal Matthews, Jr.

Playing stuff: Virtually any simple pop song with largely diatonic harmony, perhaps a couple of secondary chords, and a straight-forward modulation is a likely candidate for the Nashville Numbering System. But what about more complicated tunes? Here's a Nashville chord chart for a bebop-jazz version of "I Got Rhythm" changes. Just specify the key (normally B♭) and away you go. Notice the "°" symbol for the diminished chord. If you want to experience the expediency of the system, go ahead and rewrite all of the chords in the keys of B♭, E♭, C, and G, using actual chord names. Enjoy the writer's cramp.

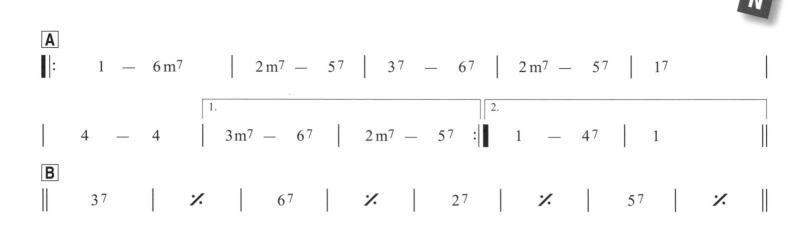

NECK

General stuff: The neck is where the fingerboard is mounted—the surface where most of the playing takes place. It stands to reason that the neck should be checked frequently and kept in optimal condition. Most problems with the neck involve the action and intonation and are attributable to some sort of distortion or twisting of the wood. These are usually corrected by adjusting the truss rod.

Technical stuff: Players regularly use expressions like "This one has a great neck!" What do they mean? Take a survey and you'll get a wide variety of answers and opinions. Most of the time, the neck preference refers to the shape of the back (the other side of the fingerboard) and the overall thickness/width. Eric Clapton prefers a V-shape on his signature Fender Strat and on his Martin acoustics. Stevie Ray Vaughan's Strat has an early sixties–style "oval shape," while Jeff Beck has had a large, extra-deep C-shape on his nineties model and a softer, thinner C-shape on his current Strat. Eric Johnson's signature Strat begins with a soft V-shape at the first fret and graduates to a wider C-shape at the twelfth fret. And James Burton favors a U-shaped neck on his Tele. You get the point. It comes down to how well a particular shape fits the individual's hand.

Playing stuff: The feel and size of a neck affects the way a player responds in performance. Some guitars are sought after and prized for their neck shapes and sizes. Some vintage fifties Gibson Les Pauls have clubby necks, while others are noticeably slimmer and flatter. That holds true for ES-335s, SGs, and various archtop electrics. If you're a beginner or novice who's shopping for a guitar, take a knowledgeable guitar-playing friend or your teacher along to evaluate the neck and how it fits the hand. Of course, everyone's hand is different, thus leading to a range of opinions and confusion. Nonetheless, a second opinion is invaluable and gets you into the ballpark.

NINTH CHORD

General stuff: A ninth chord is a seventh chord with an added second degree (7+2=9). The ninth chord is written in charts and notation as a "9" after the letter name, as in G9, Cmaj9, Dm9, etc. The ninth chord is called an "enriched" or "extended" chord and is idiomatic to many music styles, including blues, jazz, funk, fusion, pop, and country.

Technical stuff: The most common ninth chord adds the ninth degree to a dominant-seventh chord. The C9 chord is spelled: C–E–G–B♭–D. A ninth degree can also be applied to major-seventh chords and minor-seventh chords. In those cases, the chords would be called and written "C major 9" (Cmaj9) or "C minor 9" (Cm9), respectively. The ninth degree is often *altered* in dominant-seventh chords. Two common forms are the flatted and raised 9th, which are called and written "G7 flat 9" (G7♭9) and "G7 sharp 9" (G7♯9), respectively.

Playing stuff: Blues harmony makes prominent use of dominant-ninth chords. This phrase depicts a typical guitar application, courtesy of Mr. T-Bone Walker. Notable are the two common shapes and the characteristic slurred articulation. This type of ninth-chord figure is often found in slow-blues turnarounds.

TRACK 28

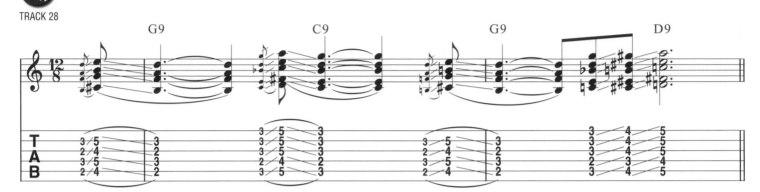

Funk music has its share of vamps and rhythm patterns that exploit the ninth chord. Since much of the style derives its harmonic content from jazz, it only follows logically that the ninth chord would appear often in the funk context. This riff is based on two common shapes. Note the addition of a 13th (C) to the E♭9 to make E♭13, an enrichment of an enrichment.

TRACK 28
(0:13)

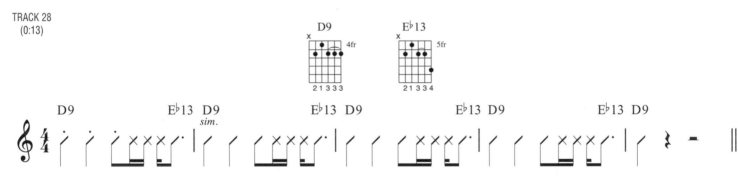

Jazz harmony abounds with enriched chords, particularly varied ninth chords. This ii–V–I progression in G major is a case in point. Every voicing is some sort of ninth chord, depicting the application of 9ths to minor, dominant-seventh, and major chords. Notice the altered 9th in D7♭9♯5 and the use of the 9th and 6th in the rootless G6/9/B sonority.

TRACK 28
(0:26)

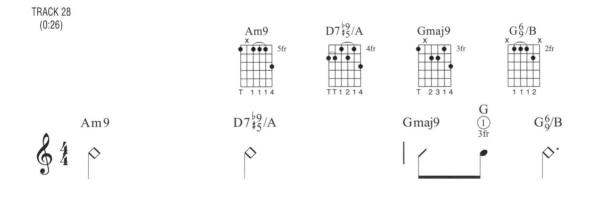

72

NUT

General stuff: The nut is the point at which the strings extend from the fingerboard to the tuning keys. The nut is located on the head of the guitar and is the point at which the vibrating part of the string ends. Originally, a nut was made of bone, ivory, or hardwood. Today, it is usually made of some sort of plastic or synthetic material.

Technical stuff: The nut is a slim piece of material that has grooves cut into it. This is where the strings sit. The depth of the grooves is determined by the *curvature of the fingerboard*. The depth of the grooves is the first crucial aspect when determining action. See *Action* (p. 9). If the grooves are cut too deep, the strings will have an inferior tone, less sustain, buzz, and may even fret out. If the grooves are not deep enough, the strings will be more difficult to press down at the first fret and higher and may affect intonation. The grooves must also provide the correct *string spacing*. The strings should be equally spaced over the fingerboard as they pass from bridge to nut.

The *roller nut* was developed to alleviate tuning problems that are inherent to stock nuts on Strat-style guitars with standard vibrato-bar systems. The most famous type was built by Trev Wilkinson and was featured on the first-edition Fender Jeff Beck Strat. The technology involved replacing the plastic nut with a metal fixture that used needle bearings in the path under and over the strings and did not grip the string tightly. The Wilkinson model led to the smaller LSR, which is currently used by Jeff Beck and others.

What do you do if a nut is too low or buzzes because the grooves are too wide? A nut groove can be temporarily shimmed with thin pieces of paper in the grooves under the strings. This simple solution often suffices on the gig, until a visit to a repair shop. If you are adept at guitar repair, the nut itself can be removed and shimmed with thin strips of metal, plastic, or wood.

standard nut

roller nut

O

OCTAVE

General stuff: An octave is an interval span of twelve half steps. Consider the chromatic scale, beginning on the note C. The interval from C to C, in either direction, is an octave. Depending on direction, there is a lower octave and a higher octave. Several riffs exemplify this motion. Three that immediately come to mind are the Knack's "My Sharona" (low-to-high octave leap), Led Zeppelin's "Immigrant Song," and the Spencer Davis Group's "Gimme Some Lovin'." Moreover, countless classic bass lines use the melodic walking-octave effect of broken octaves moving stepwise.

Technical stuff: An octave encompasses the beginning and repeat of a diatonic seven-tone scale. Put another way, an octave is the eighth step from any given tone. For example, the C major scale is spelled: **C**–D–E–F–G–A–B–**C**. The bold notes are the octave interval. An octave can occur on any step of the scale and in any scale, and is not subject to the major, minor, diminished, or augmented quality of other intervals.

Sonic stuff: An octave can also be played as a *dyad*, or two-note "chord." In this application, two notes that are an octave apart are sounded together. Wes Montgomery remains the undisputed master of playing entire improvised jazz solos in parallel octaves. His style influenced virtually every guitarist who's played octaves since, including most of his jazz colleagues and a plethora of rock and blues players such as Jimi Hendrix ("Third Stone from the Sun"), Stevie Ray Vaughan ("Chitlins Con Carne"), Eric Johnson ("East Wes"), Eddie Van Halen, Steve Vai, the Edge, and Dave Navarro.

Octave technique involves fingering the two-note octave shape and muting all of the other strings. Most of the time, these shapes are strummed with the thumb or pick. These are the octave forms Wes Montgomery used. There are two basic shapes that occupy four possible arrangements on string groups. It is vital to "lock" the fingers into these shapes for fluid parallel motion. Note the different muted strings in each grid. These X's are muted with fret-hand finger sides or tips. See *Muting* (p. 67).

Some players prefer to use the following octave shape. This form is often fingerpicked or hybrid-picked, as strumming runs the risk of sounding the two idle strings between fretted notes. George Harrison played this shape with pick and fingers for the octaves in the main riff of the Beatles' "Please Please Me" and in the coda of "This Boy."

George Benson has filled in those forms with diatonic 3rds to harmonize melodies in octaves with harmonic content. These forms illustrate the previous shapes, augmented with a major- or minor-3rd interval below the top note. The small amount of harmonic information makes these forms very malleable and well-suited to a number of applications. For example, the first shape (if fingered in first position) could imply F6, Dm, B♭ major, Gm7, Bm7♭5, F°, E7♭9, G7, etc.

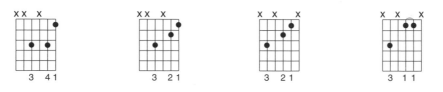

Playing stuff: This quintessential octave phrase exemplifies the style of Wes Montgomery. This characteristic jazz lick makes the point with a bebopping ii–V–I phrase in parallel octaves. Mute every string that is not fretted in every octave shape. And strum these octaves with your thumb for a Wes-approved effect.

TRACK 29

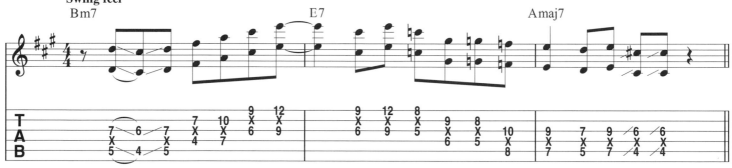

Muting is essential in this hard-rock octave lick. This phrase is delivered with wah-wah pedal colorations and is largely rhythmic. Here the octaves are played with a distorted tone and vigorously
TRACK 29 strummed throughout, emphasizing their textural nature.
(0:09)

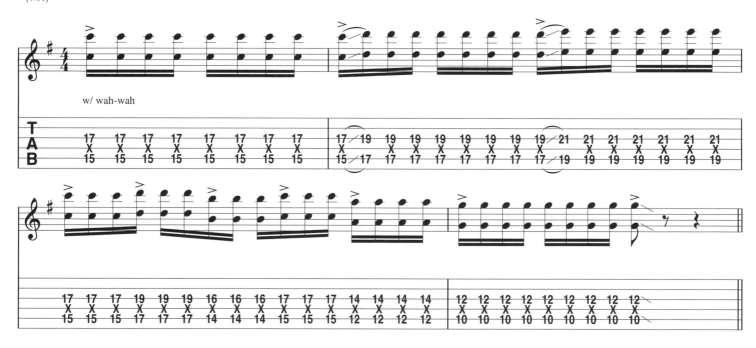

OPEN TUNINGS

General stuff: Open tunings are alternate tunings wherein the strings of the guitar are tuned to the notes of a chord, usually with a major or minor harmonic structure. That leaves a lot of room for possibilities; indeed, there are innumerable tunings, from cliché to obscure.

Historic stuff: The most common open tunings are Open G and Open D (tuned to G major and D major chords) and their higher counterparts, Open A and Open E (tuned to A and E major chords). Countless blues, folk, rock, and pop guitarists have harnessed the sounds of these tunings, including

Eric Clapton, Keith Richards, Robert Johnson, Muddy Waters, Johnny Winter, Ry Cooder, John Lee Hooker, Joni Mitchell, Kurt Cobain, Jimmy Page, James Taylor, and Duane Allman.

Other less common but highly effective open tunings include Open C (John Fahey), Open C Minor (Lawrence Juber), Open F♯ (Norman Blake), Open C♯ Minor (Will Ackerman), Open D7 (Joni Mitchell), Open Dm7 (Richie Havens), Open D Minor (Bukka White), Open G Minor (John Renbourne), Open E♭m7 (Smashing Pumpkins), Open A9 (Chet Atkins), Open E7 (Phil Keaggy), Open E Minor (Skip James), Open Emaj7 (Alex de Grassi), Open F (Jimmy Page), and Open F Minor (Albert Collins).

Open G (D–G–D–G–B–D) and Open D (D–A–D–F♯–A–D) are major chords, as are Open A and Open E. Keith Richards and Eric Clapton use Open G, while Bonnie Raitt and the late Duane Allman prefer the same intervallic arrangement a whole step higher (i.e., Open A). Similarly, Elmore James, Joni Mitchell, and Kurt Cobain are proponents of Open D, while its higher equivalent, Open E, was favored by Robert Johnson and Duane Allman.

Technical stuff: This chart depicts standard tuning and deviations from standard tuning: Open G, Open A, Open D, and Open E. Note the tuning changes of whole steps (1) and half steps (1/2).

	⑥	⑤	④	③	②	①
Standard tuning:	E	A	D	G	B	E
Open G:	D ↓ 1	G ↓ 1	D	G	B	D ↓ 1
Open A:	E	A	E ↑ 1	A ↑ 1	C♯ ↑ 1	E
Open D:	D ↓ 1	A	D	F♯ ↓ 1/2	A ↓ 1	D ↓ 1
Open E:	E	B ↑ 1	E ↑ 1	G♯ ↑ 1/2	B	E

Playing stuff: The rationale and strategy behind open tunings is to facilitate chord sounds as a barre or open strings. In the following examples, the tunings of Open G and Open D are first played as a chord of open strings, then arpeggiated in ascending order, and, finally, followed with a I–IV–V progression. Note the use of barred shapes for the IV and V chords. This advantage exemplifies the utility of open tuning.

In Open G, barring all six strings results in a second-inversion voicing (5th in the bass). This aspect has led Stones guitarist Keith Richards to initially avoid the sixth string of his guitar, and, later, remove it altogether. With this step, all of the barred chords in Open G are in root position.

TRACK 30

Open G Tuning:
(low to high) D–G–D–G–B–D

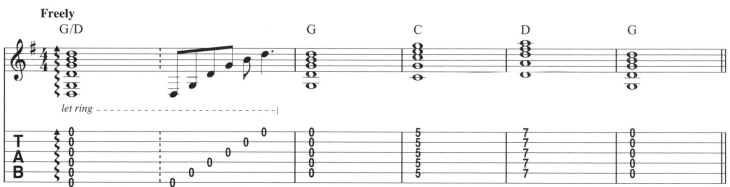

In Open D tuning, it is possible to play I–IV–V progressions as all-barred patterns. The tuning is built from the root, D (lowered sixth string).

TRACK 30
(0:21)

Drop D Tuning:
(low to high) D–A–D–F♯–A–D

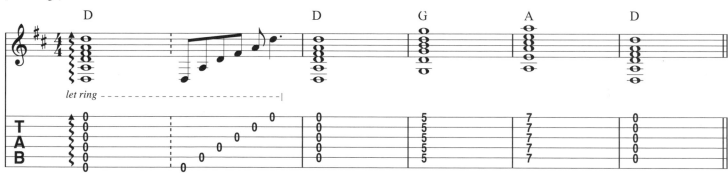

PEDALS

General stuff: Electronic pedals have been in common use by guitarists for decades. Prime among these are the wah-wah pedal and the volume pedal. Practically every electric guitarist has owned or played some sort of a wah-wah pedal. Vox and Crybaby models are the most common and desirable, but companies like Mutron, Foxx, Dallas-Arbiter, Electro-Harmonix, Ibanez, Schaller, Colorsound, Sound City, Marshall, and Morley have gotten into the act and made their own, often viable, units over the years.

Sonic stuff: The *wah-wah pedal* is based on the principle of a tone control with an emphasized Q point that can be operated by the player's foot. The effect is similar to the hand-operated Harmon mute of a trumpet. The rapid or gradual shift in emphasis from treble to bass frequencies produces its distinctive wah-wah sound. The wah-wah is generally placed first in the signal path (sometimes distortion precedes it) to receive the guitar's unprocessed signal for manipulations and tone-shaping.

Technical stuff: Many players use the wah-wah pedal to produce unique polyrhythmic effects. Often, as in the case of "Wah-wah" Watson, who used the wah effect so extensively that he was synonymous with the sound, the guitarist will strum muted strings in a steady sixteenth-note (or eighth-note) rhythm while manipulating the pedal at a different rate to create a second, implied rhythm through accent and tone change. These fluctuations are both syncopated and metric, depending on the desired phrase feeling.

Playing stuff: This funky rhythm part is a common R&B application of the wah-wah pedal. "Shaft" is a landmark riff that launched a thousand (maybe more) spin-offs and affected rock, pop, blues, and fusion genres. Here a sixteenth-note strum pattern of muted strings is subjected to the rhythmic opening and closing of the wah pedal.

TRACK 31

Randomly open and close wah-wah pedal.

Rock players such as Jimi Hendrix, Eric Clapton, Jeff Beck, Robin Trower, Steve Vai, Joe Satriani, and Slash have used the wah-wah pedal to shape lead licks. This telling phrase is made of single-note blues-rock melodies that are colored with wah-wah rhythmic manipulations.

TRACK 31
(0:09)

The wah-wah pedal is also used as a tone-shaping device in a *fixed position*. Here the player leaves the pedal parked at a specific point in its travel to emphasize certain frequencies and harmonics in the melody. Michael Schenker and Randy Rhoads are two of the most well-known guitarists associated with the sound; however, it is ubiquitous in rock, metal, fusion, and modern blues.

TRACK 31
(0:19)

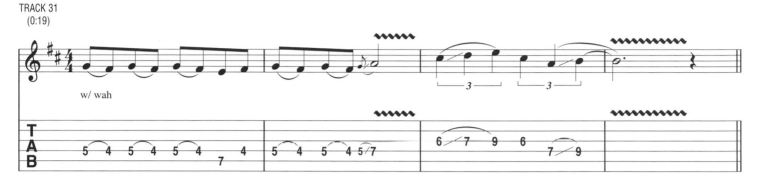

w/ wah

General stuff: The *volume pedal* is another common resource in the arsenal of electric guitarists. This is essentially a potentiometer that is mounted in a floor pedal and designed to control the guitar volume.

Sonic stuff: The volume pedal is used to control overall level to the amp or effects without using the hand to turn knobs. It is generally placed last in the signal path to control the volume of the fully processed guitar sound and to reduce the overall noise level of multiple stomp boxes. The volume pedal is also used to control gain and feedback through boosting and attenuating the strength of the output signal. And it can be applied to a melody to create interesting volume-swell effects that are comparable to "whale sounds." Larry Carlton is the undisputed master of phrasing with the volume pedal, but many other guitarists have made good use of this approach.

Playing stuff: This characteristic melody receives the volume-pedal treatment. Here the pedal attenuates the attack of the notes, swelling in as the notes are sustained. Whale sounds, vocal effects, and quasi–bowed violin emulations are accessible with this application of the volume pedal.

TRACK 31
(0:29)

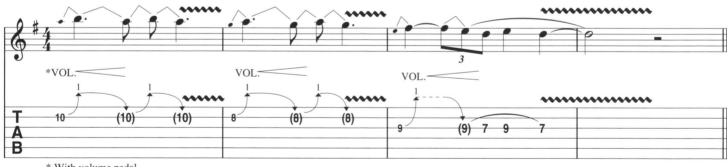

* With volume pedal

General stuff: A more recent entry into the world of pedals is the *modulation pedal*. This foot-operated device controls the rate, and sometimes the depth and feedback, of an effect like a phaser, flanger, vibrato unit, or rotating-speaker simulator. Notable examples include the Uni-Vibe, Mutron Bi-Phase pedal, Digitech Whammy Pedal, and the Dunlop Roto-Vibe. Modulation pedals are usually placed in the center of the effects signal path relative to other processors like fuzz, distortion, echo, and reverb. Use your ear and experiment.

PENTATONIC SCALE

General stuff: The pentatonic scale is a five-note pitch collection that is arguably the most pervasive melodic pattern in the world. Pentatonic scales are found in Oriental music and American blues. They have been heard in indigenous African folk music, as well as post-bop avant-garde jazz and country genres. Pentatonic scales abound in the repertories of B.B. King, Eric Clapton, Jimi Hendrix, Lynyrd Skynyrd, Albert King, Leslie West, Stevie Ray Vaughan, Kenny Burrell, John Coltrane, John McLaughlin, Robben Ford, and Slash.

Technical stuff: Pentatonic scales are, by definition, *five-note scales* (penta=five, tonic=notes). Pentatonic scales, compared with diatonic scales, are gapped scales; that is, the scale contains gaps that create skips in the pattern rather than strict stepwise motion. Beyond the notion of five discrete notes is the quality of the pentatonic scale—namely, its major or minor quality.

The *minor-pentatonic scale* is commonly used in blues, jazz, pop, folk, R&B, and other music. This pentatonic scale has a minor sound due to its minor-3rd interval. In the key of A, the tonic minor-pentatonic scale is spelled: A–C–D–E–G. Note the missing second step, B, and the missing sixth step, F, as well as the minor-3rd interval, A–C. These are the elements that distinguish the quality of the scale. The letter names and the most common "blues box" shape are presented in this diagram. When this scale is used with an A7 chord, a distinctive blues sound (minor on major) is produced.

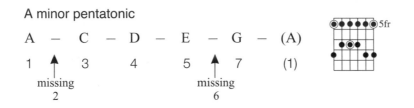

A minor pentatonic

Many players, including Albert Collins, Larry Carlton, and Robben Ford, are fond of using an alternate minor-pentatonic scale with a major 6th interval replacing the more typical 7th step. In the key of A, this scale is spelled: A–C–D–E–F♯. This alternate pentatonic has a more sophisticated sound. The F♯ yields a tritone in the scale (F♯–C), as well as a generally sweeter quality that is preferred by swing- and jazz-oriented blues players. The alternate minor pentatonic scale's elusive nature has prompted some to refer to it as the "secret blues scale."

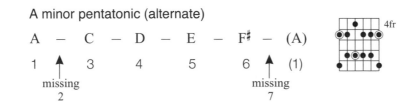

A minor pentatonic (alternate)

The major-pentatonic scale has the same shape and melodic content as its relative minor-pentatonic scale. If A is the minor pentatonic scale in question, the relative major is C. This diagram reveals the common tones and shape of the major pentatonic scale in C, spelled: C–D–E–G–A. Note the missing fourth step, F, and the missing seventh step, B. It's the same as the relative minor pentatonic but with a different reference point (i.e., the C key note).

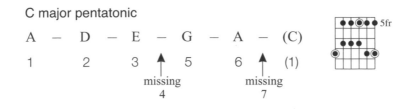

C major pentatonic

PENTATONIC RIFFS AND LICKS

General stuff: Pure scalar playing and exercise patterns can sound exceedingly stiff, formulaic, and contrived in a real-world setting. Knowledge of where the scales are on the fingerboard and the chops to pull them off technically is only half the story—maybe less.

Technical stuff: It is of paramount importance for the creative player to insert the generic language of a style—its characteristic riffs, licks, and melodies—into the network of fingerboard shapes. Indeed, the decisions one makes in choosing what to insert is the beginning of what creates a personal style. Do you want to mix up some B.B. King and Kenny Burrell with a dash of Van Halen? Or does your ear lead you to a combination of John Coltrane and Eric Clapton?

Playing stuff: This minor-pentatonic lick in the key of E is played largely in triplet rhythm. The electric-blues lexicon contains many such pentatonic melodies. Note the use of string bends, legato phrasing, and indispensable clichés like the opening three-note figure.

TRACK 32

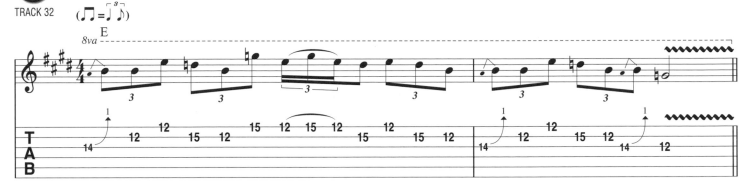

The major-pentatonic scale has a sweeter, more melodic quality. Compare this phrase in E with the previous lick. Many blues and rock players mix this sound with the minor-pentatonic scale for variety.

TRACK 32
(0:07)

Note the string bends and emphasis on the pivotal major-3rd and major 6th tones.

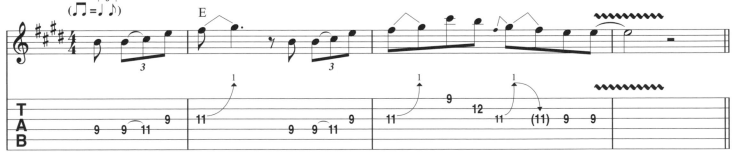

The **Mixolydian pentatonic scale** is a common pattern found in rock, fusion, and metal, though you won't find it in most instructional books. The sound has been heard in the music of Jeff Beck, Gary Moore, and Randy Rhoads, among others. The Mixolydian pentatonic scale is a sort of combination of the major and minor pentatonic. The simplest way to perceive the scale is as a minor-pentatonic scale with a raised 3rd; in the key of E: E–G#–A–B–D. It is closely based on the dominant-seventh chord (E7: E–G#–B–D). This lick exploits a typical triplet pattern and a definitive G#–E–D melody at the

TRACK 32
(0:15)

phrase's ending.

PICKING

General stuff: A string can be picked with a piece of plastic or nylon, the finger, or the thumb. The pick, or plectrum, comes in many shapes and sizes. It is usually constructed of plastic, celluloid, nylon, or tortoise shell. The common *flat pick* varies considerably, from small teardrop jazz models to large triangular types.

Sonic stuff: No particular style of pick is right for a particular style of music. Steve Lukather and Jimmy Bruno use small jazz picks, while Carlos Santana and Charlie Christian favor large triangles. Jazz guitarist Pat Martino has resorted to ultra-heavy picks made of ebony and stone, while another master picker, Jeff Watson, uses a stainless-steel pick. Yes's Steve Howe favored thick Plexiglas picks in the seventies. The choice of pick shape, its gauge (thickness), and material are matters arrived at through years of experimentation and are at the core of each player's articulation and physical tone. Start your explorations now.

Some players prefer a *thumb pick*. This is a semi-circular piece of plastic that is formed to fit the thumb. The thumb pick allows the player to have the rest of the fingers free for plucking. Country pickers Chet Atkins and Merle Travis used thumb picks, as have Johnny Winter, Scotty Moore, Scotty Anderson, and Muddy Waters.

General stuff: Picking is the act and technique of striking the string(s). There are many ways to pick the string, and various theories abound regarding pick angle and pick-hand position. Pick angle and position vary considerably from player to player, and are often manipulated during a performance for specific musical effects. George Benson favors an angled attack, 90 degrees from the typical posture. Stevie Ray Vaughan consistently played with the round end of his pick, while Pat Martino uses the same technique judiciously for ballads to simulate a thicker thumb-like tone. Eddie Van Halen holds his pick between his thumb and middle finger, leaving his index finger free for tapping.

Technical stuff: *Picking techniques* can be broken down into categories: alternating picking, unidirectional picking, sweep picking, and economy picking. It behooves a plectrumist to become familiar and fluent with each technique, as each serves a specific musical purpose. *Alternating picking* is strict down- and up-strokes, alternating with each attack. Al Di Meola uses this approach. *Unidirectional picking* refers to the use of a single type of stroke, usually predominate downstrokes. Charlie Christian and James Hetfield adhere to this approach. Sweep picking generally involves a single downstroke for ascending melodies across strings and a single upstroke for descending melodies. The idea is to accommodate and facilitate the fingering action of the fret hand. Frank Gambale, Paul Gilbert, and Barney Kessel have incorporated sweep picking into their styles. *Economy picking* judiciously combines alternating down- and up-stroke picking with unidirectional picking and sweep picking to make string changes comfortable and efficient. For example, when picking from a lower string to a higher, adjacent string, a downstroke is used in an otherwise alternate-picked phrase.

Playing stuff: The following exercises depict the most common strokes and combinations. The first is a simple all-downstroke eighth-note pattern on a single open string (the open sixth string). Lay on the palm muting and you have a common hard-rock figure. A downstroke symbol is written as a bracket, like an inverted U shape, placed above the note or tab number in question.

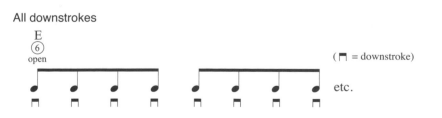

Alternating strokes (down and up) are used for faster passages that contain single notes and chords. This eighth-note figure can apply to notes and/or chords. Note the steady alternation of down- and upstrokes. This alternation is maintained across changes to adjacent strings, as well as wide skips.

This modal-jazz phrase illustrates the use of economy picking. Note the two successive downstokes in measure 1 and the two successive upstrokes in measure 2 to facilitate motion to an adjacent string in ascending and descending direction, respectively.

TRACK 33

Economy picking

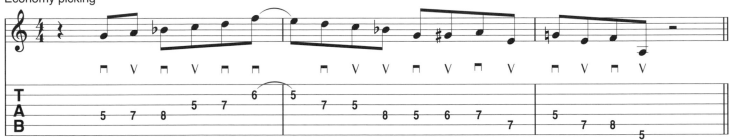

Sweep picking is generally used to attack arpeggio shapes on three successive strings, although, in lengthier passages, it can be applied to all six strings in one stroke. This phrase exploits arpeggios based on a diatonic progression, Fmaj7–Em7–Dm7–Cmaj7, and upstroke sweeps. In a passage like this, the fingers are lifted after each note to maintain a distinct articulation.

TRACK 33
(0:06)

Sweep picking

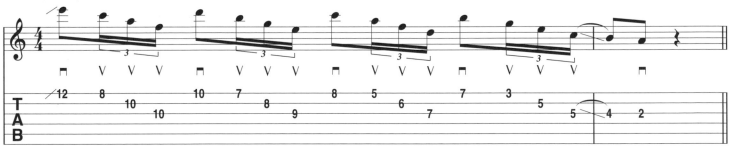

Sweep or economy picking techniques are often written as either ⊓ or V, followed by a broken line over/under the notes in question. It is generally preceded with the word "rake," a variant on the term sweep. This example zooms in on the first arpeggio of the previous phrase to depict the sweep, or rake, technique in its most common written form.

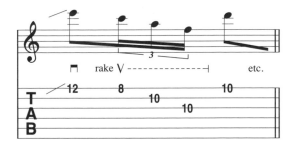

POWER CHORD

General stuff: The term *power chord* is used in rock and pop parlance to specify root-5th voicings on the guitar. Power chords are ubiquitous in hard rock and metal and are heard in virtually every modern style, including contemporary country, blues, Christian rock, R&B, and jazz-rock fusion. Power chords are frequently employed in place of standard major, minor, or seventh chords in many rock-oriented styles.

Technical stuff: The typical power chord is a *dyad* that is played on the lower strings. It is comprised of two notes, the root of the chord and its 5th degree. For example, an A power chord contains A and E, the root and 5th. In modern guitar nomenclature, A5 specifies the power chord built on an A root. This diagram depicts the steps of the scale in the key of A, from which the root and 5th are located and extracted, and two common guitar forms of the A5 power chord.

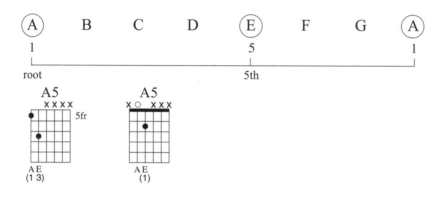

Power chords are often played as a voicing with the root tone doubled. Here are the three-note counterparts of the previous figure's dyads.

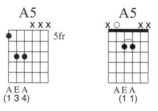

Power chords can also be inverted. Because a power chord contains only two tones, only two forms are possible: root-5th and 5th-root (5th in the bass). This inverted power shape was used by Jimi Hendrix in the chord riff of "The Wind Cries Mary." The inverted power chord has a different musical character than the typical root-position form.

Inverted power chords that are situated in the guitar's mid-range give rise to dyad-style rock riffs like "Smoke on the Water," "La Grange," and "Can't You Hear Me Knocking." These typical dyad shapes are played on the middle four strings of the guitar, often harmonizing the pentatonic or blues scale, and are generally barred with one finger, mixed with 3rds on the third and second strings, and have yielded countless memorable rhythm guitar figures.

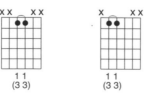

Playing stuff: Power chords reign supreme in rock rhythm styles. The Chuck Berry comping pattern is nothing more than the alternation of power chords with their "cousins," root-6th and, occasionally, root-7th dyads. This characteristic rhythm figure illustrates a familiar pattern.

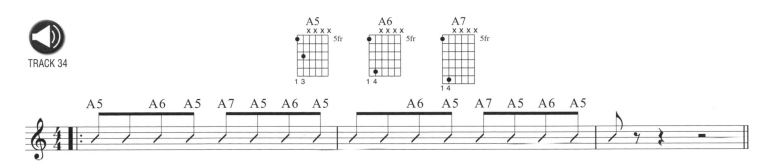

TRACK 34

Power chords are often played in parallel progressions (i.e., the same shape moved verbatim to different chord positions). Metal, punk, surf, blues, rock 'n' roll, and all manners of pop have made use of this guitar-oriented device. This rock rhythm riff is based on three power chords that share the same physical form and string group.

TRACK 34
(0:08)

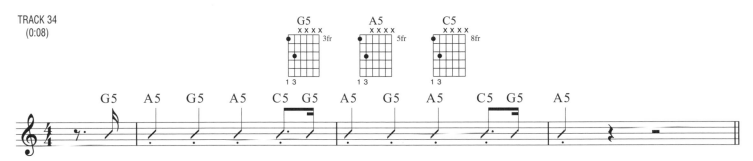

PRACTICING

General stuff: The fine art of practicing the guitar is a cultivated taste and a necessary indulgence. In this age of instant gratification, the notion of working for hours, days, weeks, and months to master one component of what will someday become music may seem antithetical to some, maybe even off-putting. But, make no mistake about it, there is no substitute. When we filmed Larry Carlton's instructional video for Star Licks back in the mid-eighties, Larry underscored the point with an inspiring sermon to guitarists that contained the simple, often-quoted phrase, "Hard work gets the job done." Truer words have yet to be spoken.

Effective practicing requires the advancing player to make several important decisions and to set concrete goals before he or she enters the woodshed. Among these are defining objectives such as improving technique, polishing repertory, learning and memorizing new material, developing greater improvisational abilities, studying theory, sight-reading music, and working with play-along tracks. Some of these objectives can be met in step time; others must happen in real time. Some will change as you progress, and some will be replaced when a real-world gig presents new demands. Speaking of real-world gigs: Joe Pass never practiced anything he wouldn't play in a performance, but practiced improvisation whenever he touched the guitar. Welcome to the woodshed.

Technical stuff: Time management must be considered at the outset. If you have one hour per day to practice, it had better be well-managed. Barney Kessel, a consummate professional, went further. He developed and advocated a system of rotation in which he focused on skills and materials seasonally, dividing his practice time and regime into yearly quarters and specific subjects.

Time management maxims: The greatest benefits come from *daily practice*. It is better to have several short sessions (20–30 minutes) than one long session. One half hour of conscientious, focused practice is preferable to a whole day of directionless, sloppy playing. Indeed, the latter may only reinforce bad habits. Spend 10 minutes warming up with familiar material before plunging into 30 minutes of concentrated new study. Punctuate practice sessions with rest periods.

Practicing at a regular time each day is ideal, though many pros are basically practicing, in one form or another, all day in segments. A log or practice diary is recommended for diligent students with serious goals. And, if possible, avoid serious practice when you're tired, nervous, or mentally distracted. Practice should balance warm-up time, learning new material, reviewing and polishing repertory, technical etudes, and concentrating on pre-determined musical priorities (these can vary considerably). A certain amount of rote practice of specific licks and pieces of the player's generic language (jazz, blues, rock, country, etc.) is necessary to develop and maintain the motor skills and motor memory of improvisers. Moreover, some professional players purposely practice with distractions like the TV to fine-tune their ability to focus and perform effectively in noisy or chaotic environments.

It is advisable to enhance and offset structured practice sessions with recreational free-jamming or "noodling," listening to music, and visual or mental practice without the guitar. In the latter category are techniques like visualizing new chord shapes and progressions, spelling interval structures of chords individually (build a D13♭9♯11 in your mind), and scat-singing rhythmic phrases along with solos.

> *"If I don't practice for one day, I know it. If I don't practice for two days, the critics know it. If I don't practice for three days, the audience knows it."*
>
> —Ignacy Jan Paderewski, famed concert pianist

> *"I never practice anything I wouldn't play on the gig."*
>
> —Joe Pass

> *"I don't practice the guitar. I just open the case once in a while and throw in some raw meat."*
>
> —Wes Montgomery

PROGRESSION

General stuff: The term *progression* is generally used to designate a sequence of chords in a particular order. In formal music study, the word progression may apply to melody (i.e., melodic progression), as well as chords (harmonic progression). Harmonic (or chord) progression, the advancement of one chord to another, is the one that concerns us here. See *Twelve-Bar Blues* (p. 132).

Historic stuff: Some songs are characterized solely by their chord progressions. These include 12-bar blues progressions, the "I Got Rhythm" changes of jazz, two-chord modal vamps of funk and R&B, standard gospel changes that are shared by numerous hymns, and repetitive I–IV–V patterns that abound in rock 'n' roll and pop. Many of these give rise to lasting popular contrafacts across genres.

The contrafact is common in blues, jazz, country, and rock. This is the practice of composing a new song on pre-existing, and often well-known, chord progressions. Whoever wrote the first 12-bar blues created the most often-accessed chord structure of the last century. We get numerous contrafacts and variants from the 12-bar blues structure: Robert Johnson's "Ramblin' on My Mind" (country blues), Howlin' Wolf's "Killing Floor" (urban blues), Benny Goodman's "Wholly Cats" (swing jazz), Chuck Berry's "Johnny B. Goode" (rock 'n' roll), Charlie Parker's "Billie's Bounce" (bebop jazz), "Wipe Out" (surf), and James Brown's "Papa's Got a Brand New Bag" (soul/funk).

Playing stuff: Any chord change generates a progression. With the smaller harmonic lexicon of folk, country, rock, and blues, many progressions are based on different patterns of the most common I–IV–V changes. This chord progression harnesses those three chords, but in a different order. It can be perceived as a V–IV–I pattern in the key of E or a I–♭VII–IV in B (a modal pattern). The I–IV–V progression has yielded innumerable spin-offs and variants, such as "Back in Black," "Can't Get Enough of Your Love," "Gloria," and "White Room."

TRACK 35

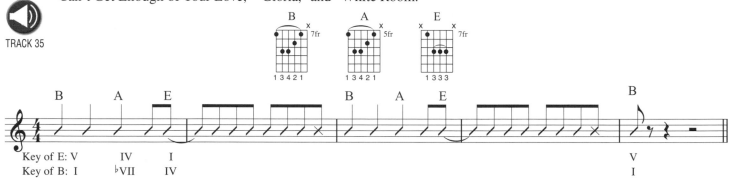

In the larger harmonic lexicon of jazz, chord progressions tend to be more complex, fluid, and multi-faceted. The "Rhythm Changes" bridge, originally heard in the B section of "I Got Rhythm," is just such a pattern. This progression has survived since the twenties in countless versions, like the famed "Flintstones Theme" contrafact of modern pop culture. In this progression, a pattern called the cycle of 4ths is used. Each chord in the four-chord progression is a perfect 4th step away from the last: D–G–C–F. Moreover, each chord is a dominant seventh, which dilutes any sense of traditional resolution to a tonic I chord; it is the paragon of a fluid progression.

TRACK 35
(0:13)

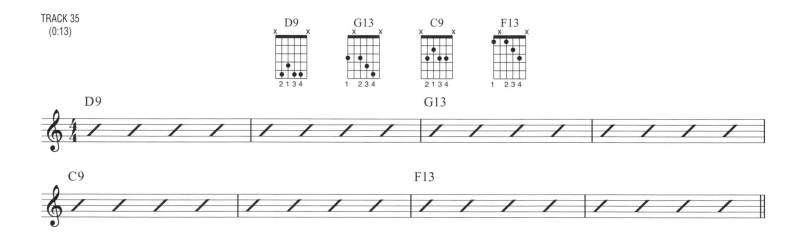

QUARTER NOTES

General stuff: The quarter note is the basic rhythmic division in 4/4 meter. The time signature 4/4 means there are four quarter notes in a measure, dividing the time span into four equal rhythmic parts called beats.

Technical stuff: In 4/4 meter, the quarter note gets the beat and is counted as the primary unit in 4/4: "1, 2, 3, 4, 1, 2, 3, 4," etc. Within these divisions is the placement of accents. *Accents* can stress the strong beats, 1 and 3, or the weak beats, 2 and 4.

Sonic stuff: Quarter notes, as they pertain to the guitar, are epitomized by *four-to-the-bar rhythm patterns*. Four-to-the-bar rhythm patterns are ubiquitous in classical, Latin, rock, swing jazz, country, and pop. This is particularly true in several notable guitar figures. Consider Andy Summers' guitar groove in the Police's "Roxanne" and most of Freddie Green's rhythm-guitar parts with Count Basie. The common denominator is the deliberate quarter-note pattern. Green's rhythm parts are often played as straight quarters (literally four quarter-note strums per measure), as is Andy Summers' staccato rhythm figure.

Playing stuff: This typical Freddie Green rhythm part exemplifies the straight-quarter approach. Here the quarter-note strums are maintained through all manners of chord progressions and sequences of voicings and inversions.

TRACK 36

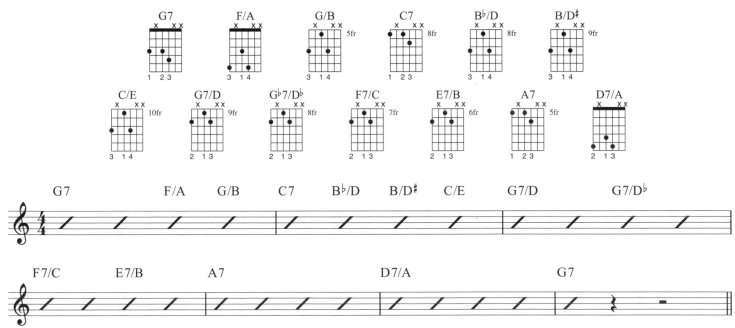

The term *backbeat* refers to an emphasis on beats 2 and 4 of a straight quarter-note pattern in 4/4. The typical backbeat figure involves using space (rests) on beats 1 and 3 (the normal strong beats) and playing emphatic strums on beats 2 and 4. Rhythm guitar parts like this are called "chinks" in pop parlance. The strums, or chinks, are purposely played short and staccato, often with up strokes, to provide rhythmic punctuation in the overall 4/4 structure. Backbeat patterns are prevalent in R&B, pop, rock, blues, and funk—so much so that session man Joe Messina was called on countless Motown studio dates to play just the backbeat chinks.

TRACK 36
(0:13)

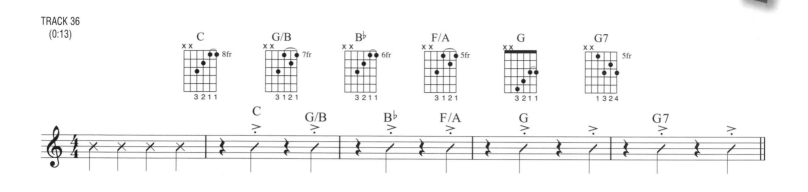

READING MUSIC

General stuff: Reading music is the ability to interpret and perform written music notation. Sight reading is the ability to perform from written music without preparation. But is that really true? A sight reader's ability to perform necessitates countless hours of unseen practice, preparation, and experience.

A guitarist has additional complications when sight reading due to the physical nature of the instrument itself, with its many positions, unison notes, varied fingering options of chords, intervals, and melodies. Only extensive experience and preparation enable the guitarist to compete with wind, brass, string, and other ensemble players in situations in which real-time sight reading is required.

Many great performers have adequate reading abilities yet are not great sight readers. They have enough background to access the music they will ultimately memorize and externalize. This is comparable to the modern guitarist who can interpret tablature well enough to master songs and licks but cannot play from written notation. However, it is advisable to learn basic note-reading skills and develop the ability to sight-read a chord chart if one will, in any way, use written music in professional life.

Technical stuff: The ability to read notes on the guitar requires thorough knowledge of where the notes are found on the fingerboard and to quickly determine which *position* (group of notes in a particular location) is best for a phrase. This presupposes *reading ahead* to reckon the ending notes relative to the starting note. Also significant and vital is the ability to read wide intervals and to determine key centers. A practical preliminary exercise for guitarists is to randomly name any note on any string and then finger it on the fretboard. With practice and repetition, the process grows increasingly faster and builds instrumental confidence in the budding reader.

Good readers have the experience to effectively scan a piece of music and glean the following information in a few seconds: the key and key changes (or modulations), the time signature and deviations from the signature (e.g., 3/4 measures in 4/4 meter), the form (including repeat symbols), sections and endings (e.g., D.S., D.C., Coda), repeated rhythm patterns and chord progressions, written chords, high and low ledger lines (i.e., notes above and below the staff), complicated rhythm figures, interval skips, dynamics, phrasing, changes in clef (treble and bass clef), and directions for effects use and/or idiosyncratic guitar sounds.

Playing stuff: Test yourself. This real-world chart contains a myriad of typical directions and challenges. Note the following points: First, the chart calls for an alternative-rock sound à la U2. It's played at a moderate tempo (160 beats per minute), is in the key of F major, and is in 6/4 meter. Second, the guitar plays a two-bar single-note riff with the synth and no accompaniment in measures 1–4. Note the syncopations in 6/4 and determine what position you would play the melody. It only has three notes (an A minor arpeggio) but it contains high ledger lines, and the rhythm is complicated. Think about phrasing it like a violin player. Third, note the clef change in measure 5. Here the direction calls for "band in" and an F chord. Because the music has a heavy-metal/Celtic feel, play it as an F5 power chord and use the written rhythm figure for a strummed part. Note, too, that the guitar lays out in measure 13, the 3/4 meter at measure 20 (count while resting), and that you and the band re-enter at measure 21.

Alternative Rock (U2 style)

REVERB

General stuff: Reverb is short for *reverberation*. The dictionary defines reverberate as "to re-echo and resound; to be reflected many times as sound waves from the walls of a confined space." And this is what reverb strives to do, electronically. Reverb is a complex resonant sound and has an attractive expansive effect on acoustic instruments.

Historic stuff: Some sax and brass players have purposely practiced in tunnels or under bridges to make use of the ambient reverb effect. But how did electric guitarists avail themselves of the much desired sound? Enter Leo Fender. Though various tape-echo units were available in the fifties, there was still no processor that could produce the resonant, cavernous sound of a large concert hall. The genesis of modern electric-guitar reverb is attributed to Fender and Dick Dale, the King of the Surf Guitar. In the early sixties, Dale, working closely with Fender, requested a reverb effect that he could use on his voice. The outboard reverb unit was born in 1961, when Fender licensed the famous Hammond organ spring reverb and created the classic Fender Reverb model 6G15.

Following the success of the Fender Reverb with guitarists, the reverb effect was built into many amps of the sixties. Who invented built-in reverb amps? Ampeg had introduced the Reverberocket, Echo Twin, and B-12X a year before Fender marketed their first, the 1963 brown-tolex Fender Vibroverb. In any case, other models followed quickly in the mid-sixties, including the Fender Twin-Reverb, Super-Reverb, Deluxe-Reverb, Vibrolux-Reverb, and Princeton-Reverb, as well as those by Ampeg, Vox, Gibson, Gretsch, Guild, Rickenbacker, Standel, Supro, Alamo, Kustom, and Acoustic.

Nowadays, reverb comes in many forms for the guitarist: the classic tube units, built-in spring reverb and digital reverb in amps, studio-quality digital-reverb rack units, and in numerous stomp boxes and multi-effects processors.

Sonic stuff: The Fender Reverb boasted that it was "designed for all amplification systems." Its small cabinet, about the size of a shoe box, housed a tube-driven Hammond spring-reverb circuit with three controls: Dwell, Mixer, and Tone. Dwell controlled the depth of the reverb effect, the Mixer balanced the amount of wet versus dry signal (or reverb level), and Tone modified the sound, from bass to treble emphasis.

Most amps with built-in reverb combine two of the three reverb parameters (depth or dwell and tone) into a preset and allow the guitar-to-reverb mix to be adjusted with a single control on the front panel, usually marked "Reverb" (Fender) or, occasionally, "Echo" (Ampeg). The current Heritage Kenny Burrell model amp is an exception, employing the original Dwell, Tone, and Level parameters in its control panel.

Modern digital reverb units have additional parameters. These commonly include a choice of reverb type (spring, room, gated, or plate sounds) and room size (from small spaces and moderate room sizes to large arenas), reverb level and dwell (adjusts reverb circuit, not output), reverb tone or shape (adjusts high frequencies in the reverb sound and decay with gated reverb), reverb sustain (amount of time that the reverb resounds), and reverb diffusion (adjusts decay quality, from sparse and irregular to dense and smooth).

Playing stuff: Reverb is a central component to countless styles. In modern bop and post-bop jazz (post 1960), as well as blues, country, pop, and R&B, reverb is a crucial part of a guitar player's live sound. In jazz, this is a subtle, organic type of sound in which reverb enhances an already warm clean tone. The ideal is an effect that envelopes the guitar tone without undue gimmickry. This characteristic jazz line exemplifies the typical reverb sound of players like Wes Montgomery, Pat Martino, and George Benson.

TRACK 37

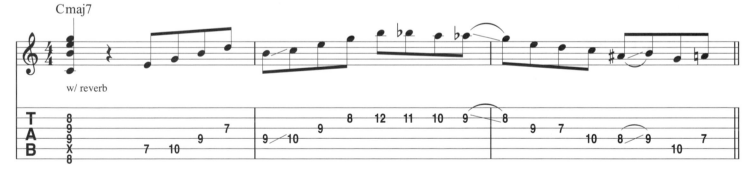

Reverb in its most extreme form was heard often in the wet sounds of 1960s surf music. Many players of the genre followed Dick Dale's lead, sought out the outboard reverb unit and applied copious amounts of reverb to their twangy guitar tones. This phrase features the surf reverb effect with dwell cranked high enough to make a splashy ostentatious sound that emulates crashing waves of the Banzai Pipeline.

TRACK 37
(0:07)

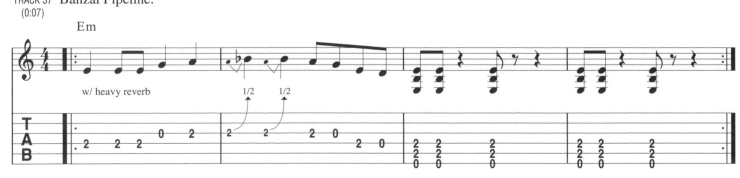

RHYTHM GUITAR

General stuff: *Rhythm guitar* is a generic term usually describing a strummed, largely chordal accompaniment approach. Though it is characterized in some genres by strict strumming, it can also apply to heavy-rock power-chord riffs, percussive arpeggiations laced with modulation effects, or spacey textural washes.

Historic stuff: Rhythm guitar has had many faces. It is epitomized by Freddie Green, Allen Reuss, and Steve Jordan in swing jazz, Robert Johnson, John Lee Hooker, and Stevie Ray Vaughan in blues, Jimmy Nolen, Curtis Mayfield, Steve Cropper, Ray Parker, and Al McKay in R&B, Paul Simon, Don Everly, and James Taylor in pop, Jerry Reed, Buck Owens, and Jimmy Rogers in country, and Keith Richards, John Lennon, Andy Summers, James Hetfield, Malcolm Young, and The Edge in rock.

Technical stuff: Rhythm guitar has many musical approaches and disciplines. Rhythm guitar in jazz can vary from Freddie Green's straight, four-to-the-bar chord strumming (see *Quarter Note*, p. 88) to varied on- and off-beat comping and emulations of big-band horn figures and piano punctuations. In blues, rhythm guitar can range from loose acoustic accompaniments, boogie patterns, and Chuck Berry–style comping to the expressive improvisatory lead/rhythm approach of Jimi Hendrix. In metal and hard rock, rhythm guitar encompasses all types of power chording, ensemble riffs, textures, pedal-point figures, and various dyad patterns. The well-rounded guitarist should be conversant with these and more.

Playing stuff: Nothing says *rhythm* guitar like Stevie Ray Vaughan's blues comping in tunes such as "Pride and Joy" and "Cold Shot." This approach is similar to the skank style of R&B rhythm guitar with the use of fret-hand muting and the alternation of fretted chords, single notes, and muffled textures. The basic technique involves synchronization of the hands: the synchronizing of consistent continuous strumming (pick hand) while damping unwanted notes and chord partials or creating purely percussive muted sounds (fret hand).

TRACK 38

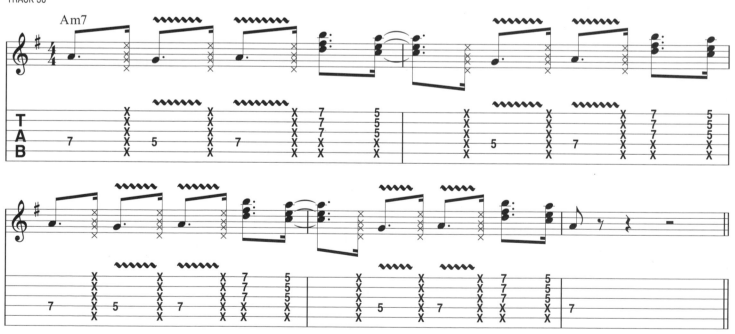

In rock, rhythm guitar is personified with the driving riffs of Keith Richards. This next particular figure is in Open G tuning and uses typical Stones-approved barred triad shapes to produce the requisite magic. Keith's time-tested formula for rock rhythm guitar: "5 strings, 3 notes, 2 fingers, and 1 a--hole."

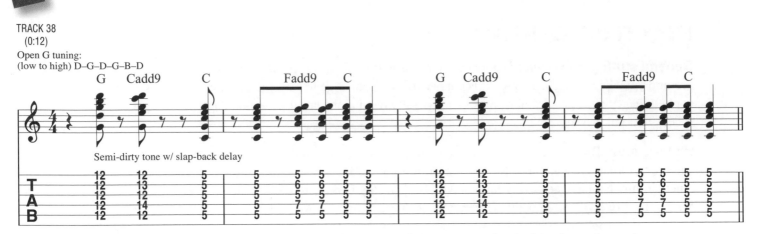

Open G tuning:
(low to high) D–G–D–G–B–D

Semi-dirty tone w/ slap-back delay

Harmonic minimalism, pedal point, drones, and forward motion come together in this alternative-rock rhythm-guitar figure. Ambiguity with respect to chord type and progression reduces the unusual sonorities to their lowest common denominator: pure rhythm. Chord names are of secondary importance here; the main event is the driving eighth-note rhythm, textures, and the shifting accents.

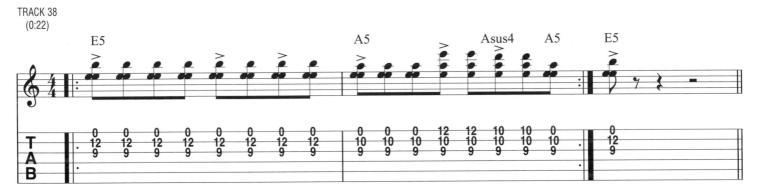

RIFF

General stuff: Riff is a contraction of the words *repeated figure*. The term is synonymous with the concept of repetition in popular music. According to the dictionary, riff is both a noun and a verb. A riff is a melodic phrase, often constantly repeated, forming an accompaniment. To riff is to perform riffs. So when Jimi Hendrix plays a repeated lead lick for the umpteenth time, he is riffing. And when James Hetfield lays down the heaviest power-chord ostinato pattern, it's a riff. Charlie Christian locked into a repeating lick with Benny Goodman is a swing riff. Got that? It all comes down to *repetition*, the magical procedure that makes all things comprehensible to the average listener and transcends genre and style.

If you play something once, it often goes flying over the heads of the audience. Play it twice and the listener begins to take notice. Repeat and you draw listeners like a magnet. That rule was made clear to Pat Martino when it came from the lips of mentor Les Paul. Martino's music is filled with some of the most exciting riffs in improvised jazz guitar. There's a premium on repetition and riff consciousness in modern jazz. Buddy Guy uses the same idea to mesmerize a roomful of blues aficionados. And Nigel Tufnel can riff by bowing his guitar with a violin while strumming a second guitar with his foot!

Historic stuff: In rock and metal, the riff is not only essential, it is often central to the music. Many songs are recognized immediately upon hearing the main riff—or a mere fragment of it. In this group are unforgettable riffs like "I'm Your Hoochie Coochie Man," "Jailhouse Rock," "Day Tripper," "Satisfaction," "Sunshine of Your Love," "Smoke on the Water," "Crazy Train," "Super Freak," "I Wanna New Drug," "Louie, Louie," "Whole Lotta Love," "Beat It," "Pretty Woman," and "Come as You Are." And those are just the tip of the iceberg.

Playing stuff: Riffs are prevalent in blues and rock. This riff has been found in both genres. A simple figure—and simplicity is part of the package—is repeated, forms a phrase structure, and defines the time span. Here the compact four-note melody is offset with rhythmic muted strings.

TRACK 39

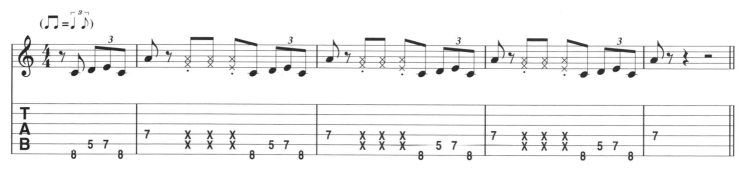

ROCKABILLY

General stuff: Rockabilly is a distinct branch of early rock 'n' roll music and a genre that has remained truest to its fifties roots through its numerous revivals and reappraisals of the past 50 years. The name reflects a combination of rock 'n' roll and hillbilly styles, but the sound is something more—a case of the whole being greater than the sum of the parts.

In rockabilly, we hear the tell-tale elements of early rock: blues riffs and actual repurposed blues songs, honky-tonk piano licks, boogie-woogie patterns, and guitar improvisations that borrow liberally from the playbooks of Chuck Berry, B.B. King, and T-Bone Walker. We also hear plenty of references to southern country music and western swing, with strummed acoustic rhythms, Chet Atkins and Merle Travis guitar picking, jazzy ninth and thirteenth chords, and Charlie Christian–inspired single-note runs. This rock/country duality is at the heart of the style.

Historic stuff: In its earliest incarnation, rockabilly is the Sun recording legacy of Elvis Presley, Carl Perkins, Johnny Cash, Roy Orbison, and Jerry Lee Lewis. It is also Eddie Cochran, Gene Vincent's Blue Caps (with Cliff Gallup), Dale Hawkins, and Ricky Nelson (with James Burton). These artists are considered essential listening to this day. The eighties rockabilly revival was spearheaded by the Stray Cats, who were led by guitarist Brian Setzer, the leading exponent of rockabilly guitar today. In this period, rockabilly affected artists like Dave Edmunds and bands like Queen ("Crazy Little Thing Called Love"). In between, there are enumerable references to rockabilly in the music of the Beatles, CCR, Tom Petty, Paul Simon, and countless others—even Jimi Hendrix covered "Blue Suede Shoes." On a related tangent, the classic instrumental "Guitar Boogie Shuffle" (The Virtues) is a rockabilly tune without lyrics that cracked the Top 10 in 1959 and influenced many subsequent pop guitar players.

Sonic stuff: The classic rockabilly guitar sound is distinguished by archtop electric guitars, usually a Gibson (Scotty Moore, Hank Garland) or a Gretsch (Eddie Cochran, Brian Setzer), a semi-distorted tube amp, and distinctive tape-echo effects. Generally, the echo unit is set to produce a single, tight slap-back delay (around 100ms) with only one repeat. Some guitarists, notably Carl Perkins, James Burton, and Cliff Gallup, preferred solidbody guitars, and due to their influence, the Fender Telecaster and Gretsch Duo-Jet are also viable rockabilly tools.

> *"Rockabilly is blues with a country beat."*
> —Carl Perkins, *Rolling Stone*

> *"[My lead guitar solos with Elvis] were primarily my own inventions. A lot was a combination of old blues licks, some Travis, some Atkins, a combination of thumb and finger—just whatever I could make work. I was listening to Atkins, Travis, Barney Kessel, Tal Farlow, and B.B. King."*
> —Scotty Moore, *Guitar Player*

"The record that made me want to play guitar was 'Baby, Let's Play House' by Elvis. I just heard two guitars and bass and thought, 'Yeah, I want to be part of this.'"

—Jimmy Page, *Guitar Player*

Playing stuff: Several essential rockabilly ingredients are depicted in this exemplary accompaniment phrase. Note the boogie-woogie bass-register riff, which is delivered with staccato articulation. This riff is palm-muted and saturated with echo. The arpeggio-type melody, with emphasis on the 6th tone, C♯, is definitive. In measures 3–4, a typical Travis-picked cadential figure, B7–C7–B7, is found. Also check out the palm-muted bass notes (downstemmed), the loose polyphony, and sustained chord partials.

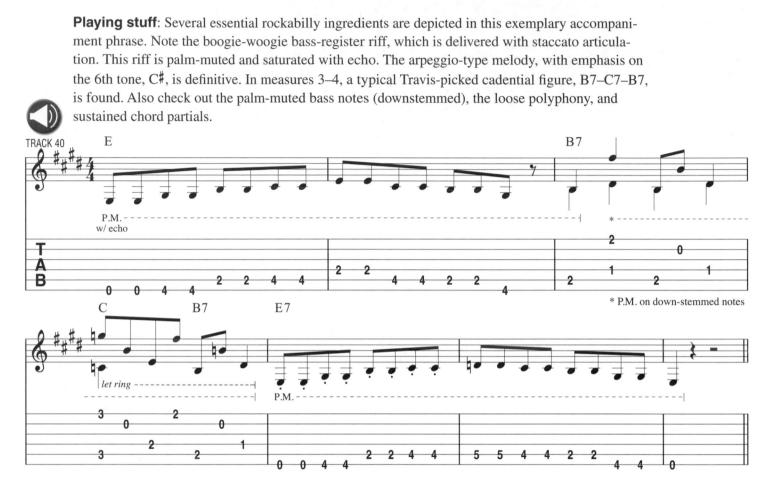

The lead side of rockabilly is presented in this multifarious lick. Note the tritone dyad that is bent a quarter tone (T-Bone), the use of Berry-style double stops, a quick single-note riff that exploits the 6th (C♯) of western swing, the bluesy minor/major polarity of G–G♯, and a swinging Charlie Christian–based line as a potent phrase ending.

SCALE

General stuff: A scale is a collection of related notes in consecutive order. There are many forms of scales, each with different pitch content. Scales are generally determined by the quality of their steps—that is, the different orders and relationships of half and whole steps in most diatonic scales and modes. These relationships result in perceptions like minor versus major tonality. Moreover, there are five-note scales (pentatonic), seven-note scales (diatonic), six-note scales (hexatonic, whole-tone, and blues scales), eight-tone scales (diminished and bebop), and many other synthetic constructs.

Technical stuff: A guitarist's directory of must-know scales include the minor and major pentatonic scales, the blues scale, the hexatonic scale, the major scale, the Aeolian mode, the Dorian mode, the Lydian mode, the Locrian mode, the Phrygian mode, the diminished scale, the whole-tone scale, the altered scale, the dominant bebop scale, the major bebop scale, the harmonic-minor scale, and the melodic-minor scale.

Playing stuff: The scales in this chart are all based on the keynote C, also called the root, or tonic. This system places all of the scales in the same key and aids in hearing and viewing their unique interval arrangement and melodic effect. It also provides instant back-to-back comparison of scale type.

What about their usage? Note the difference in qualities. Initially, the major or minor 3rd interval presents a clue as to usage, followed by minor versus major 6ths (m6–M6) and 7ths (m7–M7), and then by their diminished and augmented quality (written as "♭5" and "Aug," respectively).

Check out other peculiarities, like the ♭2nd step in the Locrian, Phrygian, Altered, and Phrygian-dominant scales, the *augmented 2nd* interval (1½ steps) in the harmonic-minor and Phrygian-dominant scales, and the chromaticism in the bebop scales. Moreover, note the modes of the ascending form of the melodic-minor scale. These include the *synthetic scales*, the altered scale, and the Lydian-dominant scale.

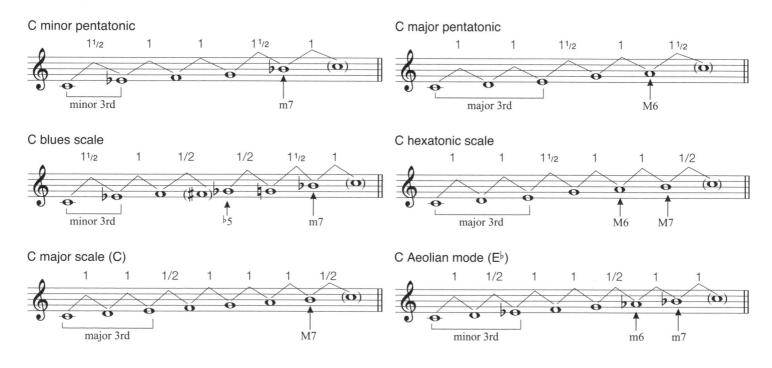

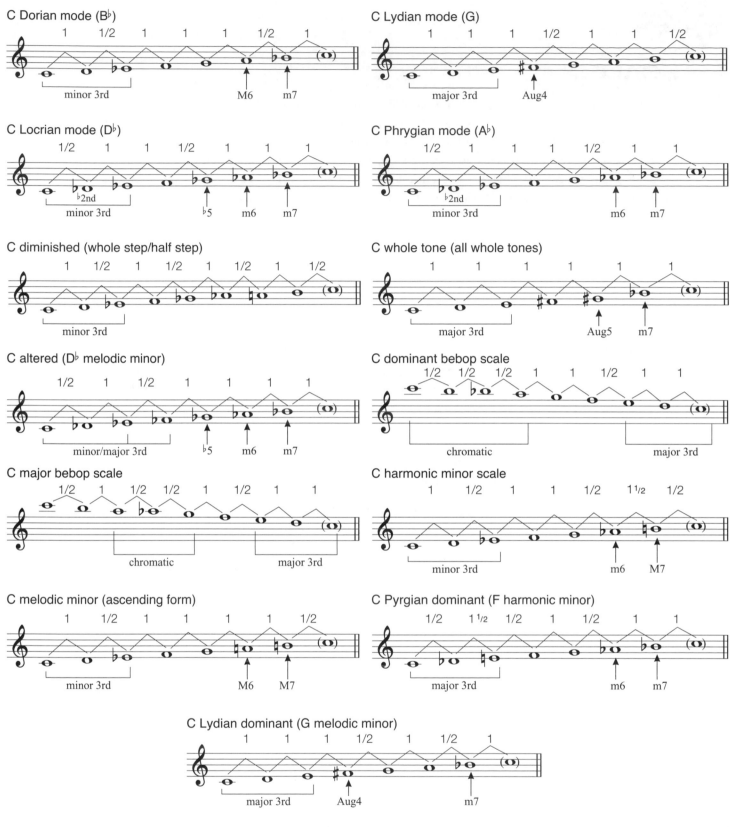

SEMI-HOLLOW GUITAR

General stuff: The semi-hollowbody electric guitar was developed in the fifties as a response to the increasing volume levels of rock, blues, country, and jazz and the feedback of hollow-body electrics. Prior to the late fifties, hollowbodies were fine for most players, as long as the amp wasn't too close and the music wasn't too loud. John Lee Hooker, B.B. King, Chuck Berry, Les Paul, Jimmy Nolen, Merle Travis, Keith Richards, Larry Carlton, Lee Ritenour, and Robben Ford all used large hollowbody archtop electrics in the early stages of their careers.

Historic stuff: Who invented the semi-hollow guitar? Gretsch began chambering their "solidbody" guitars—the 6121 Chet Atkins model, White Penguin, and Duo Jet—back in the early fifties. These guitars were routed substantially under the surface for wires and controls and had a superficial appearance of a solidbody. Technically, they are referred to as "semi-solid" and are usually considered to be a step in the direction of the true semi-hollow guitar.

In 1958, Gibson introduced the ES-335 to their new thin-line series. This was the first production guitar to feature hollow wings (with F-holes) on the upper and lower bouts and a solid wood block in the center, under the pickups, bridge, and tailpiece. By 1960, Gibson expanded their semi-hollow line with the ES-345 and 355, and other major guitar companies quickly followed suit. Other entrants include the Guild Starfire, the Epiphone Sheraton and Riviera, and the Fender Coronado. Recent variations on the semi-hollowbody theme are represented by the Gibson Lucille, Pat Martino, and Paul Jackson models, as well as the Fender Telecaster '69 Thinline reissue, Espirit, and Robben Ford models.

Sonic stuff: Over the years, many prominent players have relied on the distinctive tone and response of semi-hollow guitars. Among the most prominent are B.B. King, Keith Richards, Pat Martino, John Lee Hooker, Freddie King, Larry Carlton, John Scofield, Robben Ford, Alvin Lee, John McLaughlin, Lee Ritenour, Jonny Lang, Johnny Marr, Otis Rush, Jimmy Rogers, and John Abercrombie. Even devout Strat cats like Eric Clapton, Stevie Ray Vaughan, Eric Johnson, and Buddy Guy have turned to semi-hollow guitars for alternative sounds.

> "[I was attracted to the 335 because] *I needed a guitar that I felt comfortable on, that I could play the way I liked to play—which was coming from a 175 [Gibson ES-175 arch-top] approach with a more contemporary sound. I needed something real versatile."*
> —Larry Carlton, *Guitar Player*

SEVENTH CHORDS

Gibson ES-335   Pat Martino   Fender
                                            Coronado

General stuff: A seventh chord is formed by adding the interval of a 3rd to the top of any triad, creating a four-note structure. The most common seventh chord is the *dominant-seventh chord*. The dominant seventh's structure is a major triad plus a minor-7th interval. For example, C7 contains the C major triad, C–E–G, and the minor-7th interval B♭, a ♭3rd above G in the triad.

Technical stuff: The dominant-seventh chord, like many seventh chords, has a tendency to resolve due to the active nature of the 7th interval. With a dominant seventh, this is more emphatic due to the *diminished-5th* interval in its structure; in the case of C7, this would be E–B♭. In fact, in many forms of comping, the use of active seventh chords is based purely on these tones—the chord's 3rd and 7th degrees. In blues and jazz comping, as well as funk and rock, the dominant-seventh chord's 3rd and 7th degrees become shell voicings and are often played in sequential patterns.

Playing stuff: This chain of similar shapes demonstrates a progression of dominant-seventh chords that moves in a cycle of 4ths.

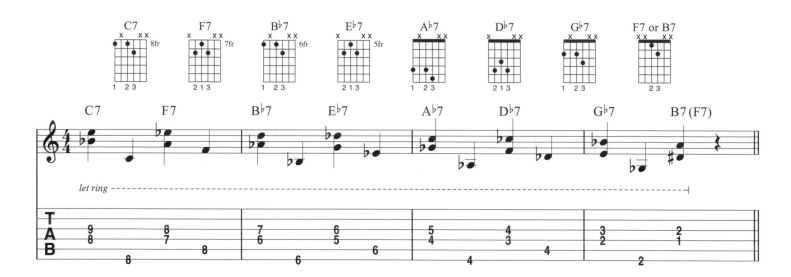

This progression is in the keys of C major and its relative minor, A minor. It contains diatonic seventh chords and secondary seventh chords that are built on steps of the C major scale. In this sequence of 4th-related chords, every type of seventh is used: dominant seventh, minor seventh, and major seventh. Note the use of *secondary dominant sevenths*, E7 and A7, which are not diatonic to the key and resolve to their own temporary tonic, A minor and D minor, respectively.

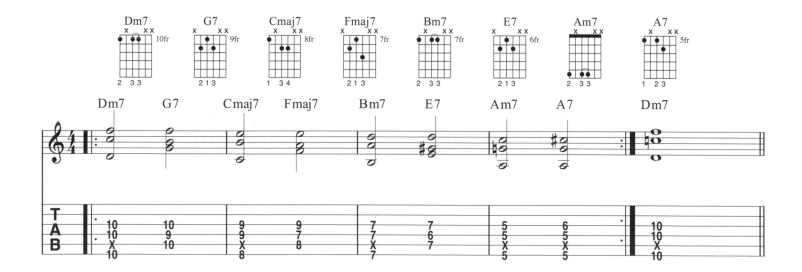

SHUFFLE

General stuff: The shuffle is a triplet-based rhythm pattern common to blues, jazz, rock, pop, and country music. The shuffle is ubiquitous and inescapable. You can't have a loping boogie-blues piece like Stevie Ray Vaughan's "Pride and Joy," the lilt of a Bob Wills western-swing rag, or an irresistible Count Basie jazz swing groove without the shuffle. In fact, the central rhythmic pulse of an improvised jazz or blues line is almost always a swung shuffle pattern, even when the overall rhythm feel played by an ensemble is straight eighth notes or a slow rubato ballad.

Technical stuff: A shuffle rhythm is produced when an even triplet is subdivided to form an oblong quarter-note/eighth-note pattern on each beat. Here's how it works. First, imagine the three separate notes of a triplet group. Next, picture the first two notes tied together to form a quarter note in the triplet. Finally, see the triplet converted to an uneven two-beat unit. Count: "long-short, long-short," etc.

Playing stuff: Mathematics notwithstanding, a shuffle is better felt than calculated and determined.

To feel a shuffle, first consider this blues comping figure, which is played in a straight eighth-note rhythm. This phrase is rendered without the shuffle feel and comes off like the strutting rock groove in "Bang a Gong."

TRACK 41

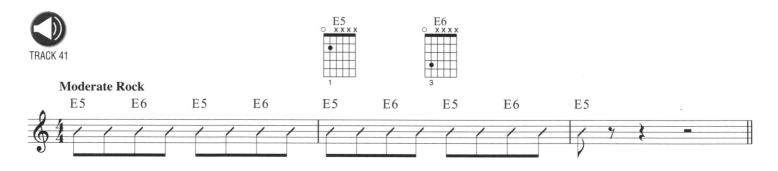

When the same comping figure is subjected to uneven triplet rhythms (*long*-short, *long*-short, etc.) a shuffle groove is produced. Note that the strum pattern of the eighth notes is identical to the previous phrase. But look closer. The music calls for a "Moderate Shuffle" and contains a symbol in parentheses that specifies that two eighth notes equal the uneven triplet. Get used to scanning music to look for this direction in your favorite transcriptions.

TRACK 41
(0:08)

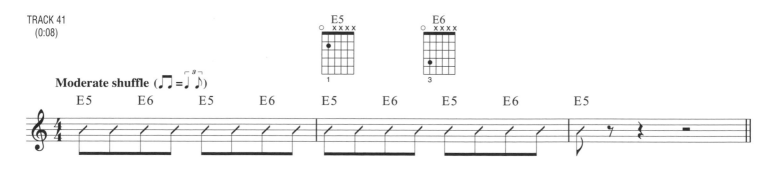

SLASH CHORDS

General stuff: Slash chords specify the chord names of inversions and polychords in chord charts, written guitar notation, and transcriptions. While it is unlikely that anyone will ever ask you to play a "slash chord" on a gig—unless, of course, you're in a Guns N' Roses cover band—it is absolutely essential to be familiar and conversant with the idea and its usage.

Technical stuff: Put simply, a slash chord indicates a note in the bass other than the root, or tonic. Slash chords are notated with two letter names that are separated by a forward slash. The first letter symbolizes the chord name; the second tells us what note is in the bass. Therefore, a *first-inversion triad* would be written as follows: chord name/3rd of the chord in the bass. For example, C/E is the first-inversion C major triad.

Playing stuff: This series of C major chords illustrates the use of slash-chord notation to specify inversions. Note the C triad, followed by C/E and C/G, first and second inversions, respectively.

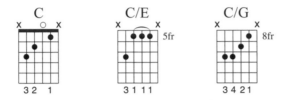

Slash chords are often used in chord progressions to indicate bass movement and chord types. This classic gospel progression puts slash chords to good use. Note the C/B♭ (a C7 with the seventh tone in the bass) resolved to F/A and Fm/A♭ (F major and minor chords in first inversion). C/G and F/G share the G common tone in the bass. G is the 5th of the C major chord (second inversion); however, F/G is a different animal, the other slash chord. Here the bass note is not a member of the triad; instead, it is the second step added to the voicing and played in the bass. This type of slash chord yields a more sophisticated dominant-seventh sound (G11) and is prevalent in fusion and jazz.

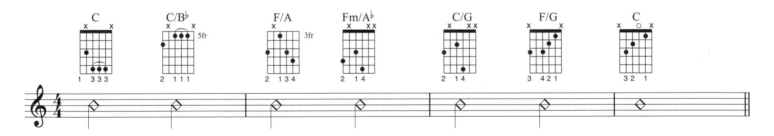

Slash chords are frequently applied to *pedal-point* progressions. In this diatonic example in the key of G, C major and D major triads are posed over an A pedal point. A is the prevailing bass note for the entire sequence and is not a member of the triads in the pattern.

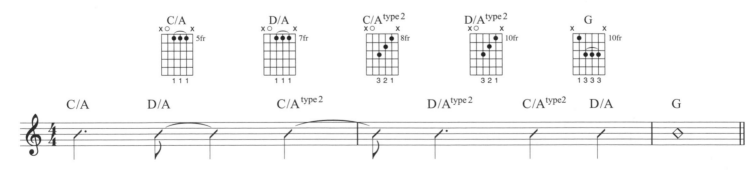

In jazz harmony, slash chords often imply complex *rootless seventh chords* and other sophisticated sounds. This example illustrates the concept with three complex chords of varied dissonance, all without their tonic tones, in a ii–♭II–I progression (Dm7–D♭7–C). These chords make for a more interesting color and have the added advantage of not doubling the bass player's notes.

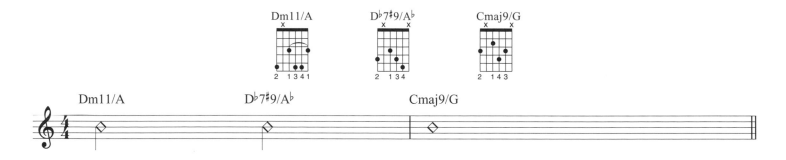

SLIDE GUITAR

General stuff: Slide guitar is a sound and a style. The sound is created by the use of a glass bottleneck or metal tube on the strings. The style, in its most common form, is based on the blues approach, idiomatic phrases, and open tunings of players like Charlie Patton, Robert Johnson, Elmore James, and Muddy Waters.

Slide guitar is played on acoustic or electric guitars. The acoustic sound is personified by Robert Johnson, Son House, Tampa Red, Bukka White, Fred McDowell, Blind Willie Johnson, and Eric Clapton. Electric slide is epitomized by Muddy Waters, Elmore James, Duane Allman, Ry Cooder, Bonnie Raitt, Johnny Winter, Sonny Landreth, and Derek Trucks. On a separate tangent, guitarists like George Harrison, Jimmy Page, and Jeff Beck have pursued a different yet very attractive form of slide playing in standard tuning with a scalar, or linear, "non-blues" melodic conception.

Sonic stuff: Many pro guitarists set up specific instruments for slide playing. This involves using higher action at both the bridge and the nut and heavier strings. Some players, like David Gilmour and Jeff Baxter, alternatively use a Hawaiian or country-style lap-steel guitar for slide. Others prefer to use a single guitar with a compromised set-up: slightly heavier strings and slightly higher action that would still not hamper regular playing.

> *"If you really want to develop your own voice as a slide player, you're way better off having a guitar that's set up solely for slide. The trick for me is having the strings high enough that the slide will float easily on them yet low enough that I'm able to fret notes in tune behind the slide. For me [a nearly flat fingerboard] is another crucial element of a good slide setup because it makes all the strings level with each other, allowing you to play slide cleanly on all six strings at once."*
>
> —Sonny Landreth, *Guitar Player*

Technical stuff: Judicious muting by both hands is essential to clean slide guitar playing. Sonny Landreth and Arlen Roth are two among countless slide players who have developed effective muting techniques to control the noise and strings' ringing—and so should you. Landreth, a skilled slide player, erases unwanted slide noises by muting strings with the pick hand. Each finger mutes an unwound string while the thumb damps the bass strings. Players also mute with the fret hand by resting lightly on the strings behind the slide, thereby canceling unwanted errant notes and noises at the other end. One last point: The slide creates a properly tuned note when positioned directly over a fret rather than between frets, as in conventional guitar playing.

Sonic stuff: Authentic vintage electric slide sounds require old-style guitars that are generally fitted with a fixed bridge (i.e., hardtail) and low-output pickups—though they are noisier, many players prefer single-coils—married to an amp with a fair amount of overdrive. The signal is often enhanced with appropriate mid-range boosting and compression for more sustain and evenness of tone. For traditional slide guitar, it is generally not advisable to employ a "shred guitar" with low action, light-gauge strings, super-distortion pickups, and a whammy bar. Pick the right tool for the job. The choice of glass bottleneck or metal tube, its length, and what finger it is worn on varies from player to player.

> *"First, I'd get a bottle that I'd think was going to fit my finger. Then I'd wrap some string around the neck and soak it in kerosene and light it and let it burn till it go out. Then you just rap it and it breaks off just right. It's a short slide…I play single strings mainly."*
>
> —Muddy Waters, *Guitar Player*, 1983

> *"I use a metal slide. It's a pipe that I got at a plumbing-supply place. I bought a 12-foot piece and had it cut into pieces a little over an inch long."*
>
> —Johnny Winter, *The Guitarist Book of the Blues*, 2003

> *"I would just get a suspension bush from a car because it was just the right length; nobody was cutting up microphone stands back then."*
>
> —Jimmy Page, *The Guitarist Book of the Blues*, 2003

> *"I like a glass slide as opposed to a metal one. The weight is important—not too much but not too light."*
>
> —Peter Green, *Heroes of the Electric Blues*, 2004

> *"I use a pick and fingers when I play slide, and I vary the slides. Sometimes, I use a Coricidin bottle on my ring finger or my pinky or I'll use a brass slide if I'm playing a National. The sound of glass is smooth and sweet, and brass and copper are very harsh. Steel is a good compromise, and socket wrenches are ideal. They're fantastic but you need very heavy strings."*
>
> —Rory Gallagher, *Heroes of the Electric Blues*, 2004

Playing stuff: This familiar slide-guitar phrase is typical of the acoustic-blues genre and exemplifies the role of the resonator guitar in the style. The music is in Open D tuning, makes use of characteristic barred shapes, and is played with slide or bottleneck. The use of the slide-guitar lead line and boogie comping in the lower register is a staple of the Delta country blues style.

TRACK 42

Open D tuning:
(low to high) D–A–D–F♯–A–D

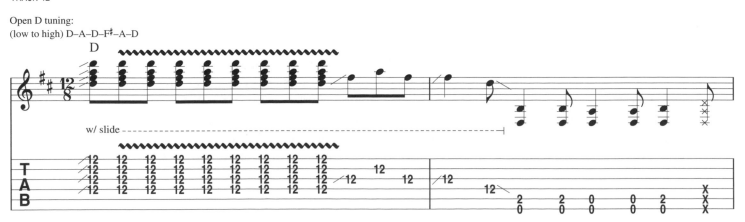

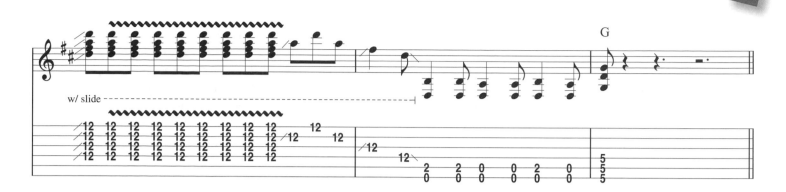

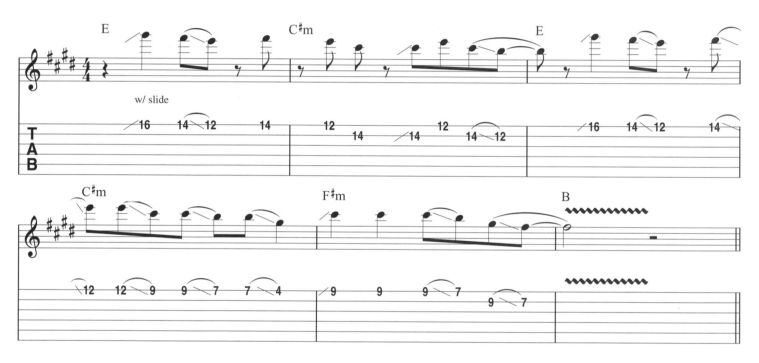

Slide guitar is also played in standard tuning. George Harrison and Jeff Beck are two of the leading players in this style. Many rock and pop standard-tuned guitarists prefer to play melodic figures laced with abundant slurs and legato passages facilitated by the slide. This phrase is exemplary and has little to do with the slide clichés of traditional blues and country.

TRACK 42
(0:15)

SPEAKERS

General stuff: The speaker is the final aspect in shaping and delivering the voice of a guitar amplifier before it goes out to the microphone and human ear. Speakers come in many types and sizes, and discerning players know that each imparts its own sound and response.

Guitar-amp speakers typically range between 8–15 inches in size. Arguably, the most common is the 12-inch speaker, which is found in most Marshall stacks and combos, as well as in similar models such as Fender Twins and Deluxes, Vox AC-30s, Polytone Mini-Brutes, and Raezer's Edge Stealth-12 cabinets. Alternatively, numerous notable amps are equipped with 10-inch or 15-inch speakers. The classic tweed Fender Bassman and the blackface Fender Super-Reverb, as well as the Acoustic 134, have four 10-inch speakers, while the Fender Pro, 1964 Vibro-Verb, and the 1952 Gibson GA-75 all have a single 15-inch speaker. The 1950 Gibson GA-50 has the unusual mixed configuration of an 8-inch speaker and a 12-inch speaker. The more recent Polytone 102 is equipped with two 8-inch speakers and one 12-inch speaker.

Sonic stuff: Many players have been very specific about their speaker preferences. Why? It comes down to tone. Cone size, paper thickness, flexibility, types of magnets, and materials used all affect tone. While most heavy rockers of his era stayed with stock Celestions, metal-innovator Randy Rhoads preferred Altec Lansings in his Marshall cabinets for a brighter tone. Mark Knopfler loaded his 4x12 Marshall cabinets with 12-inch Electro-Voice speakers, while Frank Zappa opted for JBLs (James B. Lansing). Pat Metheny put 10-inch JBLs in his Acoustic 134 combo, while Carlos Santana favored a single 12-inch Altec speaker in his Mesa Boogie combo. Moreover, players vary in their preference for speaker wattage and resistance. Joe Satriani and Eddie Van Halen like 25-watt Celestions in their Marshall cabs, while their colleague Steve Vai uses 30-watt Celestions. Tone-maven Eric Johnson goes further, rewiring his Marshall cabinets (for dirty rhythm) to 8 ohms instead of the customary 16 ohms. And on and on it goes. Bottom line: Use your ear.

Technical stuff: The speaker is a simple electrical system that is made of a voice coil (wire wound around a hollow form) and a magnet in the center, mounted in a frame. When the assembly is electrically charged, it develops a north-south polarity that shifts according to the notes played by the guitar. The paper of the speaker cone, which can easily be damaged by accidental puncture, moves in response to those frequencies. Keep sharp objects away! Rock-guitar lore has it that some players, like Link Wray, purposely poked holes into the cone to make them "fuzz out," but this is generally not a recommended procedure!

Speaker care comes down to a little info and lot of common sense. The paper in the cone should be protected from dampness, moisture, and excessive heat, including prolonged direct sunlight. Evaluate the safety of long-term storage (i.e., no leaky garages). Transport an amp carefully; jarring the amp can loosen the fasteners that hold the speaker, causing all sorts of unpleasant sympathetic vibrations and buzzing when you play. In most cases, place a speaker cabinet or combo amp face down in a trunk.

Playing stuff: Don't be tempted to use a shielded guitar cable as a spare speaker cord. This acts as a capacitor. Keep a spare high-quality speaker cable in your gig bag or accessory case. A higher-quality cable with thicker wire and proper insulation has lower resistance and provides more output and better low-end tone.

Don't blow it. A speaker can be blown with a sudden, loud, transient sound spike. Turn down the volume or use the amp's standby switch when plugging in or changing guitars. Generally, a clean percussive sound is a sharper spike and will more easily damage a speaker than a compressed distorted sound.

A fully blown speaker gives you no sound. After checking speaker response with a 9-volt battery (hooked up to the terminals) you may have to replace or re-cone it. A partially-blown speaker produces a scratchy, unpleasantly distorted sound. Besides a spike, a power mismatch can cause a blown speaker. Make sure your speaker can handle what the amp delivers. If you have a 100-watt head, don't use a single 50-watt speaker. Upgrade to a 100-watt speaker, two 50-watt speakers, or four 25-watters. Again, common sense.

STRINGING

General stuff: The way you string a guitar affects the way the instrument will sound, perform, respond, and stay in tune. Indeed, an improperly strung guitar can suffer chronic string slippage, faulty intonation, and other subtle-to-glaring problems. Stringing is not self-evident and common-sensical. Many guitarists have given the process little or no thought and simply hope for the best— sometimes to their dismay. Bottom line: Stringing is worthy of coverage in any serious book about guitar stuff. It may well make for a far more enjoyable playing experience.

Here are a few basic points: The stringing procedure should be evaluated relative to the guitar being strung. A Strat with a stock tremolo system is strung differently than a Les Paul … if you want to be in tune. A guitar with a locking-nut system is strung differently than an archtop. And a nylon-string classical guitar is strung differently than a steel-string acoustic. The process, however, has some universal commonalities. First, the string should be measured (eyeballed) before it is cut, and often not cut until after the string is in place. Second, avoid stringing in any manner that may result in slippage. Third, avoid sloppy wraps around the post with all guitars. Instead, strive to keep wraps even and consistent like a coiled rope.

Technical stuff: The basic stringing procedure that is most common applies to steel-string acoustic guitars, solidbody guitars without a vibrato bar, and archtop guitars with or without a Bigsby-type vibrato bar, and is as follows:

Step A

The string is anchored at or through the tailpiece and passed over the appropriate groove at the bridge, over the fingerboard, into the groove in the nut, and to the post on the headstock. Leave some slack for winding. With tricky tailpieces—for instance, certain trapeze types on archtops—the slack string's ball end will continually slip out of position while you are trying to thread it through the post's hole. A useful tool is the surgical clamp, which can be positioned to lock the string in place at this point. (Take care not to damage the guitar's finish though!)

Step B

The string passes through the hole and is wound around the post. Generally, the string passes over the post at 12:00, into the hole or slot at 9:00, and back out at 3:00. Many pros bend the string at a right angle at the exit side of the post hole during the first wrap for extra security. The slackened string is then wound to tightness. Keep the windings uniform and separate with no overlap, starting with the string break at the bottom. Imagine a coiled rope on a floor.

Step C

Wind the string counterclockwise with the tuning key. FYI: A string winder is a helpful tool that saves time and trouble. How many wraps? This can vary somewhat from player to player. It is generally best to have three or so full wraps around the post to keep the string secure—unless you lock the string. After stringing, the string should be stretched and rechecked for tuning. This may take several attempts before the string is sufficiently stretched and stable.

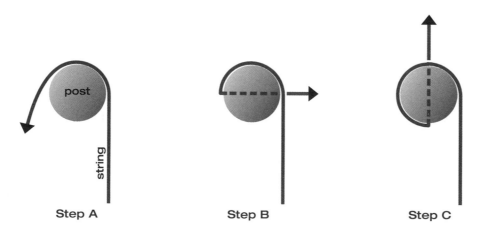

Step A   Step B   Step C

Some guitarists use fewer windings and the "loop lock" trick. This guarantees minimal slippage with fewer windings, ideal for stock non-locking vibrato-bar systems. The four steps of the loop-lock procedure are depicted on the following page.

Step A

The string is threaded into the post hole, entering at 6:00 and exiting at 12:00.

Step B

The end of the string is wound clockwise, making a turn under the string at 6:00. This is the start of loop lock.

Step C

The string makes a 180-degree turn back over the string to end the loop lock.

Step D

The tuning key is tightened over the loop. This holds the looped string into a locked position. Use a full turn to wrap the string around the post at least once. In many cases, this is sufficient to lock and hold the string in place, even for aggressive vibrato use and string bending.

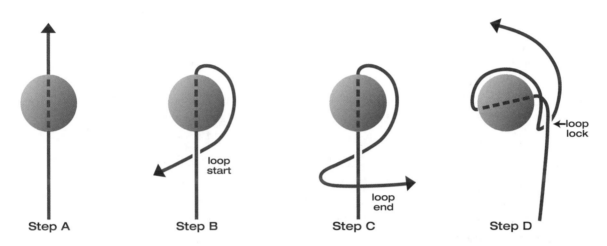

The final step of both procedures involves wrapping, cutting, and bending. After the wrapping is completed, the end of the string should be trimmed to a desired length. Leave enough string length to be able to quickly remove it. Many players prefer to bend the end of the string to avoid pricking the finger tip during a performance. George Van Eps once expressed this concern to me. His finger tip was punctured during a concert, making it difficult to play all his marvelous music. Subsequently, he mounted plastic "peanuts" (from old-style flash bulbs) on the end of his strings. Another way to accomplish this is with a bend and tuck. This two-step process is shown below:

Step A

Cut the string end to approximately one inch in length.

Step B

Using needle-nose pliers, bend the string in half, at a right angle, toward the post. Squeeze the bent string into a rounded shape so that its end cannot be touched and tuck it into the post shaft, out of harm's way. Be careful not to scratch the headstock surface during this procedure.

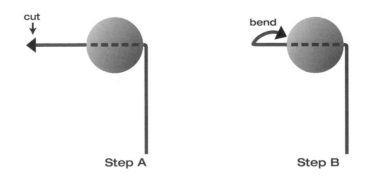

STRINGS

General stuff: Guitar strings come in many different types and gauges. There are round-wound, flat-wound, and semi-polished (half-flat), or "ground wound," strings. There are guitar strings made of nylon or steel cores, wrapped with windings of stainless steel, nickel, nickel alloy, copper, bronze, brass, or even gold. Each has its own tone, response, level of durability, and resistance to sweat and corrosion. Additionally, some modern strings are coated with a synthetic compound that fights corrosion. What makes a player choose a particular string?

Sonic stuff: While acoustic guitars can be strung with nylon or steel strings bearing any type of winding, only certain types will work with the magnetic pickups of electric guitars. These are generally of the "white metal" type (steel or nickel wraps); bronze and brass-wrapped ("yellow metal") strings generally have an inadequate magnetic response. Acoustic guitars can be strung with bronze-, brass-, nickel-, or steel-wrapped strings with differing results. John Lennon of the Beatles strung his acoustic-electric J-160E alternately with Pyramid flat-wounds or normal round-wounds.

The choice of round-wound versus flat-wound strings is a personal decision and often reflects the musical tastes of a player. Jazz guitarists use both types. Consider the tone and dynamic quality of various players. Howard Roberts, Barney Kessel, Johnny Smith, and Chuck Wayne favor the lively acoustic-oriented sound of round-wounds, while Wes Montgomery, Kenny Burrell, Grant Green, Pat Martino, George Benson, and Pat Metheny prefer the mellow, darker tone of flat-wounds. Fusion player John Scofield arrived at a compromise. His ES-335 is strung with round-wounds with an unwound G, while his main guitar (Ibanez AS200) has flat-wounds with a wound G.

Most country, pop, funk, blues, and fusion players, and virtually all rock guitarists, use round-wound strings. This type of string accentuates high frequencies, twang, and upper-partial harmonics.

Choice of string gauge varies with musical genre and a player's style. Jazz players usually prefer a medium to heavy–gauge set, beginning with a .012 to .014 high E. Pat Martino and Howard Roberts have gone further, opting for an ultra-heavy .016 high E. Why? The general rule is: the heavier the string, the better the tone. However, in blues and rock styles, light-gauge strings are necessary for the string bending and fluid wide vibrato of many stylists. Nonetheless, the blues king of the modern age, Stevie Ray Vaughan, strung his Strat with a custom heavy set (.013 to .058). Moreover, many rock players prefer a big bottom, using heavier gauges on the three wound strings. Eric Johnson's set-up is exemplary: (from high to low) .010, .013, .018 and .026, .038, .050.

STRING BENDING

General stuff: String bending is the art and technique of pushing or pulling strings on a guitar to change pitch. A central aspect of blues, rock, country, and pop, string bending is now a universal and pervasive sound found in the playing of Eddie Van Halen and Eric Clapton, as well as B.B. King, Albert Lee, Albert King, Kenny Burrell, Mike Stern, and Larry Carlton.

Historic stuff: String bending is a staple of modern electric guitar playing. Popularized by T-Bone Walker in the Forties, string bending entered the mainstream with classic cuts like "Stormy Monday" (1947), "T-Bone Boogie" (1945), and "T-Bone Shuffle" (1949).

Second-generation electric blues guitarists like B.B. King and Albert King elevated string bending to a high art form, often using it to emulate the microtonal quality, wide intervals, and legato phrasing of blues singing. Eric Clapton, Jeff Beck, Jimmy Page, and Jimi Hendrix followed the lead of their blues heroes. Subsequent rock and metal players built on the contributions of modern blues guitarists and, since the late sixties, made string bending a vital part of pop music.

Technical stuff: An important aspect of string-bending technique is *reinforced fingering*. Here, more than one finger is used to push the string, reinforcing and supporting the primary fretting finger. Commonly, a third-finger string bend is reinforced by the index and middle fingers. Moreover, the fret-hand thumb acts as an anchor and pivot point to further assist in the string-bending process.

reinforced string bend

> *"One* [finger] *might do, but you might use two, depending on what context the bend is in. The bend might be a slow blues, in which case you'd want to get your whole fist around the neck."*
>
> —Jeff Beck, *Guitar Player*, 1980

String bends are notated with specific graphic symbols in modern guitar transcriptions. The most widely used symbols are the bent lines that connect the note heads of the starting pitch to the note heads of the ending pitch. A line with an arrow is used in the tab staff. The number at the point of the arrow specifies the interval distance of the bend.

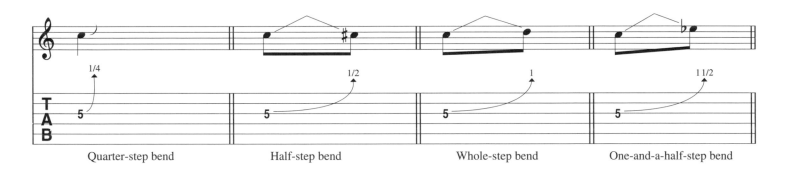

| Quarter-step bend | Half-step bend | Whole-step bend | One-and-a-half-step bend |

Lengthier string-bending passages are indicated by the continuation of the bent line over the note heads. The first figure is a legato bend-and-release. Note the bent line that connects bent and unbent pitches. The second passage can be played with the same bends, but with every note picked. This is an *articulated* bend and release. A different, yet common, articulation in string-bending technique involves the pre-bend. This is indicated with a small note head in parenthesis that precedes the bent note. The note in parenthesis is the starting pitch. The action is as follows: Bend the string a whole step, and then pick it. Compare this symbol with the standard bend, which is written in the second measure. In the tab staff, note the straight, vertical bend line, which indicates the pre-bend.

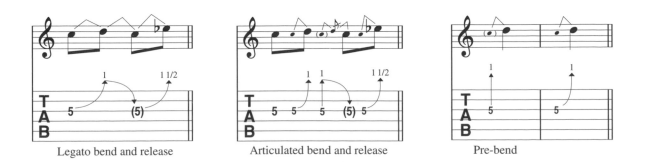

| Legato bend and release | Articulated bend and release | Pre-bend |

Playing stuff: This rock phrase contains a number of typical string bends. Note the articulated bend in measure 1. Here the whole-step bend is released, in rhythm, to a half-step bend and then returned to pitch. Moreover, check out the wide string bend of a major 3rd (four steps) in measure 2. The final measure contains another typical mannerism. The whole-step bend is held and bent another half step (1½ steps).

TRACK 43

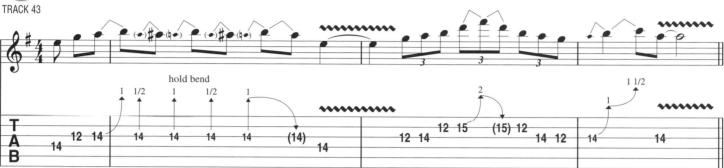

SUSPENDED CHORDS

General stuff: Suspended chords are chords that contain suspensions. Suspensions abound in all forms of chord-based music, from classical music and jazz to rock, pop, folk, R&B, and metal. The suspended chord has ample color and has enlivened the compositions of Bach, Beethoven, Tchaikovsky, and Stravinsky, as well as the Beatles, the Rolling Stones, the Who, the Police, U2, and Rush. In fact, Pete Townshend once commented that the suspensions of the Baroque Era (Purcell, Bach, Handel, et al) inspired many of his chord figures and riffs on the Who's first album.

Technical stuff: In classical music, a suspension is a theoretical expression that is applied to the retention of any note(s) from a preceding chord. The most common suspensions are the suspended 4th and the suspended 2nd (sus4 and sus2, respectively). Since it is not part of the prevailing chord, the suspension is a non-harmonic tone and is considered a dissonance.

The suspension is of two types: prepared and unprepared. This distinction describes the way the suspension is approached and resolved. The prepared suspension begins as a tone of one chord, which is held over into a second chord and then resolved. If the suspension does not appear in the preceding chord, it is unprepared.

This progression contains two prepared suspensions. The suspended chord is expressed as a sus4 or a sus2 chord; it is named by its root and followed by the suspension's interval. Here the B7sus4 retains the suspended tone, E, from Cmaj7, and Asus2 holds B over from E7. The E resolves to D in Bm7, and the B resolves to A in A5. The first example is based on a 4–3 suspension; the second, a 2–1 suspension.

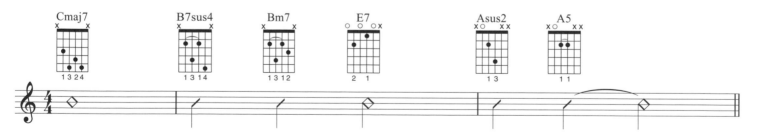

In contemporary music—rock, pop, jazz, R&B, country—the unprepared suspension, also called *suspended chord*, is frequently exploited in idiomatic chord progressions. Some of the most common suspended chords are depicted in the following collection. You'll recognize that many of these voicings are ingredients of your favorite songs, chord-melody patterns, or rhythm figures. Note the brackets, which connect the suspension with its resolution.

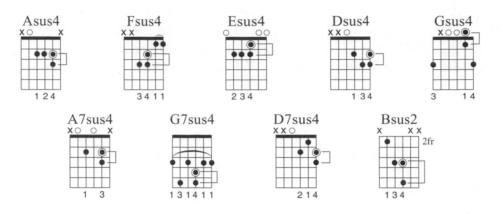

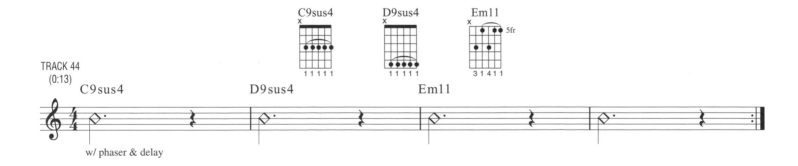

Playing stuff: This lively rock figure exploits the most typical suspended chord, resolving to its consonant counterpart. Here the riff pattern is a suspended chord to a major chord (Bsus4–B). The figure receives a propulsive sixteenth-note strum rhythm characteristic of the Townshend style.

TRACK 44

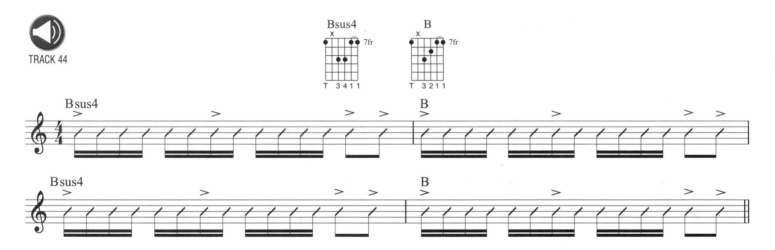

This modal chord progression revels in the ambiguous quality of suspended chords. Here the suspensions are added to more complex chords, such as dominant ninths and minor sevenths. This application harnesses the exotic color of jazz voicings, combined with modal chord movement, and subjects it to an alternative-rock groove. This progression is reminiscent of Andy Summers' imaginative work with the Police.

TRACK 44
(0:13)

w/ phaser & delay

SWING

General stuff: The term *swing* has a two-fold definition. The performance aspect of swing transcends style and is based on a feel, whereby a *shuffle rhythm* is applied to a composition, arrangement, groove, chord progression, or melodic line. The swing rhythm is heard in blues, pop, country, rock, jazz, and other music.

Swing is also used to describe the popular musical style that dominated the late thirties and forties. To jazz historians, swing bridges the gap between classic jazz of the twenties and the modern jazz styles of bebop and cool jazz. Yet swing was certainly not confined to jazz genres. Swing manifested itself in country form as western swing, a highly influential subgenre. At the dawn of rock 'n' roll, rockabilly regularly employed many stylistic elements of swing music. And with respect to groove, harmony, riffs, and even melodic material, blues has been inextricably linked to swing. Moreover, many pop songs have borrowed telling elements of the swing style.

Historical stuff: The Swing Era had its beginnings in the music of composer/arranger/bandleaders Duke Ellington and Fletcher Henderson. In fact, music history chronicles Ellington's 1932 song "It Don't Mean a Thing If It Ain't Got That Swing" as the first significant expression of the word in pop usage.

In 1935, swing caught on with the masses. Benny Goodman and his big band ushered in an era of hot dance music that remained popular into the mid-forties. Other important swing groups of the era include big bands led by Count Basie, Artie Shaw, Tommy Dorsey, Glenn Miller, and Woody Herman. Lester Young, Art Tatum, Roy Eldridge, Harry James, Gene Krupa, rhythm guitarist Freddie Green, and guitar virtuoso Charlie Christian are some of the most significant and influential instrumentalists of the swing style.

By the late forties, many of swing's prominent bandleaders broke up their big bands as smaller combo groups began to dominate jazz, vocalists began to dominate pop music, and young jazz players gravitated to the new bebop style. Nonetheless, the swing feel, riff-based tunes, and harmony continued to affect many subsequent developments in country, pop, dance music, and rock 'n' roll.

Technical stuff: Swing is a rhythmic feel that is based on the subdivided triplet group for a beat of music, often called a *shuffle rhythm* (see *Shuffle,* (p. 101)). At moderate tempos, these shuffling patterns have been called *swung eighth notes* and are most evident in jazz and blues melodies and boogie rhythm figures.

The swing rhythm is most often indicated in modern music notation as two even eighth notes, an equal sign, and the long-short pattern of a subdivided triplet. Each pattern applies to one beat of music. At slower tempos, sixteenth notes become the basic unit of time.

At the beginning of a piece of blues, rock, country, or pop music in swing feel, the directions usually include the tempo and feel, as well as the appropriate symbols. For example, the words "Medium Shuffle" and the metronome mark are included at the top of the music, with the swing symbols in parenthesis. In many jazz scores, the swing rhythm symbols are omitted (the experienced player already knows how to interpret the swung eighth notes) and only the words "Medium Swing" are needed to designate feel. Swing and shuffle are generally interchangeable to the performer of a swing rhythm.

In older times, swing rhythm was often incorrectly written as a dotted-eighth-and-sixteenth subdivision of the beat. This jerky rhythm is seen in old-school piano/vocal sheet music of pop songs and is reproduced when the sheet music itself is copied into fakebooks without editing, such as the reprinting of "You Go to My Head" in the unofficial *Golden Standards of the 1900's*. More often than not, the composer suggests that swing rhythm is to be applied to eighth notes but, as a rule, it should not be taken literally. Other, more savvy arrangers of sheet music have depicted the melody as straight eighth notes, assuming a player will swing them during performance.

This: ♩ ♪, not this: ♩. ♪

Playing stuff: The essence of swing is *feeling*. Many players are recognized by their personal sense of swing. It fact, it is incumbent on a well-rounded performer to develop a sense of swing. Where to start? This simple aural demonstration is worth a thousand words. Here a straight rhythm is applied to a typical swing-era melody line and then immediately contrasted with the same phrase, this time as swung eighth notes. One glance at the notated swung version, with all of its fussy triplet rhythms, argues the case for simply posting the *swing symbols* and performing all straight eighth notes as shuffle rhythms.

TRACK 45

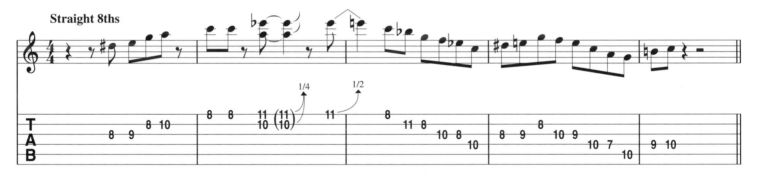

TRACK 45
(0:09)

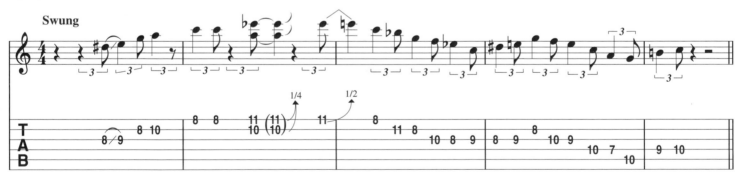

TAPPING

General stuff: Tapping, or bi-dextral (two-handed), technique involves fretting notes on the fretboard with the pick hand in conjunction with normal fretting action. In the hands of imaginative players, the use of the bi-dextral technique can create impossible wide-interval lines, intricate classical keyboard sounds, unusual sound effects, and dazzling cascades of notes.

Historic stuff: Prior to the rock age, the idea of using the pick hand to play melodies was limited to brief coloristic passages in flamenco guitar and atypical early experiments by jazz guitarists like Tal Farlow and Barney Kessel in the fifties. Surprised? Most are. But check out the tapped line in Kessel's intro to his 1953 recording of "Tenderly."

Though rock musicians Jeff Beck, Harvey Mandel, Steve Hackett, Larry Carlton, and Billy Gibbons were tapping sporadically, a young guitar player from Pasadena, California, made the sound popular worldwide. As a result of Eddie Van Halen's influence in the late seventies, tapping became a codified must-know technique by the eighties. Essential listening for aspiring tappers includes definitive pieces like Van Halen's "Eruption," "Spanish Fly," and "Mean Street," as well as riffs and solos by Randy Rhoads (with Ozzy Osbourne), Joe Satriani, Steve Vai, Stanley Jordan, Jennifer Batten, Jeff Watson, and Steve Lynch (with Autograph).

Technical stuff: Most bi-dextral licks require one finger (in Van Halen's case, the right-hand index finger) to tap the operative notes. Other players, like Steve Lynch, Jeff Watson, and Jennifer Batten, use several fingers of the tapping hand within a single phrase to achieve a cascade of notes across the strings. Some guitarists tap with the pick's edge for a different, brighter sound.

No matter how many fingers are employed or which finger(s) are preferred, the basic tapping technique involves three actions: preparation, attack, and recovery. The tapping finger is poised above and aimed at the string and fret to be tapped (preparation). The next step is the attack. The pick-hand finger makes contact with the string, striking the note in a firm, committed motion. As the finger recoils from the attack, it pulls off sideways to a fretted note or an open string. Which way? Van Halen taps with his index finger and pulls off toward his body. Other players tap with the middle finger and pull off away from their body. The pull-off action sends the finger into the *recovery* step. In recovery, it is important to lift the finger slightly to avoid sounding an adjacent string as an unintentional note. In recovery, the finger returns to the original position to prepare for the next note to be tapped.

Anchoring on the edge(s) of the fingerboard is an essential part of tapping technique. Some guitarists, like Steve Lynch, rest the fret-hand thumb on the upper edge of the fingerboard. Others, like Eddie Van Halen, grip the bottom edge of the fingerboard with the pinky, using the upper edge for additional support.

What happens to the pick? Most players who tap with the middle finger hold the pick with the index finger crooked into the palm. What about the maestro? Van Halen taps with his index finger and lodges the pick between the first and second joint of the middle finger.

In modern guitar notation, the tap-on is indicated with a "+" over the note in standard notation and a "T" over the equivalent note in the tablature staff. Steve Vai regularly uses more than one finger for tapping and favors a code that ascribes different symbols for each finger. In this system, a circled note indicates a middle-finger tap, a diamond shape specifies an index-finger tap, and a square is used for a ring-finger tap.

Playing stuff: The classic tap-on statement is the coda to Van Halen's "Eruption"—hands down. This phrase depicts the idea. Note the use of a pick-hand tap-on, plus a hammer-on that is played with the fret hand. The cascade of notes is based on shifting arpeggios. The smooth voice-leading of the harmony and continuous three-note patterns connote a classical keyboard-like impression.

TRACK 46

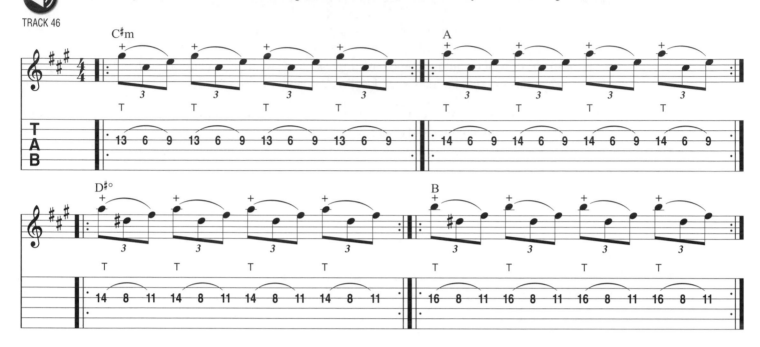

Tap-ons are frequently used with string bends. Players like Billy Gibbons, Larry Carlton, Jay Graydon, Steve Vai, and Randy Rhoads have gotten considerable mileage out of this simple refinement of the tap-on technique. In this idiomatic phrase, a string bend is held while the fret hand taps higher notes on the same string. Later in the line, a trill is applied to a held-and-released bend. This is a standard rock effect and should be part of every guitarist's bag of tricks.

TRACK 46
(0:12)

*tapped trills

THUMB FRETTING

General stuff: Guitarists of all stripes employ the thumb-fretting technique. What was once taboo is now *au courante* and, indeed, essential in the guitarist's tool box. Thumb fretting is the use of the thumb to fret bass notes on the low string(s) of the guitar. Players associated with the technique include rockers Jimi Hendrix, George Harrison, Jeff Beck, Jimmy Page, and Ron Wood, country pickers Merle Travis and Chet Atkins, and jazz players Howard Roberts, Wes Montgomery, Tal Farlow, and Kenny Burrell.

Technical stuff: Effective thumb fretting takes practice. Why bother? When the thumb joins the other digits in performance, the other fingers are freed up to play otherwise impossible chord voicings and polyphony. A logical first step in the development of thumb fretting is to convert conventional fingerings with bass notes on the sixth string into thumb-fretted versions.

Consider a typical third-position G barre chord. Play the first form and then compare it with the thumb-fretted version. The thumb should wrap around the neck in a "broom handle" posture to fret the root tone, G, on the sixth string. It is essential to play with a relaxed grip, which will allow for quick, fluid position shifts. The second chord is a G7 that has been converted to its thumb-fretted counterpart. Note the half barre across strings 2–4. This form frees two fingers to play additional melody notes, suspensions, or extensions.

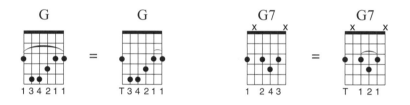

Here are several typical thumb-fretted chords in common usage. They vary in types, from minor seventh and dominant eleventh to altered dominant thirteenth and minor-major ninth.

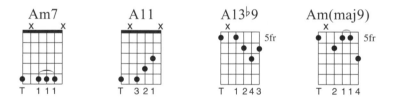

The thumb is also used to fret two notes in the bass register. Generally, the thumb presses both the sixth and fifth strings while maintaining four notes in the upper structure, utilizing all six strings of the guitar. Here, three common jazz voicings are presented to depict the technique.

Playing stuff: Master picker Merle Travis was one of the leading advocates and exponents of the thumb-fretting technique. This typical country-swing phrase employs his thumb-fretted chords and the Travis-picking approach, a powerful combination punch. Note the use of two thumb-fretted notes in the D9 chord.

*P.M. on 5th and 6th strings throughout.

Thumb-fretted chords are prevalent in jazz guitar. Why? Simple arithmetic: The more freed fingers, the more possibilities for extensions, alterations, or color tones. Savvy jazz players like Howard Roberts and Barney Kessel have used enriched harmonic passages like this one to good effect in their music, which are made possible with thumb fretting.

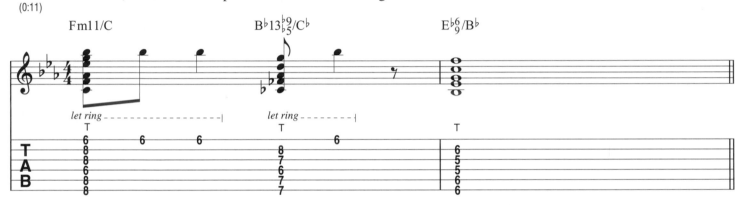

Jimi Hendrix was one of the most renowned thumb-fretters in rock. As a corollary, many rock disciples began to employ the technique post-1967, and now it permeates all forms of the genre. This characteristic phrase demonstrates Hendrix's thumb-fretting approach and blend of rock and R&B ingredients. Note the use of embellishment, passing tones, and melody patterns that are facilitated by having freed fingers.

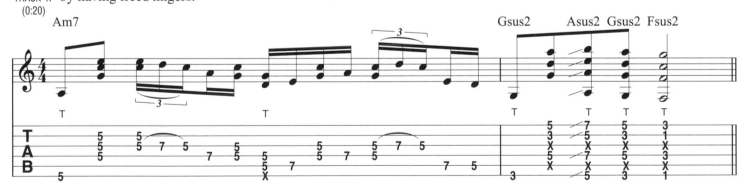

TONE

General stuff: Tone…. We know what we like and we know it when we hear it. But what is it, exactly? The dictionary defines tone as "the quality of sound; e.g., good tone, harsh tone, brittle tone." That's a serviceable starting point.

On the guitar, there is acoustic tone and electric tone. Moreover, there is a wide range of timbres that are produced on both electric and acoustic guitars by varied degrees of attack and different placements of the picking hand. Electric guitarists spend a lifetime finding ideal timbral combinations of guitar, amp, and effect. Acoustic players continually refine their physical embouchure, selecting a particular instrument to convey their tone.

Tone is one of the most debated topics in guitardom. Why? Tone is more than the sheer attack and type of instrument. Tone is a statement of the player's persona—the first step in establishing their "voice."

> *"More important than anything—the fame, the bread, the prestige—is to be able to get a tone out of your hands."*
> —Carlos Santana, *Guitar Player*, 1995

> *"Tone is basically in the hands and heart. Line up 90 guys and have them play the same blues lick; you'll get 90 different readings in terms of touch, tone, intensity, and authority."*
> —Steve Lukather, *Guitar Player*, 1995

Sonic stuff: On some instruments, electric guitar tone is affected by the volume control because it engages the circuit's capacitor. This applies to clean, traditional jazz-guitar sound, as well as hard rock. Tone is also affected by judiciously applying the timbre of neck, bridge, and middle pickups and combinations thereof.

> *"I generally like to keep a little* [volume] *in reserve because an electric guitar's tone is improved one-hundred percent by not pushing the volume up all the way and just saving that little bit of volume for when you might need it for a solo."*
> —Keith Richards, *Guitar Player*, 1977

Technical stuff: Tone production is determined by a guitarist's plucking relative to the bridge. Picking close to the bridge produces a smaller, brighter sound; picking near, or over, the end of the fingerboard results in a mellow, broader sound.

Tone is also affected by the use of fingers or a pick. Playing with the fingers produces a warmer, more personal sound with greater nuance but is not as facile and consistent as the flat pick. Classical and flamenco players play exclusively with their fingers. Many blues guitarists, notably Hubert Sumlin and Albert Collins, prefer the use of fingerstyle on electric guitar. Stevie Ray Vaughan, Eric Clapton, Keith Richards, Robben Ford, Eddie Van Halen, Larry Carlton, Eric Johnson, Buddy Guy, and many others alternate freely between pick and finger playing. Jeff Beck, Mark Knopfler, and Robby Krieger are among the most recognized rock players to pick solely with their fingers on the electric guitar. Famed jazz guitarist Wes Montgomery preferred the tone of his thumb. Blues master Albert King shared this approach. For more information, see *Picking* (p. 82).

Playing stuff: Ultimately, tone comes down to the way a player hears their music. The choice of embouchure and plectrum thickness, type of equipment, and use of thumb and/or fingers are personal decisions, informed by years of listening, experimenting, and application in the real world. Where to start? Here are three possibilities for future exploration of electric-guitar tone. In this section, the same blues phrase is played with three different timbral approaches, each varied electronically and physically.

This first example exemplifies the stereotypical jazz-guitar tone. It's played on an archtop electric with humbuckers and heavy strings and plucked with the thumb, Wes style. The amp sound is clean, warm, and set to emphasize the mid-range. The neck pickup (on a two-pickup guitar) is selected with the volume on 7 and the tone on 5.

TRACK 48 Here the same phrase is played with a brighter semi-clean amp tone on a Strat-style solidbody
(0:10) guitar with single-coil pickups. The fingers are used to create a sound with greater nuances and
dynamic shadings. This option generates an increased range of timbres, from mellow thumb-
plucked notes to a twangy percussive tone. Bridge and middle pickups are selected, resulting in the
classic "phased" sound. The amp is a moderately overdriven vintage Fender combo model that still
allows the guitar voice to speak clearly. This tone is associated with everything from rock, pop, and
blues to smooth jazz and R&B.

TRACK 48 In this example, the sample phrase receives a fully distorted tone and is attacked with an extra-
(0:21) heavy pick. These decisions reflect the timbres of hard rock, fusion, electric blues, and some metal.
Notice the emphasized harmonics, which are accentuated by greater amp overdrive and high gain.
The guitar is a solidbody that is equipped with humbucking pickups. The bridge humbucker is
selected with tone and volume controls on 10. The amp is a classic Marshall-stack type with a
closed-back 4x12 cabinet.

TRANSPOSING

General stuff: Transposing is the process of writing or performing music that was originally written in another key. Many songs are written in another key for convenience (i.e., to favor a vocalist's
natural range or to facilitate instrumental performance). Transposing should be part of every savvy
guitarist's basic training.

Transposing and the guitar go hand in hand. In fact, the guitar is a *transposing instrument*. Guitar
music is generally written in only the treble clef and is transposed up one octave to accommodate a
single staff. If it was written in actual pitch, the guitar's range would have to occupy two staves, like
the piano. Some guitarists, like Johnny Smith, advocate the practice of applying a two-staff system
for guitar notation; however, the idea never captured the mainstream audience of players. Most
prefer to deal with the established convention (i.e., its ledger lines and octave transposing) rather
than to relearn how to read music.

Historic stuff: In earlier times, a song conceived and recorded in a guitar key, like the Beatles' "Nowhere Man" (written in E major), was transposed by the sheet-music arranger into a
piano-friendly key, like E♭ major. Consequently, guitarists learning songs from traditional sheet
music were confounded and frustrated by the discrepancies between what they were hearing and
the "official" printed form. Guitarists working from the printed source were compelled to transpose
back to the original key.

Technical stuff: Transposing on the guitar is a straight-forward process. Any song or piece of
music learned using discrete chord forms can be physically transposed by simply moving the hand
and the basic chords to another location on the fingerboard.

Playing stuff: Physical transposition is demonstrated by taking the three-chord riff of "Louie, Louie" and transposing the figure to any other key. In this example, the riff, presented in the key of A, is transposed to the key of C. Note that the chord shapes and fingerings remain identical, though three frets apart. Transposing the figure from A to C was accomplished by simply moving the hand and chord forms from the fifth position to eighth position.

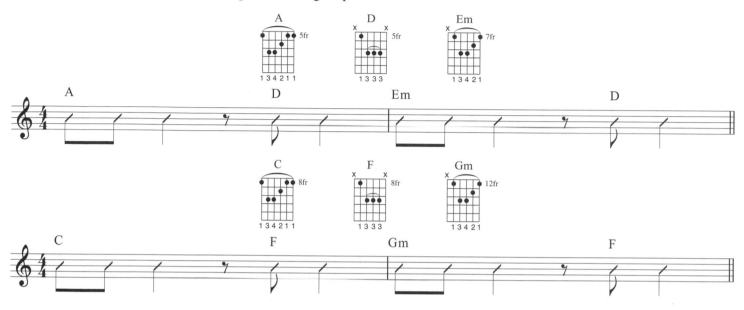

In the same way, a lick or melody can be transposed by using physical relocation. This standard jazz lick, in A minor, is transposed to the key of C (up a minor 3rd, or three frets). Note the same principle at work, whether transposing simple rock riffs or complex jazz lines.

TREMOLO

General stuff: *Tremolo* is an Italian word that comes from the Latin root *tremulus*, literally meaning "to tremble" or "trembling." In the guitar world, tremolo is a physical technique and an electronic effect, like its sonic counterpart, vibrato.

The physical tremolo technique involves a fast, continuous reiteration of a tone(s). This can vary considerably in application, from a single note to a full chord. Classical and flamenco guitarists achieve the tremolo effect through the rapid alternation of free strokes with the index, middle, and ring fingers, generally on a single string, like the *a–m–i* arpeggiation that is applied to a single string.

Fingerstyle jazz, rock, pop, and blues guitarists use a finger tip or the thumb to strum a string in alternating strokes. And plectrum players of all stripes use the flat pick and alternating strokes to strum chords or pluck single-note melodies.

Tremolo picking is heard throughout the guitar repertory and in diverse genres. In the nineteenth century, Francisco Tarrega wrote a famous tremolo etude for classical guitar called *Recuerdos de la Alhambra*. Dick Dale used the technique for his surf solos, and rockers like Eddie Van Halen, Kirk Hammett, and a host of others have applied tremolo picking to modern hard-rock and metal licks.

Sonic stuff: Bo Diddley made the electronic tremolo sound part of guitar lore and rock 'n' roll in the fifties, followed by Duane Eddy, Link Wray, and a slew of imitators. Electronic tremolo, which is a fluctuation of *volume* (or amplitude), is often confused with vibrato, which involves a fluctuation of *pitch*. See *Vibrato* (p. 140). The most common tremolo effect is a pulsation of an electronic signal in an on-off cycle with no discernable pitch change.

Tremolo was a sought-after effect in the fifties and sixties and was built into several notable amplifiers by Magnatone, Fender, Gibson, Vox, and others. Ampeg doctored their tremolo effect with enough modulation so as to produce a sufficiently different, vibrating phased result that could be called vibrato by nit-pickers. The electronic tremolo effect on amplifiers is usually divided into two self-evident parameters, speed and intensity, and is adjusted by the user via knobs on the control panel.

Tremolo largely fell out of favor in the seventies and eighties—with exceptions like Pink Floyd's "Money"—but was revived in the "retro music" phase of the nineties. Many alternative acts began to exploit the effect on hit songs, epitomizing the "so old it's new" premise. The market responded, and tremolo units began to appear in the effects rosters of Boss, Jim Dunlop, and others. Moreover, many amp manufacturers made concerted efforts to reissue classic tremolo-equipped pieces in their original editions.

Technical stuff: The physical tremolo effect is indicated in written music as three (sometimes two) diagonal lines drawn below or above the note in question, through its stem. In modern guitar notation, the same symbol is transferred onto the tablature staff. Oftentimes, the words tremolo pick (or its abbreviation, *trem. pick*) are added to the system, between the music and tab staves, and accompanied with a broken line and bracket that show the duration of the effect.

Playing stuff: The most common and familiar picked tremolo was popularized in the age of instrumental-rock music. Surf musicians like Dick Dale and surf bands like the Chantays exploited tremolo prominently on their biggest hit records (Can you say "Misirlou" and "Pipeline"?) This phrase depicts the tremolo-picking technique in two characteristic forms: applied to a scalar melody on the first string and to a slurred, palm-muted bass line on the sixth string.

TRACK 49

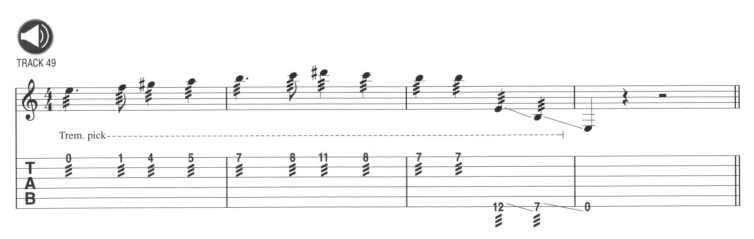

The electronic tremolo effect creates a unique wavering sound. This characteristic phrase demonstrates the sound in context, with arpeggiated chords and a single-note blues-scale lick. The effect is indicated between the staves by the term "w/ tremolo."

TRIADS

General stuff: Triads are three-note chords. The triad is one of the pervasive and inclusive resources in guitardom. Triads and sounds based on triads unite guitar players as diverse as Keith Richards, Larry Carlton, Eddie Van Halen, Mark Knopfler, Kenny Burrell, Albert Lee, James Taylor, John Lee Hooker, Barney Kessel, and Allan Holdsworth.

The most typical form of a triad is comprised of a 3rd interval and a 5th interval above a root, or tonic tone. Triads are of four types: major, minor, diminished, or augmented. These form the building blocks for all sorts of harmony. Practically every imaginable complex chord can be constructed by stacking triads on top of triads or by extending tones in successive 3rds above a basic triad.

Technical stuff: Triad names are determined by the quality of the 3rds and 5ths in their structure. Consider triads built on a C tonic tone. The major triad has a major 3rd and a perfect 5th and is spelled C–E–G. The minor triad has a minor 3rd and a perfect 5th: C–E♭–G. The diminished triad contains a minor 3rd and a diminished 5th: C–E♭–G♭. The diminished triad is like a minor triad with a lowered 5th tone. The augmented triad is a major triad with an augmented 5th: C–E–G♯. Like any chords, triads can be inverted. There are three tones in a triad and, therefore, three possible arrangements of those tones. This is easily understood by applying numbers to the triad tones. The root-position triad is spelled 1–3–5 (in the key of C: C–E–G, root–3rd–5th). The first inversion is spelled 3–5–1 (E–G–C, 3rd in the bass). And the second inversion is spelled 5–1–3 (G–C–E, 5th in the bass).

Sonic stuff: Like any chords, triads can be re-voiced and opened to produce wider intervallic spellings. For example, the basic root-position triad can be spelled C–G–E, with wide intervals of a 5th and 10th. This voicing is called *open position*. Here the placement and spacing of the voices (chord tones) exceeds an octave. In *close position*, the triad voicing remains within an octave.

The great chord maestro George Van Eps once presented the possibilities in a collection of forms he called the "Basic Voicing Chart for Tonic–Third–Fifth." This version shows how the tones of a C major triad can be juggled.

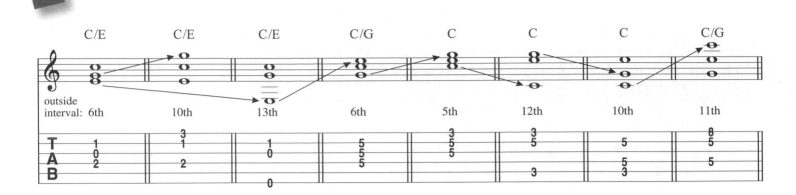

C/E	C/E	C/E	C/G	C	C	C	C/G

outside
interval: 6th   10th   13th   6th   5th   12th   10th   11th

Each triad yields a corresponding diatonic progression. Like a scale, a triad can be moved stepwise in ascending or descending order within a key—in fact sometimes this procedure is called a *harmonized scale*. This progression takes the first shape of Van Eps' voicing chart, C/E, up the C scale on the same string set. The triads in the progression are indigenous to the key of C major and are in their first-inversion forms: C/E–Dm/F–Em/G–F/A–G/B–Am/C–B°/D. The triads are voiced in close position.

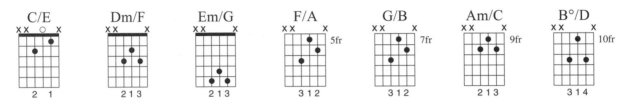

This figure includes the same progression as in the previous example, but here the chords are voiced as open-position triads. Every interval in the triad form is larger than a 3rd. Note the impressionistic effect of triads voiced with 6th and 10th intervals. Moreover, the wide interval in the inner voices is a 5th.

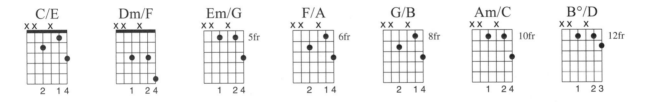

Triads are often used as components of more complex dissonant chords. These chords are often reductions of polychords and written as "slash chords." (See *Slash Chords*, p. 102.) The following forms are typical slash chords with a triad in the upper part of the voicing and an unrelated (or remotely related) bass note in the bottom.

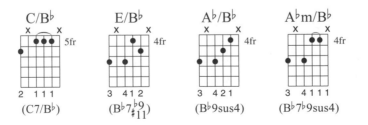

Playing stuff: Triads and rock music have been linked since the inception of the genre. Classic bands like the Rolling Stones, Beatles, Led Zeppelin, ZZ Top, Boston, and Van Halen have gotten tremendous mileage from the humble triad. This telling triad-dominated rock riff is the paragon of economy and simplicity and exploits two of the most essential guitar-friendly shapes.

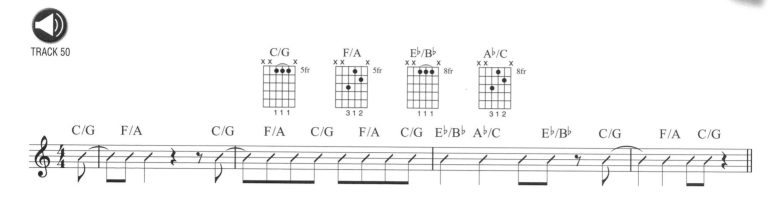

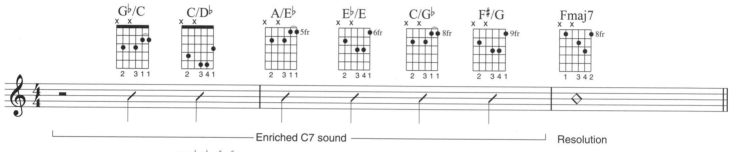

Triads figure prominently in the most exotic jazz settings. This phrase depicts the stylistic use of triads that are based on the diminished scale. Note the half-step/whole-step *symmetrical* motion and the alternation of triads in the upper structure of the altered dominant seventh chords. The passage of an enriched C7 is expressed as *polychords*. The progression resolves to an Fmaj7, which can also be seen from the triadic perspective: Am with F in the bass.

(C7♭5♭9♯5♯9: altered dominant seventh)

TRILL

General stuff: The trill is a musical ornament that involves two alternating notes repeated rapidly. The trill is a ubiquitous embellishment in guitar playing, decorating classical-guitar pieces, heavy-metal solos, jazz improvisations, and traditional blues turnarounds. Trills are found in the music of Tony Iommi, Randy Rhoads, Albert Collins, Freddie King, Buddy Guy, Jimi Hendrix, Jeff Beck, Muddy Waters, Wes Montgomery, Stevie Ray Vaughan, Eric Clapton, Pat Martino, George Benson, Christopher Parkening, Segovia, and…. Well, you get the idea.

Technical stuff: A trill is indicated in music (and tablature) notation with the abbreviation *tr* (or simply *t*) and a wavy horizontal line, usually extended above the staff for the rhythmic duration of the trill. The wavy-line symbol of the trill is as old as written music notation itself, going back to the *Neumes* of the "dark ages" (476–1000 CE).

The trill involves two notes: the principal note and its upper neighbor note (embellishment). Trills written before the eighteenth century began on the upper note. This trype of trill is used for J.S. Bach's music and pieces of the Baroque Era and early Classical Period in general. From the nineteenth century, the trill began with the principal note and is sometimes called the "modern trill." Another distinction between the two is that the older trill is played in short, measured rhythmic values (sixteenth and thirty-second notes), while the newer trill is played as fast as possible.

Unless otherwise indicated by accidentals, the trill interval is usually based on the prevailing scale. The principal note is followed by a parenthetical note, specifying which two notes are alternated. This type of trill notation is written in tablature as a principal tone, with the wavy line beginning at the grace note(s) in parentheses.

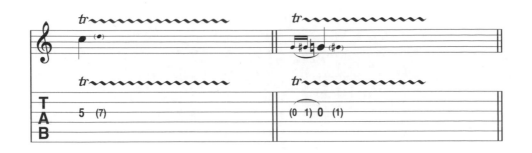

Sonic stuff: Trills require mastery of *legato technique* in its most fundamental form. On the guitar, the trill consists of a rapidly repeated series of hammer-ons and pull-offs following an initial picked note. The basic technique involves a fingered note and its upper neighbor, which is hammered on and pulled off. Practice should address the following areas: cleanliness (the trill should be precise; except for effect, the trilling finger must not activate idling adjacent strings), finger strength (the trill should have a consistent dynamic level throughout; care should be taken to assure volume of the pull-offs and hammer-ons), and consistency (the trill should be rhythmically even).

Playing stuff: This familiar blues turnaround uses two contrasting trills. The first trill, used on A7, is the "older" style and is based on beginning with the upper neighbor, or embellishing, tone; here G, the 7th of the dominant-seventh chord. The second trill leads to E7 and is the "modern" style. It is based on the alternation of minor and major 3rds, C and C#, operative tones of blues melody.

TRACK 51

This series of measured trills outlines a B arpeggio in the key of E minor. This approach is typical of the classically influenced hard-rock style and, with the D# in the melody, appropriately suggests the E harmonic-minor scale. Randy Rhoads and a host of disciples exploited similar lines in the

TRACK 51
(0:12)

neo-classical metal genre of the eighties and nineties.

126

TUBES

General stuff: Tubes, or valves, as they are called in the UK, are vital components in the electronic circuits of many popular guitar amplifiers. Perceived differences in sound between various tube amps remain much-debated topics and have defined the tone of many top players. Among tube aficionados, there is the school of hard rock and metal Marshall and Mesa Boogie players. There is also a tremendous and faithful following among savvy guitarists for classic tube amps made by Fender, Vox, Hi-Watt, Ampeg, and Gibson, as well as boutique models from Soldano, Dumble, Matchless, THD, Victoria, Fuchs, Bogner, and Bad Cat.

Historic stuff: At one time (fifties and earlier), life was simple; all guitar amps were tube amps. In the sixties, some manufacturers experimented with and marketed transistor, or solid-state, circuits. Despite some perceived advantages of the solid-state amp (e.g., reduced weight, no parts to continually replace, less heat, and its space-aged cachet) and strong publicity campaigns, many guitarists remained fiercely loyal to the tube-amp sound. This group includes players of all genres, from rock musicians Jimmy Page, Carlos Santana, Eddie Van Halen, Mark Knopfler, Yngwie Malmsteen, Eric Johnson, and Steve Lukather and bluesmen Albert Collins, Stevie Ray Vaughan, John Lee Hooker, and Muddy Waters to jazz guitarists George Benson, Pat Martino, and Kenny Burrell and country pickers Albert Lee, Scotty Anderson, Keith Urban, and Brad Paisley. In fact, the sound of tube amps working hard is part of the sound of those diverse stylists.

In time, some manufacturers, intent on finding the "best of both worlds," created the *hybrid amp*. Of these amps, Music Man (headed up by Leo Fender in the seventies) was one of the earliest and most popular. Their line featured a solid-state preamp married to a tube power amp. Today's Fender Cyber-Twin is a variation on that theme, exploiting a tube preamp with digital effects combined with a solid-state power amp.

Tubes drove the tremolo circuits of vintage tremolo-equipped amps and are also found in the classic Fender reverb units and early Echo-Plexes of the sixties. Today, tubes are employed in many overdrive and effects stomp boxes like the Chandler Tube Driver, Radial's Tonebone Trimode and Plexitube pedals, and the Area 51 tube tremolo unit.

Technical stuff: The operation of a tube is beautifully and succinctly described by amp expert Aspen Pittman in his authoritative work *The Tube Amp Book*. To paraphrase, a vacuum tube generally contains four active components that are encased in a vacuum-sealed glass enclosure: a heater (filament), a cathode, a grid, and a plate. The vacuum (air removed) in the tube keeps the parts from burning. The filament is heated to warm the cathode. When heated, the cathode (negatively charged) emits electrons that flow to the plate (positively charged). The grid's purpose is to control the flow of electrons in the tube that would otherwise flow like water rushing out of a faucet. When a signal is applied to the grid, it functions like a valve (hence, the British valve name), making related electronic changes to the cathode and plate, reacting to the guitar output and, ultimately, shaping electric guitar tone. The physical result creates a complex reaction that is perceived by many ears as a musically satisfying response.

There are at least two types of tubes in a typical amp circuit: preamp tubes and power tubes. What's the difference? Visually, the preamp tube appears smaller and slimmer, while the power tube is larger and more bulbous. The most common preamp tubes are the 12AX7
and 7025, followed by 12AT7, 12AU7, and 12AY7. These tubes are used in conjunction with various power tubes.

Power tubes are specific to the type and power rating of a particular amp. Marshall amps use various tubes: the KT-66 (many vintage models), KT-88 (200-watt Marshall Major), EL-34 (the classic British tube also found on Hi-Watt, Orange, Selmer, Sound City, and Laney amps, as well as newer Dumbles, Bogner, and Matchless amps), and 6550 (some newer Marshalls). The Vox AC-30 employs EL-84s, while many Ampegs are equipped with 7027s and 7591s. Higher-power Fender amps (like the Twin and Super-Reverb) use 6L6 power tubes, considered to produce a superior glassy tone. The popular 6L6s are also found in Soldano, Mesa Boogie, early Dumbles, Peavey's 5150 amp, Clark, Carvin, Music Man, Peavey, Rivera, Top Hat, and Gibson amps. The similarly popular 6V6 is favored for lower-power (under 30 watts) Fender amps like the Deluxe Reverb, Harvard, Princeton, and Champ, as well as some Gibsons. The unique Simul-Class/Class A power amp of some Boogie amps combines a pair of 6L6s with a pair of EL-34s.

Electronically, preamp tubes shape the initial tone of the guitar signal and determine its gain structure. The power tube is responsible for boosting the signal to full volume. As the power tube is worked harder, as in high-decibel rock, it contributes greatly to the overall guitar tone.

Some amps contain a rectifier tube. This tube converts AC power from the wall socket to DC electricity that is used inside the amp circuit. In the sixties, the tube rectifier was replaced on most amps with solid-state diodes. Though the guitar signal never passes through the rectifier tube, many players prefer the power "sag" that is produced by the tube rectifier of older amps, like the tweed Fender 4x10 Bassman, and seek out specific models for this particular dynamic response. Fender, Gibson, Marshall, and Vox amps of 50 watts or less often employ a GZ34/5AR4 rectifier tube.

Maintenance: Generally, a quality tube amp requires little maintenance, and much can be determined by using your ear and common sense. Two points are worthy of consideration: tube biasing and tube replacement. The bias control, which works like the idle of a car engine, is set internally, with the tubes removed. Unless you are knowledgeable and skilled at electronics, this is a job best left to a repair shop (it is a relatively low-priced adjustment). An under-biased amp will run hotter than optimal, causing tubes to burn out faster and possibly short out. An over-biased amp runs cool, resulting in an unpleasant distortion at any level. A properly biased amp will have a clean, tight sound at low volume and produce musical, even-harmonic distortion when cranked.

Power tube

Listen to your amp! Replacing tubes is the obvious fix when the amp sounds weak, lacks oomph, produces noise or hum, is inconsistent, drifts up or down in volume, or has an unpleasantly distorted sound when overdriven.

A few basics: Turn off and unplug the amp. Let it cool for five to ten minutes before touching the tubes. Follow the tube guide (get one if you don't have it). Replace a tube only with the type suggested or its equivalent. If your amp has them, first loosen and remove the spring clamps from the power tubes, and then remove the metal tube shields from the preamp tubes. Be careful to remove the tube itself by holding it at the top of the glass enclosure and gently moving the tube in its socket in a circular motion, gradually working it loose. Remember, the tube is made of glass—do not squeeze or force it. Make sure the tube pins line up correctly in the socket before pushing the replacement tube in its seat. The power tube has a locator notch in the center that assures proper positioning. Straighten out a bent preamp tube pin by carefully bending it back into position with needle-nose pliers or a ball-point pen case with the ink barrel removed.

Preamp tube

TUNING

General stuff: It should go without saying that tuning the guitar is an imperative skill for every guitarist. Tuning the guitar by ear is also imperative. Even in this day of electronics and gadgets galore? Yes. You may own a dozen electronic tuners. You may have one built into your pedalboard or even into your amp. But what happens if they fail, are not handy, or you forget to pack them? It comes down to pure sound and your ability to hear (i.e., tune by ear). To paraphrase pop culture: Use the (ear) force, Luke.

At the beginning of their playing career, some aspiring guitarists have trouble tuning by ear. The ear learns with practice, familiarity, and time; it develops pitch recognition and sensitivity and intonation discernment. Tuners are particularly helpful at this stage, removing doubt until the ear is trained. A tuner is a wise initial investment with your first guitar. But, ultimately, the competent guitarist must be able to tune without electronic aids.

Technical stuff: The *standard tuning* of the guitar in concert pitch is based on a particular intervallic lay-out: four perfect 4ths and a major 3rd. The strings are spelled (from low to high): E–A–D–G–B–E. G to B is the interval of a major 3rd; all the others are 4ths. In some cases, the guitar maintains this interval arrangement when lowered one (E♭), two (D), or three (C♯) half steps. Think Jimi Hendrix, Stevie Ray Vaughan, and Eddie Van Halen (E♭), and Black Sabbath (D and C♯). This is referred to as standard tuning down a half step, one step, or one-and-a-half steps.

Generally, the guitar is tuned to *concert pitch*. This means it shares the same pitch reference as other instruments in an ensemble. The current standard is A440. That means that the pitch A above middle C (first string, fifth fret) is vibrating at a frequency of 440 Hz, or cycles per second. This pitch is often played as a reference pitch when an orchestra tunes before a performance. Similarly, in many rock bands, the guitarist often plays a reference pitch to which a bass and/or second guitar tunes.

With strings loosened or out of tune, the pitch of each is brought into the appropriate tuning by turning the guitar's tuning keys, which are located on the headstock. It is advisable to lower the string one half turn if the pitch is close but out of tune. The string is then gradually brought into the correct pitch while comparing it to a fixed point, using a reference pitch, adjacent string, or the display of a tuner.

Sonic stuff: Tuning by ear generally requires a *reference pitch*. These days, a synthesizer, organ, or in-tune piano is a practical and accepted source for many guitarists, but the tried-and-proven pitch pipe or tuning fork are equally viable. Begin by comparing a note on the guitar with its equivalent reference pitch. For example, use the white key just below middle C to get the pitch of the open B string (second string), or two white keys above middle C to get the open E string (first string). You can also use a pitch pipe with a specific tone or, better still, a guitar pitch pipe with all six pitches of the guitar strings. Hint: It is usually easier to hear higher pitches when learning to tune by ear.

A number of tuning methods can be used to complete the process once the reference pitch and open string match. As you tune, keep checking previously tuned notes to ensure there is no pitch drift.

Playing stuff: The typical method for tuning by ear is based on *unison intervals*. Let's assume that we have the high E (first string) in tune from the keyboard. Follow these steps to use the *unison tuning method*.

1. First, tune the low E (sixth string) to the same pitch as the first string, but two octaves lower.

2. Next, press the sixth string at the fifth fret to produce the note A and match that pitch to the sound of the open fifth string.

3. Use the same procedure, moved over one string set, to tune the fourth and third strings, D and G, respectively.

4. The second string is tuned one half-step lower (the G–B major 3rd interval of standard tuning). Press the third string at the fourth fret (not the fifth) to sound the note B and match the open second string to that pitch.

5. Next, compare the second string, fretted at the fifth fret, with the note E, the open first string. Finally, play a few open-string chords, a scale or a lick, and some higher-register chords to evaluate the overall intonation. Is the guitar in tune with itself? If not, make the appropriate adjustments or re-check the individual strings, one by one.

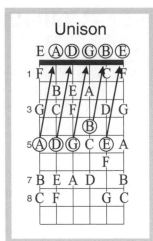

Unison

Many players employ a couple of additional by-ear methods to fine-tune the guitar. The use of *octave tuning* is useful and telling with regard to intonation. It compares fretted notes in the seventh position with their lower-octave open strings. The *octave tuning method* is as follows:

1. Compare low E (open sixth string) with its octave E, played at the seventh fret of the fifth string. Let the strings ring.

2. Compare A (open fifth string) with its octave A, played at the seventh fret of the fourth string.

3. Compare D (open fourth string) with its octave D, played at the seventh fret of the third string.

4. Compare G (open third string) with its octave G, played at the eighth fret of the second string.

5. Compare B (open second string) with its octave B, played at the seventh fret of the first string.

6. Finally, compare high E (open first string) with its two-octave low E, the open sixth string.

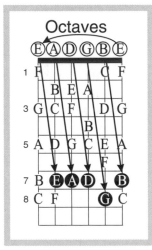

Octaves

Harmonics are also useful for fine-tuning and checking the guitar's tuning by ear. For more information, see *Harmonics* (p. 48). One popular method is to compare open harmonics with equivalent fretted notes. This tuning method is like the previous octave method, except that it replaces low open strings with open harmonics that are sounded above the twelfth fret. This produces a unison sound. Remember, harmonics are played over the frets, not between the frets as with normal fretting.

1. Compare the E harmonic at the twelfth fret of the sixth string with the fretted E at the seventh fret of the fifth string.

2. Compare the A harmonic at the twelfth fret of the fifth string with the fretted A at the seventh fret of the fourth string.

3. Compare the D harmonic at the twelfth fret of the fourth string with the fretted D at the seventh fret of the third string.

4. Compare the G harmonic at the twelfth fret of the third string with the fretted G at the eighth fret of the second string.

5. Finally, compare the B harmonic at the twelfth fret of the second string with the fretted B at the seventh fret of the first string.

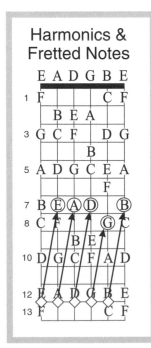

Harmonics & Fretted Notes

Another popular refinement involves using only open harmonics to check tuning. This method has the additional benefit of making the beats (pitch conflicts) very obvious to the ear in their higher octave. The use of only open harmonics necessitates that the tones be clean and precise. The *harmonic tuning* method follows these steps:

1. Compare the E harmonic at the fifth fret of the sixth string with the E harmonic at the seventh fret of the fifth string. Listen for beats. These will sound like fast, warbling vibrations between the unison high notes that are produced by the harmonics. The beats should sound like the same pitch. If you hear beats, gradually tighten the string until the beats disappear and the pitches match.

2. Compare the A harmonic at the fifth fret of the fifth string with the A harmonic at the seventh fret of the fourth string.

3. Compare the D harmonic at the fifth fret of the fourth string with the D harmonic at the seventh fret of the third string.

4. Compare the B harmonic at the fourth fret of the third string with the B harmonic at the fifth fret of the second string. This third-string B harmonic takes a little practice, as it is slightly behind the fret (toward the nut).

5. Finally, compare the B harmonic at the fifth fret of the second string with the B harmonic at the seventh fret of the first string.

Harmonics Only

TWELVE-BAR BLUES

General stuff: The twelve-bar (12-bar) blues progression is a popular and ubiquitous song form that is used in blues, jazz, country, rock 'n' roll, pop, R&B, and folk music. It is the sound of Americana.

Examples abound and cross genres without restriction. The 12-bar blues is "Crossroads" by Robert Johnson and Cream, "T-Bone Shuffle" and "Stormy Monday" by T-Bone Walker, "Sweet Little Angel" and "The Thrill Is Gone" by B.B. King, "What'd I Say" by Ray Charles, "Crosscut Saw" and "Blues Power" by Albert King, "Hide Away" and "Have You Ever Loved a Woman" by Freddie King, and "Pride and Joy" by Stevie Ray Vaughan. Moreover, it is "Johnny B. Goode" by Chuck Berry, "Lucille" and "Long Tall Sally" by Little Richard, "Hound Dog" and "Too Much" by Elvis Presley, "Papa's Got a Brand New Bag" by James Brown, "Kansas City" by the Beatles, "Ice Cream Man" by Van Halen, "Rock and Roll" by Led Zeppelin, "Wipe Out" by the Surfaris, and "Red House" by Jimi Hendrix.

The 12-bar blues is also "Chitlins Con Carne" by Kenny Burrell, "Footprints" and "All Blues" by Miles Davis, "Cousin Mary" and "Mr. P.C" by John Coltrane, "Tenor Madness" by Sonny Rollins, "Wholly Cats" by Charlie Christian, "Parker's Mood" and "Billie's Bounce" by Charlie Parker, "Sun Down" and "Cariba" by Wes Montgomery, "The Cooker" and "Clockwise" by George Benson.... The list goes on and on.

Technical stuff: The 12-bar blues form has a clearly defined structure. It is generally constructed of three four-bar phrases: 4 + 4 + 4 =12. The 12-bar blues also has a very specific chord progression and harmonic rhythm (i.e., rate of chord change). While the 12-bar blues is clearly defined and explicit, it is also malleable and open to variation.

In a standard 12-bar blues, the first four bars always begin with a major or dominant-seventh chord, the I chord (or tonic), which establishes the tonality. The second four-bar phrase begins on the subdominant, or IV chord, in measure 5 and returns to the tonic, or I chord, in measure 7. The third and last phrase moves to the dominant, or V chord, in measures 9–10 and returns to the tonic in measure 11. Almost invariably a *turnaround* occurs in measures 11–12.

Playing stuff: The 12-bar blues, in its most rudimentary form, is represented by this formal scheme in the key of C.

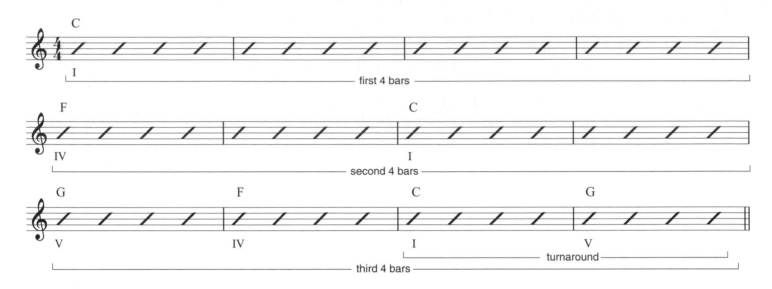

Oftentimes, the 12-bar blues form contains a chord change to the subdominant, or IV chord, in measure 2; here, F. In blues vernacular, this change is sometimes called a "quick IV" or "quick change."

Frequently, the turnaround exploits a faster-moving progression, like this typical I–IV–I–V pattern.

The harmony of the 12-bar blues progression can be perceived as dominant-seventh, minor, or major in quality. The primary chord type in blues progressions is the dominant-seventh chord. In the simplest 12-bar form, the I, IV, and V chords are played as dominant-sevenths (C7, F7, and G7) or dominant ninths. For example, the 12-bar progression above can be—and often is—played as all dominant seventh chords. Note the use of the quick IV and a turnaround with more harmonic activity.

TRACK 52

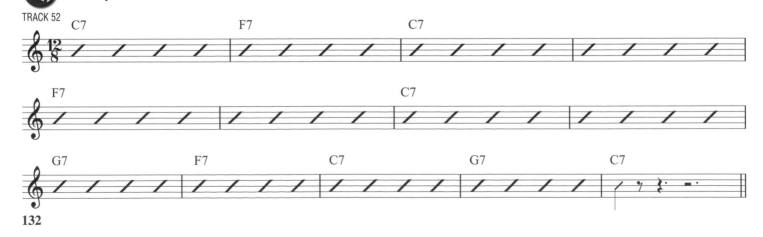

The 12-bar minor blues alludes to a parallel minor mode. That's what you hear in Otis Rush's classic "All Your Love," which was individually covered by Eric Clapton and Stevie Ray Vaughan. In this form, the tonic, subdominant, and dominant are all minor chords. For example, the previous 12-bar progression can be played as all minor chords.

Oftentimes, the strict use of parallel minor chords is musically unsatisfying—especially for the dominant, or V chord—and other harmonic alternatives are applied. More often than not, these alternatives access the harmonic-minor scale for the crucial cadence in measures 9–10 of the form. In Albert King's "As the Years Go Passing By," one of the most well-known minor-blues songs, the typical progression in C minor would be written as follows. Note the use of G and A♭ chords, the V and ♭VI, as substitutions in the final four-bar phrase and the subtle variations between the two applications.

TRACK 52
(0:56)

"As the Years Go Passing By"

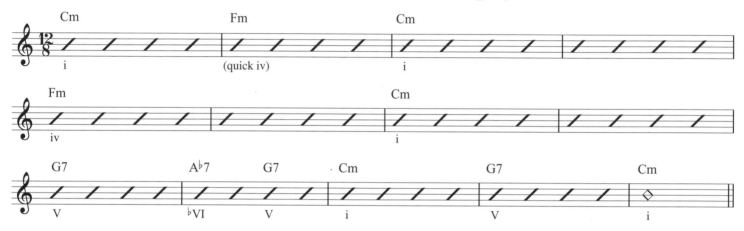

In jazz, predictably colorful harmonic variations of the 12-bar blues form are prevalent and idiomatic to the style. There are numerous permutations of the "modern" major-blues progression. This 12-bar major-blues progression has several notable gestures of the jazz language, including the the use of dominant and minor IV seventh chords in measures 5–6, the descending chromatic cycle of ii–V's in measures 7–9, the use of a ii–V for the V chord in measures 9–10, and a tritone substitute change (D♭7) in measure 4. The I–VI–ii–V turnaround is typical of the bop genre. Despite all these refinements, the basics of the 12-bar blues are retained: beginning on the I chord, the IV chord in measure 5, and the return to I chord in the turnaround.

TRACK 52
(1:52)

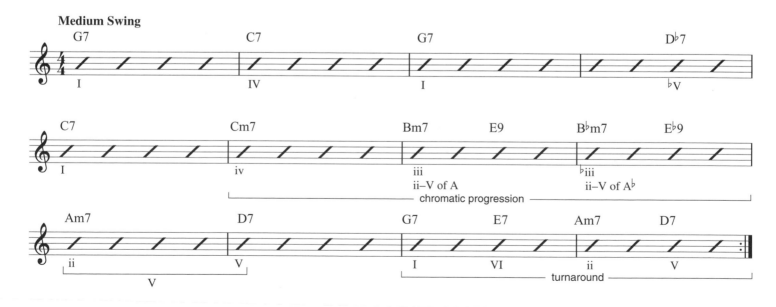

TWELVE-STRING GUITAR

Historic stuff: The 12-string guitar entered the Top 40 and the mainstream during the folk boom of the early sixties. Almost overnight, acoustic 12-strings were offered by major manufacturers like Gibson, Martin, Guild, and Gretsch, providing a high-quality alternative to the budget models that were used previously by early blues and folk musicians.

The acoustic 12-string had been heard earlier, in the twenties, in the country-blues music of Blind Lemon Jefferson, Blind Willie McTell, and Leadbelly, and, prior to that, examples of a 12-string guitar could be found dating back to the double-coursed European versions of the nineteenth century. However, it wasn't until Rickenbacker placed an experimental electric 12-string in the hands of George Harrison that the instrument attained truly iconic status in pop culture.

The Beatles' George Harrison is credited with introducing the electric 12-string to a generation in search of a new sound. From Harrison's opening fanfare on "A Hard Day's Night," we get a procession of bands exploiting the jangle-pop sound, often accompanied with a suitable folk rock–tinged repertory. Prime contenders include the Byrds, Buffalo Springfield, the Turtles, We Five, the Searchers, Sonny and Cher, Grass Roots, the Leaves, Love, the Blue Things, and the Mamas and the Papas. Even the Stones got into the act, employing the 12-string on tracks like "Mother's Little Helper" and "As Tears Go By." After the Beatles popularized the sound, electric 12-strings cropped up in the sixties catalogs of Fender, Gibson, Danelectro, Gretsch, and Guild.

Though the folk-rock era may have come and gone, the jangle-pop vibe and chiming 12-string sound lives on, surfacing sporadically in the music of Led Zeppelin, Tom Petty, Van Halen, R.E.M., Aerosmith, Boston, Kansas, Tracy Chapman, and many others.

Technical stuff: The premise behind the 12-string guitar is simple: take a standard six-string and give each string a double course. The most common arrangement involves an additional light-gauge octave string on strings 6–3: (from low to high) E–A–D–G. Generally, the highest two strings, B and E, are doubled as unisons.

Most 12-string guitars are set up with the octave string first in the course of strings 6–3, so that the downstroke attacks the octave string first. The stock Rickenbacker is an exception. These place the lower octave first. The increased tension of twelve strings has prompted some manufacturers, most notably Guild and Rickenbacker, to use a double-truss-rod system in their necks.

Sonic stuff: 12-strings come in many configurations and have their own specific jangle qualities. A miked Guild acoustic 12-string or a Gibson with a soundhole pickup doesn't sound like a hollow-body Rickenbacker 360-12. And the semi-hollow Gibson ES-335-12 is quite different in tone from the solidbody Fender 12-string or the solidbody Gibson Double 12.

Country and folk-oriented music seems to call for the acoustic 12-string, often miked. Many rockers are fond of combining a picked acoustic 12-string riff with heavily distorted electric textures, like Boston's "More Than a Feeling." Genuine folk-rock and jangle-pop screams for the chiming timbre of a Rickenbacker, as does the intro to Van Halen's "In a Simple Rhyme." Jimmy Page used a solid-body Fender electric 12-string for "Living Loving Maid." Pick the right tool for the job.

Playing stuff: The acoustic 12-string is an ideal instrument for thick, strummed rhythm parts that require an extra jangle quality. This phrase presents an idiomatic rhythm figure common to pop, rock, and country music.

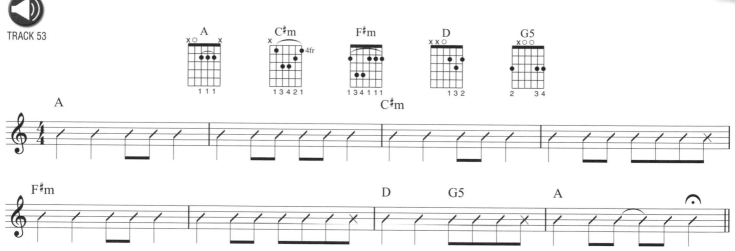

TRACK 53

The electric 12-string ups the jangle quotient with an added measure of brightness and chime. The opening Gsus4 chord of "A Hard Day's Night" sounded a clarion call for savvy rock guitarists world-wide, as did the loose arpeggiations and strummed rhythm parts in the song. The electric 12-string proved to have immense staying power and was heard in many forms of music. This example is based on the lead/rhythm figures heard in the Beatles' classic.

TRACK 53
(0:17)

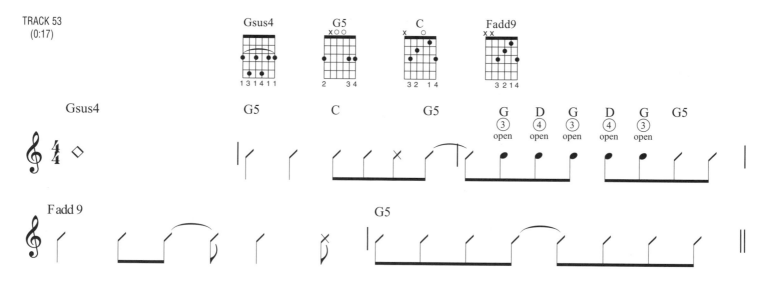

Many 12-string riffs accentuate the instrument's chiming quality with ringing arpeggiated figures. This sound is associated with the Beatles, the Byrds, Tom Petty, and legions of jangle-pop followers of the tradition. This simple triadic figure is based on a steady eight-note arpeggiation of Gsus4 and F chords, colorized with the sustaining 12-string sound.

TRACK 53
(0:31)

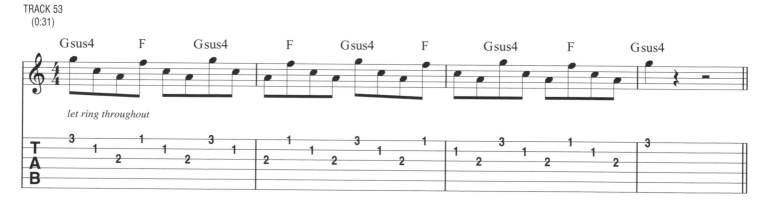

UNISON

General stuff: The term *unison* refers to the interval between two tones that share the same pitch. The unison is the smallest possible interval in music and is defined as the combined sound of two or more notes having the same pitch. When a melody line is doubled at the same pitch, it is said to be played, or sung, in unison.

On the guitar, the unison has many expressions and applications. Consider the use of unisons in the disparate styles of Charlie Christian, Howard Roberts, Chuck Berry, Allan Holdsworth, and Eric Clapton, as well as many blues and rock figures and licks used by Jimi Hendrix, Stevie Ray Vaughan, and Howlin' Wolf.

Technical stuff: The unison is considered to be a *consonant interval*, along with the octave, third, fourth, fifth, and sixth steps of a scale. If the guitar is in tune, the unison is arguably the most consonant interval possible. When a unison interval is augmented and written with the same note name, as in C–C♯, the unison is called a *prime*. Hence, the interval of C to C♯ is not an augmented unison, but rather an *augmented prime*.

Sonic stuff: On the guitar, unisons are generally played as two notes with the same pitches on different strings, often adjacent strings. In fact, one method for tuning by ear is dependant on unison intervals on adjacent strings. See *Tuning* (p. 130). There are countless instances of unison intervals in the riffs, licks, and melodies of blues, jazz, rock, and country music. These are generally played two ways: fretted on adjacent or nonadjacent strings or created by bending the pitch of one string until it matches the pitch of another.

Playing stuff: This characteristic blues phrase harnesses the power of unisons in several typical forms. Check out the familiar slur into and out of the unison E's on the first and second strings, as well as the use of unison intervals that are played as a rhythmically charged dyad in measure 3. This figure is typical of unison usage in Chicago-blues tunes like "Smokestack Lightning" and in riffs like Jimi Hendrix's opening phrase in "Hey Joe" or Stevie Ray Vaughan's "Pride and Joy."

TRACK 54

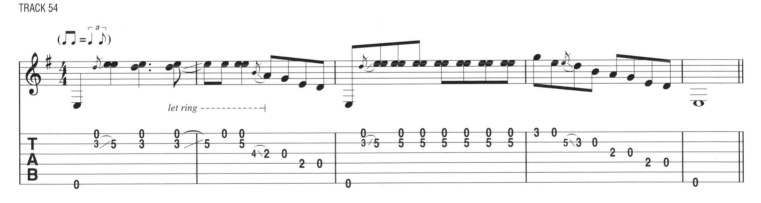

The follwing unison riff is endemic to solos of many styles. This example is based on the unison string-bending approach that is associated with Chuck Berry and many of his disciples—in other words, rock 'n' roll and blues-rock guitarists of all stripes. Here the unison becomes the center of attention—the first note of a shifting three-note rhythmic figure, which is repeated as an ostinato. The string bend from E♭ to F on the third string is played in combination with two unbent F notes on the second string. Jazz players have employed the same figure but with slides into the F on the third string, and first-generation electric blues guitarists like T-Bone Walker have used half-step bends into the F note.

TRACK 54
(0:14)

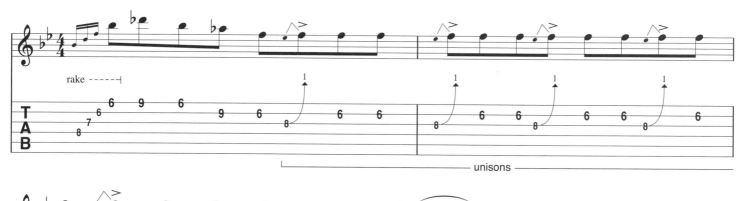

VAMPS

General stuff: The slang term *vamp* refers to extended repeated sections of music in a song or piece of music. Sometimes a vamp is part of the song form, as in an outro vamp or a repeated chord cycle behind a soloist, and often it is the basis for improvisation or solos.

Vamps are found in countless rock, funk, reggae, R&B, pop, and country songs but also occur in post-sixties jazz pieces, especially funky jazz outings, including the outros of George Benson's "Body Talk" and "Plum," as well as the solo changes in "Breezin'" and generally throughout the current genre of smooth jazz. Vamps dominate tunes like Stevie Wonder's "Superstition"; Herbie Hancock's "Watermelon Man," John Coltrane's, Kenny Burrell's, and Grant Green's versions of "My Favorite Things," Wes Montgomery's "Bumpin' on Sunset," and Larry Carlton's "Room 335." Bottom line: the vamp is ubiquitous and freely crosses seemingly incongruous genres.

Technical stuff: Usually a vamp is based on a short symmetrical section (typically one, two, or four bars), which is self-contained and open to variation and elaboration. It achieves its purpose and aesthetic value through repetition, as heard in the vamps behind James Brown, George Benson, Parliament Funkadelic, and the loop figures of hip hop. The vamp provides a stable and static background for soloists to decorate and is quite different than the chord changes of most pop, blues, jazz, rock, and country songs.

Another distinction is the harmonic content. Most vamps are harmonically spare, often confined to a simple two-chord progression that is based on a mode or tonal center, like the Dm7–G7 pattern from the D Dorian mode. This holds true for Parliament Funkadelic, as well as Wes Montgomery and KC and the Sunshine Band. In funk, harmony is often second to the "lock," the linking of contrapuntal parts that are played on guitar, bass, and drums in the repeating vamp. A general rule for vampers: the tighter the lock, the better the groove. In the groove, rhythm and the lock are of the greatest importance.

Playing stuff: The vamp riff in funk and R&B is exemplified by this simple two-bar pattern. Here, three dyads on the sixth and fifth strings are alternated with muted strings. The use of simple chords and purely rhythmic ingredients is an identifier of the style. Think of the muted strings as percussive textures that are integral to the phrasing of the vamp figure.

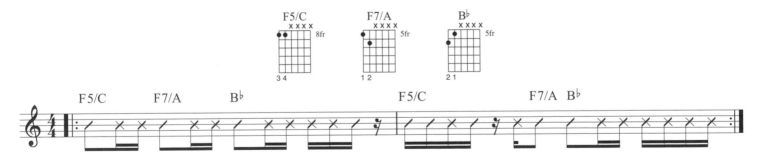

This driving vamp riff is a one-bar pattern made of the simplest harmony: one chord. This telling figure gets its rhythmic definition and forward motion from percussive elements (muted strings) and a strategic "push chord" (C#9). Many one-chord guitar patterns use similar half-step chromatic motion to embellish the static harmony and to provide variety.

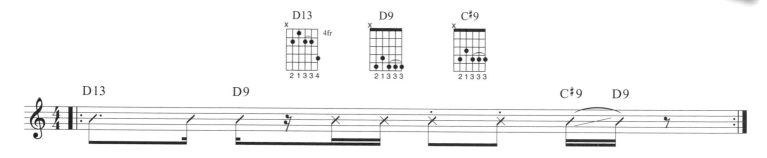

This single-note riff reveals how a simple melody can become the basis of a vamp. Here, a two-bar pentatonic lick in the key of E is looped to create an ostinato. Note the use of staccato articulation to keep things tight and funky and to yield rhythmic space for other instruments in the "lock."

VIBRATO

General stuff: Vibrato on the guitar is the oscillation of pitch that is either produced physically by moving the fretting finger on the string or through electronic means. Players use it as a basic technique to increase the emotional quality of their sound. Physical vibrato is as distinctive and personal as a fingerprint. It can be as subtle as the slight purr that is added to phrase endings of classical guitar melodies or as overt as the 3rd-interval wailing of hard-rock licks, and everything in between.

Some players can be identified by their unique hand-and-finger vibrato, including giants like B.B. King, Eric Clapton, Steve Lukather, Yngwie Malmsteen, Larry Carlton, and Les Paul. Subtle physical (how they do it) and aural (how they hear it) decisions and habits of vibrato contour, speed, and intensity vary considerably from guitarist to guitarist and is part of their musical presence and persona.

Historic stuff: The modern style of blues-based vibrato, still very much the de facto standard, is generally acknowledged to have come from the innovations of B.B. King and his disciples. The effect is definitive when used in conjunction with a bent note.

"B.B. King invented the squeezing. T-Bone was playing the neck of the guitar but when B.B. started squeezing that guitar, we all started squeezing the thing."

—Buddy Guy, *Guitar Player*

"I won't say I invented it, but they weren't doing it before I started. My ears told me that when I trilled my hand I'd get a sound similar to the sound they were getting with a bottle-neck."

—B.B. King, *Guitar Player*

Technical stuff: Physical vibrato is produced by moving a string with the fret hand. Three different motions are usually used to create the vibrato effect: vertical, horizontal, or circular. In all three types, the decision of slow or fast vibrato speed rests with the player and how they wish to express the emotion of a musical passage.

Vertical is a variation of string bending whereby the string is pushed from side to side without releasing pressure of the fret hand. This vibrato can be used with a bent or unbent note. With a bent note, the tension is released gradually and then returned to pitch to produce the wavering sound. Wide versus narrow vibrato (the depth) is determined by how far in pitch the string is bent. This action is controlled by the player during the vibrato motion. In vertical vibrato, the hand is generally anchored, with the thumb wrapped around the neck for support, and reinforced fingering is often employed. See *String Bending* (p. 109).

Horizontal is the sideways rolling motion generally used with an unbent note and is favored by classical guitarists. Many players favor an unsupported posture for this type of vibrato, with the thumb and palm not touching the neck at all. In more extreme versions of this type of vibrato, the string is pulled or pushed horizontally so far that a drop in pitch can be heard below the fretted note. Larry Carlton and Allan Holdsworth have used this type of vibrato effectively in their playing.

Circular refers to a motion that visually seems to combine the two previous forms of vibrato. The fretting hand maintains pressure on the string and assumes an arching pattern, bending above and below a central pitch with the wrist and hand moving in a lever-and-fulcrum motion.

Sonic stuff: The dictionary defines vibrato as "a pulsating effect, produced in singing by the rapid reiteration of emphasis on a tone, or, on string instruments, by a rapid change of pitch corresponding to the vocal tremolo." In singing, vibrato and tremolo are essentially the same effect, varying only in intensity and degree. On string instruments, vibrato and tremolo are two entirely different effects; vibrato denotes a pitch change and tremolo, a reiteration of an unchanged pitch or a rapid alternation between two pitches, as in a trill. The confusion of the terms initially caused amp manufacturers to incorrectly label the electronic tremolo effect "vibrato" on their front panels—and the name stuck. (Comically, the vibrato bar was also misnamed by Fender as a "tremolo bar.")

True distinction between electronic vibrato and tremolo came with the rise of modulation pedals and with renewed interest in the retro units of the past. Stevie Ray Vaughan's application in "Cold Shot" was an example from the mid eighties. The effect of pitch change that is used on vibrato pedals today aurally resembles the oscillation of rotating speakers. Units like the Dunlop Roto-Vibe pedal and the various stomp-box emulations of the Leslie cabinet are modern examples of the electronic vibrato effect.

VOICING

General stuff: The term *voicing* can be applied to theoretical and sonic aspects of the guitar. Chord voicing is one distinct area, while the voicing of an amplifier is another. The types of chords, the number and placement of tones within the chord, and the resulting harmonic motion (destination) are elements that affect and reflect chord voicing.

All amplifiers have a voicing. This is a parameter that can be controlled by the player via the tone circuit. An amplifier is said to have a "good voicing" when it produces a certain desired sound. An amplifier's voicing can be changed or improved through electronic modification.

Technical stuff: In theory, chords on the guitar are viewed as a collection of voices (tones, or notes, within a chord). In most forms of music, the motion from one chord to another is most satisfying when there is *continuity*—when the voices move logically to their intended destination as the chords change. This is most evident in the *smooth voice leading* of classical music, jazz chord-melody playing, and string and horn ensemble parts in pop arrangements. Even if a hard-rock song is dominated by parallel power chords, the string pads will usually follow the rules of smooth voice leading.

Chord voicing refers to the distribution of voices within a chord and how they are positioned. This example demonstrates the chord-voicing possibilities that exist in a garden-variety C major barre chord. The first chord is a barre-chord formation that is played in eighth position with all six strings present in the voicing. From this starting point, it is possible to derive a number of smaller, more purposeful voicings, each producing its own sound and offering different benefits to the savvy player.

The first derivative is a voicing of a triad on the top three strings plus a thumb-fretted bass note, which is ideal for the Hendrix lead/rhythm style. The second derivative is a three-note voicing that spreads the notes of an open-position C major triad (C–E–G=C–G–E). It has the desirable *10th interval* as its outside notes. This voicing is often found in classical music. The third voicing has a C major triad on the inner strings plus a low C bass note, which can be fretted with the index finger or the thumb. The latter fingering is another useful shape for the Hendrix style. All of these voicings rely on muting to cancel unwanted tones, marked by X's.

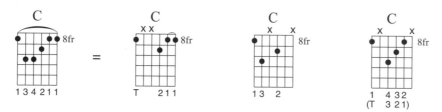

The same basic principles can be applied to seventh chords with similarly pleasing results. This example of derived voicings is based on a typical Cmaj7 chord that is played in eighth position. The first variant is played on consecutive strings in an open-position spread with the 10th interval spanning root to 3rd (C–G–B–E). This was a favorite form of Wes Montgomery. The second variant is a very wide voicing that has the compound 7th as its outside tone (C–B). This form has an "orchestral" sound that is deceptively larger to the ear than its four-note structure would suggest. It is a standard jazz voicing that is played by Kenny Burrell, Johnny Smith, George Van Eps, Howard Roberts, and many others. The final variant has five notes in the voicing. Here the root, C, is doubled. The full four-note Cmaj7 chord is placed on the top four strings in close position (low to high: C–E–G–B), with the thumb fretting the low C bass note. This shape is found in the repertory of Barney Kessel.

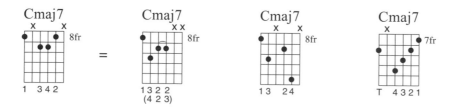

Playing stuff: Smooth voice leading is demonstrated in microcosm by the following progressions. All of these examples use the basic chromatic change D♭7 to Cmaj7. Here the voicings are enriched with 7ths and 13ths. Note the different densities of the voicings and the motion of each voice through the chord change. Look for elements like common tones and stepwise melodic movement.

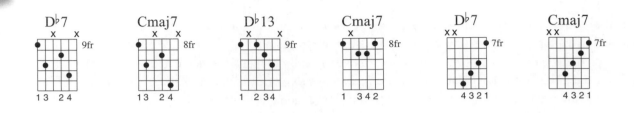

This example harmonizes a stepwise melody in the key of C through a ii–V–I chord progression with a variety of approaches. Note the following points: the use of 4th voicings for Dm7, Em7, and C6/9, the re-voicing of tones in G13 and G7♭9♯5; and the stepwise resolution of F in the bass to E, the 3rd of C6/9, in the V–I cadence (G7–C). Moreover, note the use of parallel motion (Dm11–Em11–G13/F), which is offset by oblique motion (G13/F–G7♭9♯5/F) and contrary motion (G7♭9♯5/F–C6/9/E).

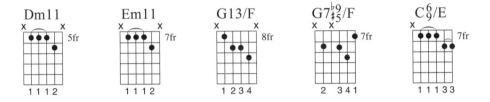

WHAMMY BAR

General stuff: Whammy bar, vibrato bar, Vibrola, Synchronized Tremolo, whang bar, wiggle stick…. Call it what you will, curse it if you must, this simple mechanical device is indispensable to rock, pop, fusion, metal, and country music, among others. The use of the vibrato bar has distinguished the repertories of Chet Atkins, Duane Eddy, Cliff Gallup, the Ventures, the Beatles, Jimi Hendrix, Jeff Beck, Ritchie Blackmore, David Gilmour, Allan Holdsworth, Eddie Van Halen, Stevie Ray Vaughan, Brian Setzer, Joe Satriani, and Steve Vai.

Historic stuff: Doc Kauffman developed and patented the first hand-controlled vibrato tailpiece, called a Vibrola, in 1932. His units were simple and practical; the strings were attached to a piece of sheet metal and manipulated with a player's sideways hand motion. His experiments led to a slew of innovations, and players could realize new levels of expression, made possible with this pioneering mechanical contraption.

Chet Atkins once mentioned to me that the vibrato tailpiece unit was a rare and most sought-after item in the forties. He first modified a custom-made D'Angelico guitar with a retro-fitted Kauffman unit before insisting his Gretsch namesake models all feature Bigsby vibrato tailpieces. Since then, a number of important manufacturers have gotten into the act—Bigsby, Fender, Gibson, Rickenbacker, Epiphone, Ernie Ball, Floyd Rose, and Kahler, to name just a handful.

Technical stuff: Vibrato tailpieces range from traditional Bigsby units and vintage Stratocaster bridges to the current double-locking Floyd Rose system, which is equipped with fine tuners and a drop-D lever.

Bigsby   Stock Strat   Floyd Rose

Tuning problems plague users of the stock vibrato-bar tailpiece. Many players prefer the tone and feel of these units, however, and have had to take extra measures to improve the intonation. Lubrication, proper stringing, removing impediments like overly tight string trees and springs, and "tuning to the bar" are among the most common remedies.

> *"I don't use any special bridge or tailpiece; I like the way Fender makes them. I've got it pretty much sewn up now by using a very light graphite on the bridge and on the nut. When the strings rock backwards and forwards and slide lengthwise along the neck, you minimize the chance of a string hang-up over the nut, which is the killer."*
> —Jeff Beck, *Guitar Player*, 1980

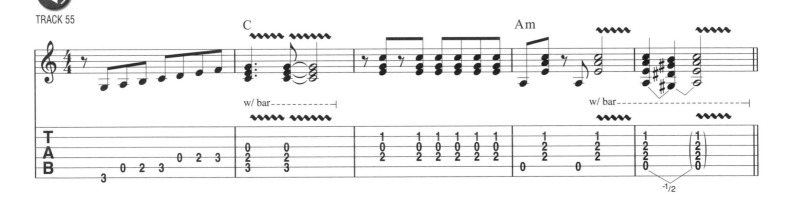

"It's a combination of a lot of things. You know those little string retainers at the top of the neck? If those clamp down, like the way Fender Strats come from the factory, the string will get caught up in there and go out of tune. The amount of springs you use in the back affects it, too."

—Eddie Van Halen, *Guitar Player*, 1978

"Some people hit the bar and just let it go. You have to pull it back up right. And then sometimes when you stretch a string too far when you're fingering it with your left hand, it'll go flat. You have to pull the bar back up to bring it back to normal."

—Eddie Van Halen, *Guitar Player*, 1978

Playing stuff: The whammy bar was a crucial part of instrumental-rock and pop styles of the early sixties, like those associated with Cliff Gallup and the Ventures. In this depictive phrase, the wham-my bar is used to provide subtle pitch bends and to vibrato notes and chords.

TRACK 55

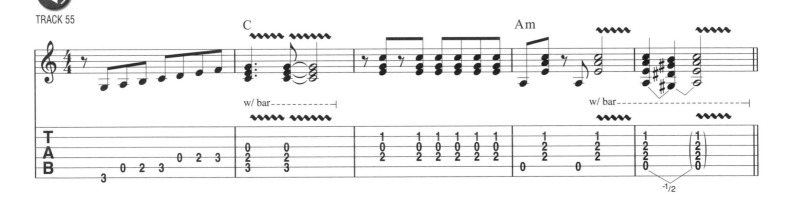

A few years later, more extreme whammy-bar techniques surfaced in the work of Jimi Hendrix, Jeff Beck, Eddie Van Halen, and Steve Vai. This characteristic lead lick has the panoply of typi-cal sounds: wide vibrato with a held bend, a legato figure that is articulated with the bar, a slow pitch-dive, and a gradual return to pitch. These whammy-bar moves are still very much in use and, indeed, are must-know aspects of the modern-rock lexicon.

TRACK 55
(0:13)

Freely

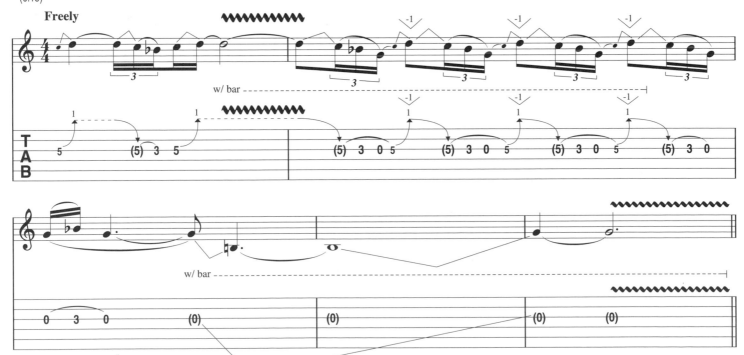

X'S (IN NOTATION)

General stuff: X marks the spot. The X symbol is used regularly in guitar notation to indicate specific techniques and sounds. Intentionally muted strings, accidentally muffled notes, and percussive ghost notes all receive the X, whether in the music staff or in the tablature staff.

Technical stuff: In music notation, the X is placed at the approximate pitch location of the muted, muffled, or ghosted note(s). In tablature, the X is placed on the particular string to be muted, muffled, or ghosted.

In this example, the pickup measure shows a single muted string. The following two measures (after the double bar line) depict a chord progression with percussive muted strings on the backbeats.

Playing stuff: This blues phrase is played as single notes and includes idiomatic muffled string jabs that act as rhythmic "place holders."

Funk players often incorporate muted strings to add texture and more activity to simple one-chord vamps. This Jimmy Nolen–inspired (James Brown) figure subjects a single E9 chord to a time-honored rhythm groove.

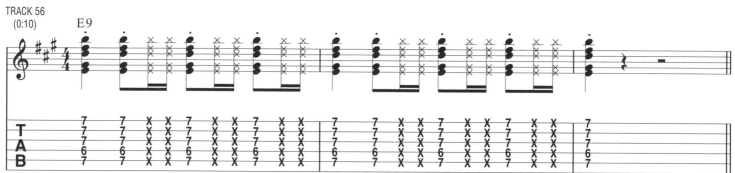

X

Another application of the X symbol is to indicate strings not included in a chord voicing. These are found on typical fingerboard grids. In this example, a D major chord, played at the fifth position, is depicted as a fingered form in the grid. Strings not to be heard in the chord are specified with X's above the top line of the grid. Here, the omitted notes are on the sixth and first strings. Finger the chord but don't play the outer strings. Instead, use muting technique when strumming all of the strings or avoid these strings altogether when plucking the chord.

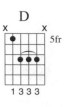

Y-CORD

General stuff: Since the sixties, Y-cords have been used by guitarists to access more than one channel of an amp or to access two separate amplifiers. With a Y-cord, the signal path leads from the guitar and then splits into a Y, with each branch leading to different destinations.

Technical stuff: Jimi Hendrix used a Y-cord to put his guitar through two separate heads of his Marshall stacks. A Y-cord can also be used to create two signal paths through effects boxes to different amps.

Y-cord

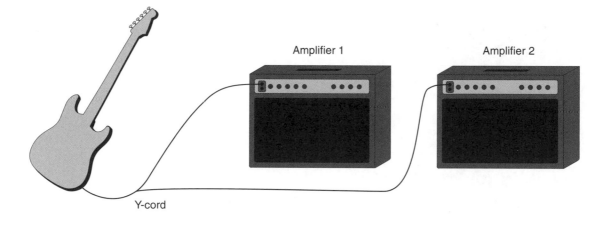

Amplifier 1   Amplifier 2

Y-cord

ZERO FRET

General stuff: The *zero fret* is an extra fret that is located on the fretboard, just below the nut. The purpose of a zero fret is to impart a fretted timbre to an open string; in theory, this assures uniform string timbre throughout the full range of the guitar's scale.

Technical stuff: The string height and scale length of the string begins at the zero fret rather than at the nut, as is the case for guitars without a zero fret. When a zero fret is installed, its height affects the action in the lower positions of the fingerboard (i.e., first through third positions).

Sonic stuff: A zero fret is found on select guitars. Fenders and Gibsons don't use the zero fret on their instruments. However, several other manufacturers offer them on their flagship guitars. A zero fret is used regularly on the Gretsch Country Gentleman, the Mosrite Ventures model, the National Glenwood, the British Burns Bison, the Italian Eko 700, and others.

fingerboard close-up with zero fret

Get Better at Guitar

...with these Great Guitar Instruction Books from Hal Leonard!

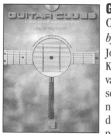

HAL•LEONARD® GUITAR PLAY-ALONG

AUDIO ACCESS INCLUDED

This series will help you play your favorite songs quickly and easily. Just follow the tab and listen to the audio to the hear how the guitar should sound, and then play along using the separate backing tracks. Audio files also include software to slow down the tempo without changing pitch. The melody and lyrics are included in the book so that you can sing or simply follow along.

INCLUDES TAB

VOL. 1 – ROCK	00699570 / $16.99
VOL. 2 – ACOUSTIC	00699569 / $16.99
VOL. 3 – HARD ROCK	00699573 / $17.99
VOL. 4 – POP/ROCK	00699571 / $16.99
VOL. 6 – '90S ROCK	00699572 / $16.99
VOL. 7 – BLUES	00699575 / $17.99
VOL. 8 – ROCK	00699585 / $16.99
VOL. 9 – EASY ACOUSTIC SONGS	00151708 / $16.99
VOL. 10 – ACOUSTIC	00699586 / $16.95
VOL. 11 – EARLY ROCK	00699579 / $14.95
VOL. 12 – POP/ROCK	00699587 / $14.95
VOL. 13 – FOLK ROCK	00699581 / $15.99
VOL. 14 – BLUES ROCK	00699582 / $16.99
VOL. 15 – R&B	00699583 / $16.99
VOL. 16 – JAZZ	00699584 / $15.95
VOL. 17 – COUNTRY	00699588 / $16.99
VOL. 18 – ACOUSTIC ROCK	00699577 / $15.95
VOL. 19 – SOUL	00699578 / $15.99
VOL. 20 – ROCKABILLY	00699580 / $14.95
VOL. 21 – SANTANA	00174525 / $17.99
VOL. 22 – CHRISTMAS	00699600 / $15.99
VOL. 23 – SURF	00699635 / $15.99
VOL. 24 – ERIC CLAPTON	00699649 / $17.99
VOL. 25 – THE BEATLES	00198265 / $17.99
VOL. 26 – ELVIS PRESLEY	00699643 / $16.99
VOL. 27 – DAVID LEE ROTH	00699645 / $16.95
VOL. 28 – GREG KOCH	00699646 / $16.99
VOL. 29 – BOB SEGER	00699647 / $15.99
VOL. 30 – KISS	00699644 / $16.99
VOL. 31 – CHRISTMAS HITS	00699652 / $14.95
VOL. 32 – THE OFFSPRING	00699653 / $14.95
VOL. 33 – ACOUSTIC CLASSICS	00699656 / $17.99
VOL. 34 – CLASSIC ROCK	00699658 / $17.99
VOL. 35 – HAIR METAL	00699660 / $17.99
VOL. 36 – SOUTHERN ROCK	00699661 / $16.95
VOL. 37 – ACOUSTIC UNPLUGGED	00699662 / $22.99
VOL. 38 – BLUES	00699663 / $16.95
VOL. 39 – '80S METAL	00699664 / $16.99
VOL. 40 – INCUBUS	00699668 / $17.95
VOL. 41 – ERIC CLAPTON	00699669 / $17.99
VOL. 42 – COVER BAND HITS	00211597 / $16.99
VOL. 43 – LYNYRD SKYNYRD	00699681 / $17.95
VOL. 44 – JAZZ	00699689 / $16.99
VOL. 45 – TV THEMES	00699718 / $14.95
VOL. 46 – MAINSTREAM ROCK	00699722 / $16.95
VOL. 47 – HENDRIX SMASH HITS	00699723 / $19.99
VOL. 48 – AEROSMITH CLASSICS	00699724 / $17.99
VOL. 49 – STEVIE RAY VAUGHAN	00699725 / $17.99
VOL. 50 – VAN HALEN 1978-1984	00110269 / $17.99
VOL. 51 – ALTERNATIVE '90S	00699727 / $14.99
VOL. 52 – FUNK	00699728 / $15.99
VOL. 53 – DISCO	00699729 / $14.99
VOL. 54 – HEAVY METAL	00699730 / $15.99
VOL. 55 – POP METAL	00699731 / $14.95
VOL. 56 – FOO FIGHTERS	00699749 / $15.99
VOL. 59 – CHET ATKINS	00702347 / $16.99
VOL. 62 – CHRISTMAS CAROLS	00699798 / $12.95
VOL. 63 – CREEDENCE CLEARWATER REVIVAL	00699802 / $16.99
VOL. 64 – THE ULTIMATE OZZY OSBOURNE	00699803 / $17.99
VOL. 66 – THE ROLLING STONES	00699807 / $17.99
VOL. 67 – BLACK SABBATH	00699808 / $16.99

VOL. 68 – PINK FLOYD – DARK SIDE OF THE MOON	00699809 / $16.99
VOL. 69 – ACOUSTIC FAVORITES	00699810 / $16.99
VOL. 70 – OZZY OSBOURNE	00699805 / $16.99
VOL. 71 – CHRISTIAN ROCK	00699824 / $14.95
VOL. 73 – BLUESY ROCK	00699829 / $16.99
VOL. 74 – SIMPLE STRUMMING SONGS	00151706 / $19.99
VOL. 75 – TOM PETTY	00699882 / $16.99
VOL. 76 – COUNTRY HITS	00699884 / $14.95
VOL. 77 – BLUEGRASS	00699910 / $15.99
VOL. 78 – NIRVANA	00700132 / $16.99
VOL. 79 – NEIL YOUNG	00700133 / $24.99
VOL. 80 – ACOUSTIC ANTHOLOGY	00700175 / $19.95
VOL. 81 – ROCK ANTHOLOGY	00700176 / $22.99
VOL. 82 – EASY SONGS	00700177 / $14.99
VOL. 83 – THREE CHORD SONGS	00700178 / $16.99
VOL. 84 – STEELY DAN	00700200 / $16.99
VOL. 85 – THE POLICE	00700269 / $16.99
VOL. 86 – BOSTON	00700465 / $16.99
VOL. 87 – ACOUSTIC WOMEN	00700763 / $14.99
VOL. 89 – REGGAE	00700468 / $15.99
VOL. 90 – CLASSICAL POP	00700469 / $14.99
VOL. 91 – BLUES INSTRUMENTALS	00700505 / $15.99
VOL. 92 – EARLY ROCK INSTRUMENTALS	00700506 / $15.99
VOL. 93 – ROCK INSTRUMENTALS	00700507 / $16.99
VOL. 94 – SLOW BLUES	00700508 / $16.99
VOL. 95 – BLUES CLASSICS	00700509 / $14.99
VOL. 99 – ZZ TOP	00700762 / $16.99
VOL. 100 – B.B. KING	00700466 / $16.99
VOL. 101 – SONGS FOR BEGINNERS	00701917 / $14.99
VOL. 102 – CLASSIC PUNK	00700769 / $14.99
VOL. 103 – SWITCHFOOT	00700773 / $16.99
VOL. 104 – DUANE ALLMAN	00700846 / $16.99
VOL. 105 – LATIN	00700939 / $16.99
VOL. 106 – WEEZER	00700958 / $14.99
VOL. 107 – CREAM	00701069 / $16.99
VOL. 108 – THE WHO	00701053 / $16.99
VOL. 109 – STEVE MILLER	00701054 / $16.99
VOL. 110 – SLIDE GUITAR HITS	00701055 / $16.99
VOL. 111 – JOHN MELLENCAMP	00701056 / $14.99
VOL. 112 – QUEEN	00701052 / $16.99
VOL. 113 – JIM CROCE	00701058 / $15.99
VOL. 114 – BON JOVI	00701060 / $16.99
VOL. 115 – JOHNNY CASH	00701070 / $16.99
VOL. 116 – THE VENTURES	00701124 / $16.99
VOL. 117 – BRAD PAISLEY	00701224 / $16.99
VOL. 118 – ERIC JOHNSON	00701353 / $16.99
VOL. 119 – AC/DC CLASSICS	00701356 / $17.99
VOL. 120 – PROGRESSIVE ROCK	00701457 / $14.99
VOL. 121 – U2	00701508 / $16.99
VOL. 122 – CROSBY, STILLS & NASH	00701610 / $16.99
VOL. 123 – LENNON & MCCARTNEY ACOUSTIC	00701614 / $16.99
VOL. 125 – JEFF BECK	00701687 / $16.99
VOL. 126 – BOB MARLEY	00701701 / $16.99
VOL. 127 – 1970S ROCK	00701739 / $16.99
VOL. 128 – 1960S ROCK	00701740 / $14.99
VOL. 129 – MEGADETH	00701741 / $16.99
VOL. 130 – IRON MAIDEN	00701742 / $17.99
VOL. 131 – 1990S ROCK	00701743 / $14.99
VOL. 132 – COUNTRY ROCK	00701757 / $15.99
VOL. 133 – TAYLOR SWIFT	00701894 / $16.99
VOL. 134 – AVENGED SEVENFOLD	00701906 / $16.99
VOL. 135 – MINOR BLUES	00151350 / $17.99

VOL. 136 – GUITAR THEMES	00701922 / $14.99
VOL. 137 – IRISH TUNES	00701966 / $15.99
VOL. 138 – BLUEGRASS CLASSICS	00701967 / $14.99
VOL. 139 – GARY MOORE	00702370 / $16.99
VOL. 140 – MORE STEVIE RAY VAUGHAN	00702396 / $17.99
VOL. 141 – ACOUSTIC HITS	00702401 / $16.99
VOL. 143 – SLASH	00702425 / $19.99
VOL. 144 – DJANGO REINHARDT	00702531 / $16.99
VOL. 145 – DEF LEPPARD	00702532 / $17.99
VOL. 146 – ROBERT JOHNSON	00702533 / $16.99
VOL. 147 – SIMON & GARFUNKEL	14041591 / $16.99
VOL. 148 – BOB DYLAN	14041592 / $16.99
VOL. 149 – AC/DC HITS	14041593 / $17.99
VOL. 150 – ZAKK WYLDE	02501717 / $16.99
VOL. 151 – J.S. BACH	02501730 / $16.99
VOL. 152 – JOE BONAMASSA	02501751 / $19.99
VOL. 153 – RED HOT CHILI PEPPERS	00702990 / $19.99
VOL. 155 – ERIC CLAPTON – FROM THE ALBUM UNPLUGGED	00703085 / $16.99
VOL. 156 – SLAYER	00703770 / $17.99
VOL. 157 – FLEETWOOD MAC	00101382 / $16.99
VOL. 158 – ULTIMATE CHRISTMAS	00101889 / $14.99
VOL. 159 – WES MONTGOMERY	00102593 / $19.99
VOL. 160 – T-BONE WALKER	00102641 / $16.99
VOL. 161 – THE EAGLES – ACOUSTIC	00102659 / $17.99
VOL. 162 – THE EAGLES HITS	00102667 / $17.99
VOL. 163 – PANTERA	00103036 / $17.99
VOL. 164 – VAN HALEN 1986-1995	00110270 / $17.99
VOL. 165 – GREEN DAY	00210343 / $17.99
VOL. 166 – MODERN BLUES	00700764 / $16.99
VOL. 167 – DREAM THEATER	00111938 / $24.99
VOL. 168 – KISS	00113421 / $16.99
VOL. 169 – TAYLOR SWIFT	00115982 / $16.99
VOL. 170 – THREE DAYS GRACE	00117337 / $16.99
VOL. 171 – JAMES BROWN	00117420 / $16.99
VOL. 172 – THE DOOBIE BROTHERS	00119670 / $16.99
VOL. 174 – SCORPIONS	00122119 / $16.99
VOL. 175 – MICHAEL SCHENKER	00122127 / $16.99
VOL. 176 – BLUES BREAKERS WITH JOHN MAYALL & ERIC CLAPTON	00122132 / $19.99
VOL. 177 – ALBERT KING	00123271 / $16.99
VOL. 178 – JASON MRAZ	00124165 / $17.99
VOL. 179 – RAMONES	00127073 / $16.99
VOL. 180 – BRUNO MARS	00129706 / $16.99
VOL. 181 – JACK JOHNSON	00129854 / $16.99
VOL. 182 – SOUNDGARDEN	00138161 / $17.99
VOL. 183 – BUDDY GUY	00138240 / $17.99
VOL. 184 – KENNY WAYNE SHEPHERD	00138258 / $17.99
VOL. 185 – JOE SATRIANI	00139457 / $17.99
VOL. 186 – GRATEFUL DEAD	00139459 / $17.99
VOL. 187 – JOHN DENVER	00140839 / $17.99
VOL. 188 – MÖTLEY CRUE	00141145 / $17.99
VOL. 189 – JOHN MAYER	00144350 / $17.99
VOL. 191 – PINK FLOYD CLASSICS	00146164 / $17.99
VOL. 192 – JUDAS PRIEST	00151352 / $17.99

Prices, contents, and availability subject to change without notice.

Complete song lists available online.

HAL•LEONARD®

www.halleonard.com

0817